Pelican Books
Tyranny

D1589914

Maurice Latey describes himself as 'a political
animal from earliest youth'. He has travelled widely
in Europe before and since the war, including
numerous visits to countries under Communist
rule, particularly the Soviet Union. He has visited
the United States on a Smith-Mundt Leader-
Specialist scholarship and in order to cover a
presidential election campaign. The son of Mr
William Latey, Q.C., author of *Latey on Divorce*,
and brother of Mr Justice John Latey, the author
says he decided two lawyers in the family were
enough; a political commentator and expert on
Eastern Europe, formerly Head of The B.B.C. East
European Service, he is now Editor of Talks and
Features in The B.B.C. External Services. Maurice
Latey has written numerous articles and book reviews
on political and historical subjects for *History Today*,
the *Financial Times*, the *Observer*, the *Sphere* and the
Listener. He is married with two daughters and a son.

Tyranny

A Study in the Abuse of Power

Maurice Latey

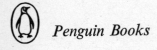 *Penguin Books*

Penguin Books Ltd, Harmondsworth,
Middlesex, England
Penguin Books Australia Ltd, Ringwood,
Victoria, Australia

First published by Macmillan & Co 1969
Published in Pelican Books 1972
Copyright © Maurice Latey, 1969

Made and printed in Great Britain by
Richard Clay (The Chaucer Press) Ltd,
Bungay, Suffolk
Set in Linotype Times

TO THE LEAST TYRANNICAL OF PARENTS

I have sworn, upon the altar of God, eternal hostility against every form of tyranny over the mind of man.

THOMAS JEFFERSON

Contents

Preface to the Pelican Edition

Three years is a short time in the life of a book spanning nearer three thousand; but it may be sufficient to establish or refute trends, and certainly in this case the course of events since original publication has confirmed the relevance and urgency of the problems examined. The winds blowing the ship of freedom and constitutional government, even of civilization and humanity, towards the rocks of chaos and tyranny have risen to gale force; and, perhaps more justly than in most other ages, men sense Doomsday, feeling that we are they on whom 'the ends of the world are come'.

What we now fear is less the tyranny of men than the tyranny of things. The sixties, as I pointed out, were bad years for tyrants; a number of familiar figures have disappeared from the scene since then – the prince of petty tyrants Papa Doc Duvalier from Haiti, and the most formidable of puppet rulers Walter Ulbricht of Eastern Germany. Indeed with the departure of Ulbricht, of General de Gaulle and of Dr Salazar of Portugal we have seen the beginning of the end of 'the class of the 1890s', that formidable group of septuagenarian personal rulers, who so dominated the post-war scene. The enigmatic figure of Chairman Mao may bestride China like some colossus from a past age, but one can hardly believe, despite his titanic efforts to secure an earthly immortality, that he will still be with us at the end of the seventies, or indeed – if history is anything to go by – that his divine image will have escaped the hammers and chisels of the iconoclasts.

What next, then? A shrewd critic of this book (Professor Bernard Crick in the *Observer*) has suggested that if this is a bad time for personal rulers, 'it is also a good time for something else perhaps more cruel and depersonalizing than personal tyrannies'. Certainly the threat of this impersonal kind of tyranny is a very real one, namely the oppression of forces and institutions rendered possible by modern forms of organization and technology, communications and transport, and rendered necessary by the need to support vast masses of people. Perhaps the greatest act of tyranny of recent years in East Pakistan is of this impersonal nature. This catastrophe was a direct consequence of the nature of military rule rather than of any personal tyranny by General Yahya Khan. He acted precisely as one would expect a military dictator to do and more constitutionally than most, since he did attempt to introduce democracy and representative government, and only sent in the army when he saw that the consequences of the election would destroy the state which he regarded it his duty to preserve. Granted the historic racial and cultural antipathies between the Punjabi troops and the Bengalis, General Yahya's simple military logic was bound to be far more destructive than any political concession. The tragic sequel bears out my conclusion in Chapter 11 that military dictatorship is by its nature tyrannical, but not the generally rather lenient judgement I made of it.

The tyranny of things, then, of impersonal forces and organizations, of collectives and oligarchies – for example the racialist domination in South Africa – may indeed be the most threatening in our time; and I have purposely framed my definition of tyranny to cover this more general type of abuse; but I have concentrated on personal tyranny not only because it is the most vivid way of illustrating the subject and because it limits an otherwise limitless theme, but also because the worst type of oppression occurs when the tyranny of a man is superimposed on the tyranny of things. The Brezhnev régime in the Soviet Union is grey and grim and impersonal, but who can doubt that it would be more terrible if its ruler were to exercise, as he still might, the personal power of Stalin?

Further, I write as a political commentator, of over twenty-five years standing, on the affairs of the two greatest tyrants of our age, Hitler and Stalin, as well as on many lesser ones; and the subject matter of the political commentator is people in action. In this book I move around in time as the current affairs commentator moves around in space. The reviewers have generally been very kind to this somewhat unusual procedure. Their chief criticism has been the lack of any general theory and the corresponding inadequacy of the remedies offered. It is indeed true that as an observer of the chaotic flux of contemporary events, I find it necessary to travel light in theory, for fear of sinking beneath the weight of some ideology or 'ism'. The political commentator knows that the more certain he feels of any theory, the more likely he is to be monumentally wrong. So I have offered a number of partial antidotes to the multiple disease, but no general theory or cure. There is in fact a general theory lurking behind the careful definition and selection of instances of tyranny. It concerns the relations of means to ends in politics and society and it points to what may be called a metapolitical problem which has, I think, become more acute and has been more generally recognized since I wrote.

I refer to the relation between politics and religion. It seems that they cannot get on together; yet they cannot get on without each other. When religion trespasses in the field of politics there is one form of tyranny – witness the relapse into old-fashioned religious communal strife in Northern Ireland and the stagnation and stultification where the priest or the Imam dominates the minds of men. Yet the worst form of tyranny comes when man plays god, and in a purely secular society it is difficult to draw the line between the things that are Caesar's and the things that are God's. For nearly two centuries the line drawn in ancient religious struggles held good, and even in those Western countries where religious beliefs had declined most rapidly, an afterglow of accepted Christian morality continued to provide that general moral consensus which is necessary for the cohesion of a free pluralist society. The afterglow is now fading; the utilitarian humanist morality which succeeded Christianity as the 'establishment code' has been progressively eroded and is rejected by the more daring spirits of a new generation. They seek strange gods – Chairman Mao, the late Ho Chi Minh,

Castro or Ché Guevara. Leaders who, by the standards of their fathers, would rate as tyrants or potential tyrants become the objects of a quasi-religious devotion among the young. The combination of a chaos of moral and social ideas and the quest for new gods is a dangerously combustible one, particularly when it coincides with a loss of nerve by the upholders of the established morality.

This loss of nerve in the western world has gone very far indeed in the last few years, particularly in the U.S.A. I wrote of Britain three years ago: 'No society, perhaps, has presented a more disreputable picture of itself to itself, since the Weimar Republic and the French Third Republic – and we know what happened to them.' Since then the Americans have far outstripped the British in public self-abasement and the position described in Chapter 13, 'The Tyrant and the Future', has deteriorated further. The present mood of despair and exasperation is understandable in a people confronted with the multiple problems of the black city ghettoes, of pollution, of inflation and unemployment, with the prospect of a demoralized army returning from Vietnam to seek work at a time when jobs are scarce and violence in the streets is growing. Yet to the outside observer this despairing mood may seem exaggerated when set beside the United States' immense human and material resources, their deeply rooted democratic traditions and habits. These should enable the great American democracy to surmount even such formidable threats, provided only that the will is there; but is it?

Without vision the people perish; can a sufficient moral consensus be restored after all the discord and disillusion? To a nation built on moral purpose and religious conviction, this is the crucial question. To ask such a fundamental question is the first small step towards answering it, and the question is increasingly being asked particularly in relation to the young. Indeed, the Western world shows a great many of the symptoms which have sometimes in the past accompanied a revolution in human consciousness. There is the frantic, often ludicrous, search after any new thing (described by Christopher Booker in

The Neophiliacs), there is the see-sawing of millennial hopes and Doomsday fears, and there is the proliferation of sects and communities mostly secular in intent but clearly religious in impulse. Some of the young leaders themselves and some of their elders (see Charles Reich in *The Greening of America*) see in their new anarchistic life styles the dawn of a new consciousness which will transform society, while others (see Duncan Williams, *The Trousered Ape*) detect in the rejection of reason and the reversal of all traditional standards the beginning of the end of civilization and even the self-destruction of Man.

Obviously, if history is anything to go by, neither of these apocalyptic expectations is likely to be realized, while a breakdown into tyranny may well be. But is history any guide? We live in a notoriously unprecedented age; further, as some critics of this book pointed out, modern historians tend to shudder at what they regard as a promiscuous selection of illustrations from the past to fit the argument. This purist attitude is not possible for the political commentator. For him history is the best training ground for judgement. And if, as Lord Acton says, the student of history is the politician with his face turned backwards, the political commentator is the historian with his face turned forward. He must, of course, recognize the differences in standards, values and practical possibilities between the different ages which he examines, just as, for example, in his daily work he takes into account the similar differences between a Communist ruler, or an Asian or African leader, or a military dictator in Latin America. Historical judgements do not differ in principle from current ones; it may well be that a British Prime Minister has more values in common with Pericles thousands of years away than with Chairman Mao thousands of miles away. The political commentator can hardly accept the dictum that 'We learn nothing from history, except that we learn nothing from history;' for him Ortega y Gasset is the better guide when he writes, 'We have need of history in its entirety, not to fall back into it, but to see if we can escape from it.'

There is, indeed, a great deal of it to escape from; and fortunately it has been researched and chronicled by a very distinguished group of historians. A study on so extensive a subject as tyranny must necessarily depend on secondary sources rather than original research; and the reader will have no difficulty in discerning my debt to the fine works of A. Andrewes, Sir Alan Bullock, Sir J. Wheeler-Bennett, Norman Cohn, F. W. Deakin, Hugh Seton-Watson, Hugh Trevor-Roper, Sir Ronald Syme, J. L. Talmon and J. M. Thompson, to mention only a few. Their work enables the political commentator to survey a wider field than most of his predecessors; and such an extensive view may bring up new truths and re-establish the old ones which tend to be nobody's business in an age of specialization.

1. The Scope of the Inquiry

We live in an age of tyrants. Our generation has had the opportunity of studying – at uncomfortably close quarters – two of the greatest tyrants the world has ever seen, Hitler and Stalin, and scores of lesser ones. Indeed scarcely a year passes without the appearance of some new dictator who may well become a tyrant.

We live too in an age when it has become a matter of life and death to study these great beasts of history, since at any moment one may arise who will have the power of life and death over all of us in the shape of nuclear weapons. This terrible power will doubtless spread; already Mao Tse-tung has it; Sukarno, before his fall, falsely claimed to have it; and other dictators aspire to it. Universal war and destruction are more likely to be launched by a tyrant unrestricted by law, by custom, or by public opinion than by any constitutional type of ruler.

We have therefore a special interest in diagnosing tyranny in its early stages before the danger becomes too great, and in seeking remedies and palliatives. The aim of this inquiry will be, as it were, to stand Machiavelli on his head. The great Florentine in his *Prince* drew on the examples of tyranny in classical antiquity and in fifteenth-century Italy in order to guide Giuliano de' Medici, to whom he dedicated his work, in the art of seizing, holding and extending power. He was not concerned with the ends for which such power should be used, although he regarded the Medici at the beginning of the sixteenth century as well placed for liberating and uniting Italy. His study was power, and he made no moral distinction between its use and abuse save in so far as abuse might lead to the loss of it.

The Prince is a handbook for tyrants, who as a rule need no such instruction, since they communicate with each other by a sort of telepathy across the centuries and the oceans and seem to grasp by instinct what they do not learn by study. It is for men of goodwill who have repeatedly down the ages been taken in by the most familiar tyrannical gambits that this inquiry is designed. Early diagnosis is the first step to a cure, and a study of past onsets of the epidemic can help in diagnosis.

The aim of this study will therefore be to parade some of these great beasts of history, to examine their characters, their various species, the conditions in which they thrive, the means by which they rise, how they maintain their course, their strength and their weakness, their attempts to perpetuate their species and the obstacles over which they stumble and fall. The attempt will be made to identify some of the characteristics which modern tyrants have in common with their predecessors and some of their distinctive features.

However, two great difficulties attend any such inquiry. First there is the difficulty of establishing the facts. The point is well made by one of the greatest historians of tyranny, Tacitus, who writes in his *Annals of the Roman Empire*: 'The reigns of Tiberius, Gaius, Claudius, and Nero were described during their lifetime in fictitious terms for fear of the consequences; whereas the accounts written after their deaths were influenced by still raging animosity.' This is a very real problem today. It is vividly illustrated by the Soviet treatment of Stalin before and since his death. In 1949 on his seventieth birthday he came as near to apotheosis as is possible for an atheist monarch; among the most fulsome eulogies was one from Nikita Krushchev, who five years later was to start the process of de-Stalinization in his secret speech at the Twentieth Congress of the Soviet Communist Party and later was to remove the remains of his great predecessor from the Lenin Mausoleum. That speech has still not been published in the U.S.S.R., although various versions of it have appeared abroad. It was certainly inspired by 'still raging animosity' and also by the political interests of its author who sought to white wash himself and inculpate his opponents. The various phases of de-Stalinization have been conditioned by the political needs of post-Stalinist Russia. With the fall of Khrushchev a more objective treatment of Stalin's part in the war was permitted, not from any attachment to historical truth, but in the political interests of Khrushchev's successors who were busy removing the name of their predecessor from the history books and condemning him to the oblivion of silence. Consequently there is no absolute certainty about some of the most crucial episodes in the great dictator's career. Did the assassination of Kirov in 1934 frighten Stalin into the great purges? Or did he himself engineer it, to put an end to the liberalizing tendencies in the Party which the Leningrad Party leader represented and as a pretext for getting rid of all possible opposition? An inquiry into the Kirov affair has long been promised but even if a new version of it emerges it is more likely to be dictated by momentary political needs than a settled regard for objective truth.

That is a recent and flagrant example of the difficulty of establishing the facts. But even in the best documented cases the difficulty exists. Napoleon Bonaparte lived on to tell his own story at St Helena, but his efforts at self-justification often cast more shade than light. Thus to many, at the time and since, the kidnapping, summary trial and execution of a foreign prince, the Duc d'Enghien, in 1804 was the first act to stamp Napoleon as a tyrant; but he disputed his responsibility and tried to thrust the blame on to Talleyrand, thus giving his champions a line of defence.

However, even greater than the difficulty of establishing the facts is the second difficulty of judging them objectively. The word 'tyrant' when it first made its appearance among the Greeks of Asia Minor in the seventh century B.C. was probably a neutral term interchangeable with 'basileus' or 'king'. But it very soon took on a derogatory colour, particularly in the hands of the aristocratic and oligarchic authors of the fifth and fourth centuries B.C. It has since been used largely as a term of abuse. Any ruler one does not like is described as a tyrant. One may speak of a benevolent despot or of a just dictator, but to apply such epithets to a tyrant would be a contradiction in terms. It is therefore an emotionally charged term and there is inevitably an element of subjectivity in the use of it. One man's tyrant is another man's hero. For many Americans doubtless King George III remains the tyrant *par excellence*; but that monarch would not stand very high on any list of tyrants drawn up in Britain. To some Englishmen, King Charles I will seem a tyrant and to others Cromwell. Indeed one of the leading experts on that great man, Mr Maurice Ashley, wrote his book *Cromwell, the Conservative Dictator* in the 1930s under the impact of Hitler and Mussolini bringing out the tyrannical aspects of his rule; and an even more convincing work in the 1950s – *The Greatness of Oliver Cromwell* – handsomely acquitting him of the charge and comparing him to George Washington. Professor Geyl writing in Nazi-occupied Holland collected the conflicting French views of Napoleon down the years in his *Napoleon – For and Against*; 'history', he concludes, 'is indeed an argument without an end'. This is particularly true of the history of great men. Our judgement of them is conditioned by our own experience. Few people nowadays peering back through the miasma raised by the dictatorships of our generation would be disposed to agree with Mommsen's description of Julius Caesar as 'the entire and perfect man'. We tend now to scrutinize great men with a beady and distrustful eye.

From the comfortable security of the Victorian age it was possible to admire such material and cultural achievements as Polycrates' tunnel, Pisistratus' recension of Homer, Augustus' finding Rome brick and leaving it marble and inspiring Virgil, the wonderful artistic harvest of the patronage of the Renaissance princes, the Code Napoléon, without considering that the good that tyrants do sometimes lives after them while the evil is often interred with their opponents' bones. We who have seen Mussolini make the trains run to time, Hitler build the Autobahns and Stalin the hydro-electric plants are much more apt to count the cost. Similarly the more leisurely and secure

Victorian age could afford to be impressed by the energy of these great men, the way they marched great armies about, won great battles and generally stirred everything up, while disapproving rather of the irregularities of their private lives. We on the other hand are more inclined to think that idleness is a virtue in a tyrant and debauchery his most innocent employment. To the barbarous Maximin, that fierce soldier, we should much prefer as Emperor his rival the younger Gordian of whom Gibbon writes: 'Twenty-two acknowledged concubines, and a library of sixty-two thousand volumes, attested the variety of his inclinations, and from the productions which he left behind him, it appears that the former as well as the latter were designed for use rather than ostentation.' Unfortunately, though perhaps not surprisingly, this amiable prince wore the purple only for thirty-six days before falling in battle.

The facts then are often uncertain, the judgements subjective. Tyrannology, indeed, is not an exact science. The men of our age are no more likely to succeed in treating the theme *sine ira et studio* – without passion or partisanship – than Tacitus, despite his heroic efforts, was able to. His vision was inevitably warped by his experiences under the Emperor Domitian and ours no less by our experiences at the hands of contemporary tyrants.

However to minimize the element of prejudice which inevitably enters into such a study we must seek a definition which will help in classification, while not pretending to a greater degree of objectivity than the subject-matter permits. Aristotle, who must be regarded as one of the best experts on the subject, both from direct experience and from deep study, defined tyranny as 'irresponsible rule over equals or betters in the interest of the ruler but not in the interest of the ruled'. This however begs all kinds of questions. Who are equals or betters? How do you distinguish between the interests of the rulers and the ruled particularly in the case of the modern tyrant who says, 'I am the state, I am the general will, I am the nation, I am the proletariat' and has at his disposal all the modern means of persuasion and coercion to make the people accept the identification? After all, every opposition party in a democracy accuses the government of ruling in its own interests and not in that of the ruled, but this does not necessarily involve an accusation of tyranny. A more sophisticated basis of classification is needed, and here Pascal helps us with one of those flashes of insight which suddenly gleam out from the *Pensées*. He writes: 'Tyranny consists in the desire of universal power beyond its scope'; and he amplifies his point by adding: 'So these expressions are false and tyrannical, "I am fair, therefore I must be feared; I am strong therefore I must be loved..." Tyranny is the desire to have in one way what can only be had in another.'

Pascal puts us on the right track; some such definition will provide a useful basis for classification in that the abuse of power is related to its scope or function which can vary according to the circumstances. The definition therefore permits the necessary degree of relativity and allows for the fact that the ruler in a revolutionary age may well have to exercise greater severity than the ruler in more settled times. It also provides for the more general usage of the term as in such phrases as the 'tyranny of the bureaucracy, of the tax-collector, of the trades unions or racial tyranny'. Thus we cannot fairly call a trade union tyrannical if it uses its powers within the law to promote the well-being of its members, however unjust this may sometimes seem to the employers and however harmful to the economy. That is the pursuit of power within its scope; but when it uses its powers to coerce its members, for example to prevent a man from doing work which would increase his well-being without harming his colleagues, the union goes beyond its scope and acts tyrannically.

However we shall not be concerned with such partial forms of tyranny in this study, nor indeed with the even more serious forms of collective tyranny, of race over race and nation over nation, although these have in fact produced and are producing some of the most monstrous abuses of power that history records. Few individual tyrants can have treated their subjects more arbitrarily than the Spartans maltreated the subject race of Helots over the centuries; and the similar apartheid policy of the South African government is a tyranny over the black population as unjustifiable in principle, though not as severe in practice. However we are not concerned with such collective tyrannies here save in so far as they tend to promote the absolute tyranny of one man, since otherwise the inquiry will extend itself indefinitely.

Nor shall we be concerned with so-called tyrannical laws, save in so far as they are used by the individual tyrant to enforce his will. We may indeed regard certain laws as tyrannical, as too strict, as Draconian in fact, but we do not for that reason classify Draco, the law-giver, as a tyrant, because tyranny carries with it the idea of being above the law or, if it works through laws, these are so drafted as to make possible every sort of arbitrary action on the part of the ruler or his agents.

Not every absolute ruler is a tyrant. Indeed since most of the human race, through most of its history has been ruled by autocrats of one sort or another, we should today be in a sorrier state than we are, if it were so. Aristotle makes this important distinction when he writes that 'Oriental despotisms have a tyrannical nature but are hereditary and according to law.' Similarly, any ruler attempting to introduce a feudal monarchy in a modern democratic society would naturally be called a tyrant; but the feudal monarchs of the Middle Ages were not such, provided they kept within the traditional limits and did not exceed them, as King John did. The first of the Greek tyrants, Pheidon of Argos, in the early seventh century B.C. was, according to Aristotle, a hereditary king who became a tyrant by exceeding the traditional royal prerogative.

Tyranny, then, is only a meaningful concept when it stands in contrast to some accepted standard of constitutional government. This standard is not fixed and absolute, but subject to development. Thus in societies where oppressive laws and customs are traditional we cannot properly call the ruler a tyrant unless he abuses even those strict laws or makes them more severe; but where more liberal standards have been introduced or are at any rate professed, the contrast between these standards and actual performance may qualify the ruler as a tyrant. The question of direction of movement must therefore also come into our definition.

It must also be recognized that there are certain conditions of emergency which in almost any society render some form of autocratic or monarchic government highly probable if not inevitable. But in these circumstances the autocrat need not necessarily be a tyrant. The Greeks, as usual, had a word for it; they called such a monarch elected to overcome an emergency or solve certain specialized problems – sometimes for life and sometimes for a fixed period – an *aisumnetes* or moderator. However since the Greeks were not much given to political moderation, the *aisumnetes* seems to have been a somewhat rare bird. Aristotle mentions only the name of Pittacus of Mitylene, who was elected to resist certain exiles who were trying to return by force and who held office from 587–579 B.C. Solon the great Aethenian reformer falls perhaps into the same category. The Roman dictatorship was of a similar character until it became debased in the first century B.C. in the civil wars between Marius and Sulla, Caesar and Pompey. Our definition should not include rulers of this sort in the category of tyrant.

Finally we must distinguish between tyranny and totalitarianism. Modern tyrannies are indeed apt to be totalitarian, exercising arbitrary power over their citizens in all aspects of their lives. But not all tyrannies are totalitarian states, nor are all totalitarian states tyrannies. The Greek city-state was in theory, if not always in practice, totalitarian, demanding total service of its citizens; and the most totalitarian state of antiquity, Sparta, which made the most exacting demands on its citizens, suffered least of all from personal tyranny, and had the longest uninterrupted record of constitutional government. On the other hand, although tyranny was endemic in the Roman Empire, the great mass of its citizens enjoyed the benefits of Roman Law and the Pax Romana for long periods, for the simple reason that with the worst will in the world the Roman Emperor could not interfere in the details of the lives of people spread over so vast an area, although it may be admitted that Diocletian and his successors made a very good attempt at it. It was the ruling classes in Rome and the provinces who bore the brunt of the tyranny. It is only in our time with modern means of transport, communication and indoctrination that totalitarian tyranny over vast super-states has become possible.

We are now in a position to proceed from Pascal's insight to a more precise definition which would run perhaps something like this. 'A tyrant is a ruler who exercises arbitrary power beyond the scope permitted by the laws, customs and standards of his time and society and who does so with a view to maintaining or increasing that power.' This restricts the field by setting the tyrant against some kind of constitutional background and takes into account the factor of progression or movement, whether from worse to better or from better to worse. However, while it is necessary to have a definition, it would be optimistic to expect much agreement about the application of it. Practically everyone nowadays would agree that Hitler was a tyrant, but on few others is there any consensus. There has even been an attempt to rehabilitate Caligula. Therefore, if the definition is to be of use in classification, the author must endeavour to show how he proposes to apply it in some typical cases ancient and modern.

2. The Classification of Tyrants

Any attempt to define and describe tyrants, to be useful, must deal not only with those monsters of history whose abuse of power is obvious and indisputable; it must also raise the cases of rulers who have achieved great things, who are justly admired for their achievements and qualities, and who have left an indelible mark on our world for better or for worse.

Let us start, therefore, with Alexander the Great. That he pursued and achieved a universal power beyond the scope of any man of his time is not in dispute. But was this power beyond the scope permitted by the laws, customs and standards of his time? He comes on the scene when the world of the Greek city-states lies in ruins, shattered by its own dissensions and unable to combine to resist the invader. His father Philip of Macedon has bequeathed to him the Empire of Greece. He secures the succession by the assassination of possible rivals, in that acting according to the traditions of his kingdom. From his first youth he proved himself an incomparable general and leader of men, his genius matched by his courage and liberality. He overthrew kingdoms and empires which were certainly more despotic than the rule which he imposed in their place. He founded great cities. Marching around with his court of philosophers and savants, he spread Hellenic civilization, which was undoubtedly in most respects the highest of its time, through the Orient. It may be argued that his rule was less that of a tyrant than a kind of Homeric kingship, a form of rule that had survived in Macedonia long after it had been obsolete in Greece. But he went further than this. When at the age of twenty-three Alexander visited the Temple of Zeus Ammon in Libya and proclaimed himself the son of Zeus, and when he attempted to make his Macedonians do obeisance in the Persian style he went far beyond the customs and standards of the Hellenic world of his time.

It is related that when Alexander lay mourning for the death of his friend Kleitos, whom he had slain in a drunken brawl, one of his court philosophers Anaxander reproached him with the words: 'This then is Alexander, the Lord of the World! He lies weeping like a slave for fear of the law and the censure of men to whom himself should be a law! Do you not know the meaning of the saying that justice sits at the right hand of God? It means that whatever is ordained by God is rightly done; and so too on earth, what has been done by the King must be thought just, first of all by the King himself and secondly by the rest of men.' This, it is true, was one of the traditional arguments in the Greek world; it was the argument put forward by Thrasymachus in Plato's *Republic* that 'justice is the advantage of the stronger', and the argument which Thucydides put in the mouth of the Athenians in the conference which preceded the extermination of the people of Melos in the Peloponnesian War: 'Of the Gods we believe, and of men we know that by a necessary law of their nature they rule wherever they can.' This is the principle on which Alexander acted and it is the principle of tyranny. Pascal remarked that more people have been made intemperate by the example of Alexander's drunkenness than have been made continent by the example of his chastity; still more perhaps have been made militarists by the glory of his conquests. He more than any other individual has given militarism a good name in the Western tradition.

The next case to be considered is a more difficult one – that of the Emperor Augustus. It can be argued that, plunged from his earliest youth into Civil War, he had no choice but violence and that the wisdom with which he exercised power outweighs and justifies the force and duplicity with which he seized it. By the time he came on the scene the structure of the Roman Republic had been shattered by the civil wars of Marius and Sulla, then of Julius Caesar and Pompey. Julius Caesar, it can be argued, had the autocracy thrust upon him by the sheer necessity of self-preservation. In the anarchy that followed his assassination his adoptive son, the young Octavian, had to act as he did. If he had not seized absolute power, Mark Antony or someone else would have done so. Rome, the city-state, with its senatorial oligarchy, could not hope to rule the Empire which Romans arms had conquered. Only an Emperor could do that and when Octavian became Caesar Augustus, he exercised his rule with moderation and set limits to the Empire, refraining from that career of conquest which is the normal course of the absolute tyrant – that 'perpetual restless desire for power after power that ceaseth only in death', and avoiding, too, that progressive deterioration of character which is one of the hallmarks of tyranny. It is further hard to say of Augustus that he pursued arbitrary power beyond the scope permitted by the laws, customs and standards of his time, since there had been a total collapse of laws, customs and standards. It was an age in which there was in Tacitus' phrase *'non mos, non jus'* – no custom, no law.

It is an arguable case, but it will not stand up to very close examination. When Julius Caesar was murdered Octavian was eighteen years old. His great kinsman had indeed adopted him as son but there is no evidence that in doing so Julius was intending to found a dynasty; he would have been the heir to Caesar's name and property but not to his Imperium. That he set out immediately to win for himself. He did it by launching a new civil war, by bribing the legions, by terrorizing the Senate, by liquidating formidable rivals in the proscriptions, by disguising beneath the constitutional forms of the Republic and of liberty an unprecedented concentration of power and by appealing to old Roman standards in order to subvert them.

The means colour the end; and for all Augustus' statesmanship, the methods by which he seized power left a fatal flaw in the foundation of his Empire which repeatedly shook the edifice and finally destroyed it. For it remained basically a military despotism; and the liberal grants with which Augustus won over the legions foreshadowed the day when the Praetorian Guard would put up the Empire for auction. A great statesman, certainly, but also, in his ruthless pursuit of power, a great tyrant.

Our next subject sought to model himself on Alexander the Great and on Augustus. He is Emperor Frederick II Hohenstaufen, *Stupor Mundi*, the Wonder of the World, who in the first half of the thirteenth century foreshadowed the modern secular state and even the modern totalitarian dictatorship. He makes the task of classification easier by styling himself the Tyrant of Sicily, though in no derogatory sense. Frederick can be represented as being pushed by circumstances along the paths of tyranny and having no choice in the matter. Orphaned in childhood by the death of his father the Emperor Henry VI, son of Frederick Barbarossa, he had from his early childhood to live by his own wits and courage. Then by what must have seemed a miraculous turn of fortune's wheel at the age of eighteen, younger than either Alexander or Octavian, he is proclaimed Emperor. When acclaimed by the senate and people of Rome, he felt 'the august spirit of the Caesars take possession of the boy'. The troubadours hailed him as the new Alexander, and he attempted to combine the Empires of the East and West, crowning himself King in Jerusalem. He gave the Germans their first code of laws in their own language and founded the Prussian state under the order of Teutonic Knights. Both in Germany and in Sicily he presided over an artistic renaissance. In Germany the Minnesänger such as Walter von der Vogelweide and Wolfram von Eschenbach flourished under him; in the kingdom of Sicily which included the whole of southern Italy, he inspired the first poetry in the vernacular. He gathered in his court the most brillaint men of his age such as Michael Scot, the astrologer. Frederick was adept in the philosophy, logic, mathematics and medicine of his time, a master in Arabic science and poetry. Fluent in Arabic and Greek, he could write in seven languages. Many of his ideas were well in advance of his time; he insisted on religious toleration for the Saracens whom he had conquered in Sicily and transferred to Lucera in

Southern Italy; he set up a sort of royal commission which refuted the stories of ritual murders by Jews so prevalent in the Middle Ages. He rejected trial by ordeal; 'how,' he asked, 'could a man believe that the natural heat of glowing iron will become cold without a natural cause ... or that because of a seared conscience, the element of cold water will refuse to accept the accused'. It is not surprising therefore that the men of his time saw in him the Wonder of the World, *Stupor Mundi*. Yet he was a thorough-going tyrant.

How he became a tyrant, whether he was forced into that position by outside circumstances is a matter for argument. He had to overcome a revolutionary situation in the island of Sicily, where law and order had totally broken down during his minority. In trying to combine the Kingdom of Sicily with the Imperial territories in Lombardy and Germany he incurred the implacable hostility of the aged Pope Gregory IX who saw in this encirclement a threat to the Papal territories and the Papacy itself. The Pope pursued the vendetta by means that were tyrannical and aggressive, exceeding by far the scope of his office and even going to the length of himself leading an army against Frederick's kingdom, of exhorting the Sultan of Egypt not to hand over Jerusalem to the Emperor, and of stirring up the Knights Templar to hand Frederick over to the Moslems. In his propaganda against the Emperor, Gregory reached new heights of apocalyptic violence. Yet by his actions the Emperor did much to justify the accusations of the Pope.

Frederick established his control of the Kingdom of Sicily by means later to be recommended by Machiavelli, conquering the most powerful of his vassals with the aid of the lesser and then sending his allies into exile and gaining control of their estates. All vassals required the Emperor's permission to marry and heirs depended on him for their inheritance. His subjects were forbidden to marry foreigners on grounds of the purity of the race. He set up the University of Naples to train his civil servants, being in the words of his biographer Ernst Kantorowicz 'the first Emperor who deliberately and consciously set himself to establish an Empire over the minds of men'. He introduced a state trading monopoly on the Islamic model and Mohammedan methods of tax collection. He centralized the whole judicial and administrative machinery, himself making appointments which had hitherto been made by election. Widely thought to be an unbeliever, he used the methods of the Inquisition to control the religious beliefs of his people. As the struggle with the Papacy proceeded, his measures came to include most of those that have disgraced subsequent tyrannies: a widespread system of informers and denunciation, the mutilation and slaughter of hostages. He employed his Saracens as a bodyguard, police and standing army. As Burckhardt puts it: 'Frederick's measures (especially after the year 1231) are aimed at the complete destruction of the feudal state, at the tranformation of the people into a multitude destitute of will and of the means of resistance but profitable in the utmost degree to the exchequer.'

Under the slogan of *Justitia*, Frederick propounded the theory of the totalitarian state and absolute monarchy. Under the slogan of peace and the return of the Golden Age, he waged implacable war against the Lombard city-states. 'All the acuteness of our mind [he wrote] was continually directed to one end ... to avenge the injury offered [by the Milanese] to our father and our grandfather and to trample underfoot the offshoots of abhorred freedom already cultivated in other places also.' 'We shall wield the sword of vengeance more cruelly against them ... and the hate that consumes us will be slaked only by their utter annihilation.' He enlisted the support of other monarchs against the Lombard League and installed his vicars-general to carry out the repression of freedom, of whom the most famous Ezzelino da Romano is said to have put to death some 50,000 people and to have exceeded in cruelty the many Renaissance tyrants who were to follow in his footsteps. Kantorowicz claims: 'All the tyrants of the Renaissance, the Scale, the Montefeltre, the Visconti, Borgia and Medici are down to the tiniest features the sons and successors of Frederick II, the diadochi of the second Alexander.'

Compared with this forerunner of modern tyrants, Oliver Cromwell born four centuries later is an old-fashioned figure – a Tudor gentleman forced into a position of supreme power by his own military genius. He stuggled desperately to control the excesses and fanaticism of the New Model Army which had put him in power and might well have made a military despot of him. A Parliamentarian, wishing to base his authority on Parliament, he yet treated successive Parliaments more high-handedly than King Charles I had. Having fought a Civil War that turned partly on the issue of arbitrary taxation, he taxed the nation more arbitrarily and heavily than the King had ever done. A champion of religious tolerance in an age of fanaticism, he interfered with personal liberty more tyrannously than Archbishop Laud. A naturally compassionate man, he ordered, in the Drogheda and Wexford massacres, atrocities that matched the horrors of the Thirty Years War, and called it 'a marvellous great mercy'. By the standards which led to the execution of Charles I as a tyrant, Cromwell was a tyrant. The rule of the Major-Generals was the most comprehensive tyranny the English people has known, even if a petty one compared with those which others have suffered before and since. It may be that a nation by suffering a petty tyranny can acquire an immunity against greater ones, and certainly Cromwell bequeathed to his countrymen an abiding distaste for his form of rule.

King Charles at his trial gave the verdict on his conqueror when he said: 'If power without law may make law, may alter the fundamental laws of the kingdom, I do not know what subject he is in England can be assured of his life or anything that he can call his own' – to which Cromwell's answer is that of any ruler in revolutionary times: 'If nothing could ever be done but what is according to law, the throat of the nation may be cut while we send for someone to make a law.'

Cromwell's rule then was tyrannical in that he exercised arbitrary power beyond the scope of the law and customs of his time, but it cannot be said that he did so with the purpose of increasing that power. He neither coveted personal power nor succumbed to its progressive corruption; although there were times when it seemed that in fits of passion he might be starting on that slippery slope, a saving moderation turned him back.

Sir Winston Churchill writes in his *History of the English Speaking Peoples* that Cromwell, although crafty and ruthless as occasion claimed, was at all times a reluctant and apologetic dictator, who recognized and deplored the arbitrary character of his own rule; Sir Winston contrasts him in this respect with Napoleon, 'the glittering adventurer of the eighteenth century. Napoleon was sure of himself. He had no scruples. He knew what he wanted to do. He intended to have supreme power in his hands, and to use that power without limit till he and his family controlled the world. He cared nothing for the past; he knew no means of governing the distant future; but the present was his prize and his spoil.'

Napoleon on the other hand, perhaps remembering the accusation of his brother Lucien that he was becoming another Cromwell, made the comparison himself, when in exile, much to his own advantage. In contrast to Cromwell he had three times been chosen by the French people in free elections; his armies had only fought foreigners and not their own people. Where then does Napoleon stand in the spectrum of tyranny?

The 90 per cent majorities in plebiscites of which he boasted in his comparison with Cromwell are unlikely to impress a generation which has seen this dictatorial device exploited *ad nauseam* by Nazis and Communists alike, although of course the plebiscite was not in Napoleon's day the machine-turned mass-produced commodity which it has become today. The defence of Napoleon's rule must be based rather on the fact that he found France weak and in chaos and rapidly restored her to order and strength, that any arbitrary action he may have taken in doing so can be regarded as trivial compared with the Reign of Terror and that, if France suffered tyranny after the Revolution, it was that of Robespierre. In the kidnapping and execution of the Duc d'Enghien and in the execution of Jacobin conspirators he did no more than was necessary for self-preservation and hence for the safety of the nation. There are estimated to have been some 2,500 political prisoners during his reign, no great number for a country emerging from a revolution and civil war. This, it can be argued, was a small price to pay for the foundation of the administrative structure of modern France and for the Code Napoléon which forms the basis of the law of France and a great part of Europe. Can such a ruler be said to have exercised arbitrary power beyond the scope of the laws and customs of his age – the age of Revolutionary France?

Vis-à-vis his own people it is arguable that Napoleon, despite the spies, informers and censors, was not a tyrant; he certainly could rely on a great deal more popular support than the régime which succeeded him. But this is to ignore the principal use to which he put his power, which was to make war. Although he came to power with the promise of peace and stabilization of the revolution, he gave his people war and Empire. He professed the revolutionary principles of freedom and equality, but robbed nation after nation of its freedom in the interests of his Empire and dynasty. His response to each new problem was to launch a new campaign. In his later years too the corruption of power became increasingly evident, taking sometimes the form of a flight from reality. A French colonel describes this scene after the battle of Borodino: 'Napoleon was riding over the battlefield beaming and rubbing his hands. "There are five Russian dead to every Frenchman", he said repeatedly and with satisfaction. I suppose he took the Germans for Russians'; and later on St Helena he was to describe Borodino, that terrible carnage, which was the beginning of the end of the *Grande Armée,* as his finest battle. The conqueror whose wars had cost nearly four million lives was able to declare at the end: 'I blame myself for some mistakes but for no crimes.' His English biographer J. M. Thompson lets Marshal Foch have the last word: 'He forgot that a man cannot be God; that above the individual is the nation; that above mankind, the moral law; he forgot that war is not the highest aim, for peace is above war.' Napoleon, in fact, came of the line of great conqueror tyrants, whose ancestor and real hero was Alexander the Great; he himself is the father of modern tyranny and the originator of the form which it most commonly takes, namely nationalist authoritarian democracy.

Of these modern cases we will for the present pass over Hitler and Mussolini whose classification as tyrants will not now cause much argument, and turn to Stalin. In countries in which oppressive laws and customs are traditional we do not call a tyrant the ruler who keeps within the scope of these laws and customs. Seen in this light Stalin may appear as a traditional Russian despot in the line of Ivan the Terrible and Peter the Great, who set about the task of modernizing and industrializing Russia in the only way in which it could be done. Moreover Lenin had already re-introduced many of the sterner features of Tsarist rule and had applied them with greater severity and efficiency than most of the Tsars; Stalin, it can be said, took over a tyrannical system and ran it according to the accepted standards of revolutionary Russia, merely continuing, as he himself always claimed, the work of the great Lenin. There is much force in these arguments, and Stalin clearly has to be judged by other standards than a ruler taking over in a settled constitutional state, a de Gaulle, for example. However, even by the standards of his own time and place Stalin must be condemned as a tyrant, since he moved from greater freedom to great servitude, from some degree of legality to almost complete arbitrariness. Although Russia had been under absolute rule more or less continually for some 500 years, new standards were beginning to emerge. There had been the 1905 Revolution, there had been the Duma with its limited parliamentary powers, there had been the nine-month interval of freedom and even anarchy after the revolution in February 1917. The Communists themselves had seized power under the democratic slogan 'All power to the Soviets'; Stalin himself on the eve of launching his most atrocious purges in 1936 introduced 'the most democratic constitution in the world' guaranteeing almost every form of freedom; it fell still-born from the press. Therefore by his own standards, he is condemned as a tyrant. In the name of the withering away of the state, he created the most comprehensive and oppressive totalitarian state the world has ever seen; in the name of national self-determination, he suppressed great nations and practiced genocide on a scale unrivalled by any other tyrant except Hitler. In the name of peace, he waged war and clamped his Stalinist system on states with altogether different and more enlightened national traditions. In him the corrupting influence of power is very clearly evidenced.

Stalin, in fact, was a very great tyrant indeed. His successors have sought to attribute the abuses of his reign to his own vindictive, suspicious and paranoiac personality and to account for his tyranny by the euphemism 'cult of personality'. But an ideology based on the assumption of an infallible scientifically proved party line and supported by conspiratorial methods will naturally tend to give power to such a personality. The rule of his successor Khrushchev was in many respects tyrannical, by western standards, but by pragmatically ignoring some of those aspects of the ideology which tend to tyranny, by curbing the secret police, he moved towards legality – even if under oppressive laws – and away from arbitrary power. He cannot, therefore, be described as a tyrant; in fact he would not have fallen from power as he did, if he had been so.

One final example of a modern autocrat who was not in terms of our definition a tyrant is Kemal Atatürk the father of modern Turkey. Succeeding to a long line of Oriental despots, his rule was as could be expected harsh and arbitrary; but he attempted by organizing an opposition party to introduce some degree of constitutional government; although he failed in this during his lifetime, he had a certain posthumous success. In the light of Kemal Atatürk's case, one is tempted to say: 'Call no man a tyrant until he is dead', but since the great object of our inquiry is to detect the symptoms of tyranny at an early stage, this safe course is hardly open to us.

3. The Conditions of Tyranny

The great tyrants have generally emerged in circumstances that appeared to make some form of autocracy inevitable. What then are the conditions which make for tyranny?

To answer this, we must study the great ages of tyranny. There are the two great waves of tyranny in Greece, in the seventh and sixth centuries B.C. and again, after the Peloponnesian War, in the fourth century B.C., there are the last days of the Roman Republic from which arose the tyrannies of the Roman Empire, there are the Renaissance despotisms and absolute monarchies which followed the decline of medieval feudal society; finally there is the French Revolution and the rise of Napoleon, the prototype of the nationalist and communist dictatorships of our time, which have followed on the decline of ancient dynasties and empires. There have of course been a number of isolated tyrannies in the intervals of these great waves, so that one may say that tyranny is endemic in the Western world.

The Greek tyrannies offer a particularly fruitful field of study. Just as the geneticist studies heredity in fruit flies because there are so many of them and they breed so rapidly, so the student of politics naturally turns to the Greek city states, because they were so numerous and because they passed with such speed through many stages of evolution. In its political development ancient Greece resembles one of those speeded up nature films in which the growth of weeks is compressed into minutes; the political tempo of our own age is similar. Further these events were analysed by some of the earliest and shrewdest political thinkers, in the shape of Thucydides, Aristotle and Plato. A final advantage is that the conditions in these tiny city states where everyone was in touch with everyone else and there was direct contact between ruler and ruled, approximate in many ways to contemporary conditions in the great modern states where radio and television and rapid communications and transport have brought people into closer contact than was possible in most of the intervening generations.

The limitation of this field of study is that we lack written contemporary records of the first wave of tyranny in the seventh and sixth centuries B.C., and either have to view it through the eyes of writers two centuries later who sometimes project back their experience of later tyranny, or to reconstruct the conditions from archaeological evidence. There is no agreement about the root causes of this first epidemic of tyranny; to mention only two theories, it has been attributed to the introduction of the coinage, which caused a great economic upheaval and put great power in the hands of those who knew how to exploit it; for example, Pheidon of Argos the first tyrant of mainland Greece has been credited – somewhat speculatively – with the introduction of the coinage. Secondly he is also said to have been the first ruler to use the hoplites, the heavily armed infantry who transformed warfare from the individualistic free-for-all between champions described by Homer. It is quite possible that some of the tyrants may have owed their power to realizing the potentialities of this new form of warfare. However it is probably wrong to be as specific as this about the causes; suffice it to say that it was an age of rapid development and social upheaval which saw the end of the hereditary tribal kingdoms described by Homer and the pastoral and peasant society of Hesiod. An aristocratic tribal system was giving way to the class structure of the city state or *polis*. Commerce was expanding and producing a new class of rich and powerful men to rival the hereditary chiefs and landowners. The economic upheavals attending the introduction of the coinage had harnessed the peasants with a load of debt which was one of the main problems of the time and a grievance which the would-be tyrant could exploit. Population was growing rapidly with the result that it was an age of Greek colonization both in Asia Minor and Sicily and Southern Italy. Commerce and colonization brought the leading men into contact with the kingdoms of the East; the intimate connection between Western tyranny and Oriental despotism which is to recur again and again in history originated in this early age. Periander the tyrant of Corinth in the early seventh century, who is said by Aristotle to have originated most of the safeguards by which tyrants maintain their power, names his nephew and successor Psammetichus presumably in honour of the contemporary King of Egypt and Herodotus relates that he sent 300 of his opponents to be made into eunuchs by Alyattes, King of Lydia.

Aristotle records that a great many of the devices of tyrants were learnt from the Persians, which is not surprising in view of the fact that the tyrants of Asia Minor were mostly more or less willing puppets of the Persian conqueror. Another issue which somewhat unexpectedly emerges as a factor in tyranny at this early stage is that of race. Most of the Greek states were of mixed origin consisting both of the conquerors and of suppressed aboriginals and previous invaders. At the beginning of the sixth century we find Cleisthenes of Sicyon launching a campaign against the Dorians – the last wave of conquerors – whose clans he calls Pigmen, Assmen and Swinemen, while his own clan is named Archelaoi or 'leaders of the people', or perhaps not too fancifully 'master-race'.

In fact, we may say that a good many of the conditions which contributed to this first epidemic of tyranny have also attended subsequent epidemics. There was the breakdown of an old social structure, with all the grievances and insecurity that attend it, the emergence of new classes, the contrast between new wealth and the increasing impoverishment of the peasants, and that class war which was to become endemic in the Greek city-state.

However, in this earliest wave of tyranny there was one current lacking that was to sweep all before it in the later floods – that of war. The earlier tyrants do not appear to have emerged as a result of defeat in war, or in response to an external threat, although this was perhaps one of the causes of the tyrannies of Asia Minor, nor were they great warriors themselves – apart from that most successful pirate, Polycrates of Samos. But this factor of war was decisive in the second wave of tyranny which swept across Sicily in the fifth century B.C. and across the rest of the Greek world in the fourth century.

Military tyranny in the Western world had its origin in Sicily, which the historian Orosius describes as 'the mother of tyrants'. This outpost of Greek colonization had to resist invasion both from Africa and Italy – from the Carthaginians and the Etruscans. The tyrant Gelon of Gela early in the fifth century defeated the Carthaginians at Himera and banished them from the island for seventy years, gaining control of half of it himself. His successor Hieron, celebrated in the Odes of Pindar, defeated the Estruscans in the battle of Cumae. The Carthaginians came back again at the end of the century and were driven out by Dionysius, the tyrant of Syracuse. These Syracusan tyrants have a special importance, because, as we shall see, in their technique for the seizure of power they deeply coloured the thought of the greatest of the Greek thinkers on tyranny, Plato, and also foreshadowed greater tyrants who were to come, such as Augustus and Napoleon.

The greatest tyrants have in fact owed their positions to two conditions, war and class war. Both were combined in the Peloponnesian War, which while it was a contest between the Athenians and the Lacedaemonians for the domination of the Hellenic world also took on the character of an ideological or class struggle. Thucydides makes clear the significance of this, when he describes the terrible *stasis* or civil war which broke out in the island of Corcyra in 427 B.C.:

So bloody was the march of the revolution, and the impression which it made was the greater as it was one of the first to occur. Later on, one may say, the whole Hellenic world was convulsed, struggles being everywhere made by the popular leaders to bring in the Athenians and by the oligarchs to introduce the Lacedaemonians. In peace there would have been neither the pretext nor the wish to make such an invitation, but in war, with an alliance always at the command of either faction for the hurt of their adversaries and their own corresponding advantage, opportunities for bringing in the foreigner were never wanting. Revolution thus ran its course from city to city, and the places which it arrived at last, from having heard what had been done before, carried to a still greater excess the refinement of their inventions, as manifested in the cunning of their enterprises and the atrocity of their reprisals. Words had to change their ordinary meaning and take that which was now given them. Reckless audacity came to be considered the courage of a loyal ally; prudent hesitation, specious cowardice; moderation was held to be a cloak for unmanliness; ability to see all sides of a question inaptness to act on any. Frantic violence became the attribute of manliness. . . . The advocate of extreme measures was always trustworthy; his opponent a man to be suspected. . . . The cause of all these evils was the lust for power arising from greed and ambition; and from these passions proceeded the violence of parties once engaged in contention. The leaders in the cities each provided with the fairest professions, on the one side with the cry of political equality, on the other of a moderate aristocracy, sought prizes for themselves in those public interests which they pretended to cherish and, recoiling from no means in their struggle for ascendancy, engaged in the direst excesses. . . . Meanwhile the moderate part of the citizens perished between the two, either for not joining in the quarrel or because envy would not suffer them to escape. Thus every form of iniquity took root in the Hellenic countries by reason of the troubles. The ancient simplicity into which honour so largely entered was laughed down and disappeared; and society became divided into camps in which no man could trust his fellow . . .

Thucydides thus describes a combination of international and civil war that has become familiar enough in our time, which often results in tyranny either of the conservative type if the ruling classes support a leader to defend their power and property against the people (e.g. General Franco), or of the radical type if the rebels defeat the governing class (e.g. Fidel Castro). War and civil war were attended as Thucydides made clear by a collapse of traditional moral standards and religious beliefs. This age also saw for the first time the rise of the intelligentsia as a revolutionary class. The Sophists with their conflicting doctrines undermined the confidence of the young in traditional standards and replaced them with a nihilistic lack of principle; many of them made considerable fortunes in the process. It was they who evolved the ideology of Tyranny ('justice is the advantage of the stronger') as expounded by Thrasymachus in Plato's *Republic*. Of course there were a number of thinkers from Thucydides down to Aristotle who diagnosed the other disease and suggested remedies. In general they dealt with yesterday's disease and ignored today's. They examined the defects in the class structure and relations between the citizens of the *polis* or city-state, but ignored the fact that from 430 B.C. onwards their mortal error was their inability to live together in peace or to combine for any great purpose.

Thus the example of Greece presents another of the conditions of tyranny: namely the imperious necessity of unity either in a common culture or a common nation and the inability to achieve it by consent and agreement. Curiously the great Greek political philosophers and historians never seem to have addressed themselves to this problem, while orators and politicians like Demosthenes and Isocrates did, but too late. When such strife and incurable disunity arises, a nation or a society becomes an easy prey for a tyrant from within or a conqueror from without. So it was that the Hellenic world fell a prey to the half-foreign tyranny of Philip of Macedon and his great son Alexander.

Many of these conditions arose again in Rome of the first century B.C., but for different reasons. Whereas defeat in war and the loss of Empire is a common enough cause of tyranny, the people seeking a leader in their humiliation and insecurity, it was a series of victories which had brought her a great Empire that paved the way for tyranny in Rome. Suddenly a small city-state based on a peasant economy and ruled by an exclusive conservative aristocracy found itself, by the prowess of its arms, the ruler of half the world. The rigid social structure and strict traditional morals cracked under the strain. Some of the rich grew richer, others ran into debt, while a new wealthy class emerged and the poor grew poorer; the spread of the great farms or latifundia, based on slave labour, the competition of cheap foreign corn imported from the Empire, drove the peasants from the land, and filled Rome with an unemployed proletariat. Flooded with slaves from the Eastern and Hellenistic world as 'the Orontes flowed into the Tiber', Rome rapidly ceased to respect the simple rustic virtues, though still paying lip-service to them. Annually elected magistrates without any permanent civil servants were clearly quite unable to govern a great Empire.

At the end of the second century B.C. the Gracchi, Rome's only democratic reformers, tried to solve the problem in terms of the philosophy of the Greek city-state. But even if they had triumphed it is clear that the Roman city proletariat would no more have been able to rule a great Empire than the narrow minded oligarchy which defeated it. Rome required a war to absorb the people of Italy into its citizenship, while the provinces became means of personal enrichment and power for Roman grandees. Even tyranny in Rome could not be contained in the framework of the city-state; this was illustrated by the conspiracy of Catiline, a destitute aristocrat who tried to seize power with gladiators as mercenaries, with the help of aggrieved Italian subjects of Rome, and by enlisting the support of other impoverished aristocrats with promises of a cancellation of debts. Even if his plot had succeeded and he had been able to terrorize the Senate by mass murder, Catiline would certainly have been swept away by the return of Pompey's legions from the East. The power in fact no longer resided in Rome. It might be necessary to bribe and terrorize the urban proletariat, through the agency of such aristocratic bravos and gang leaders as Milo and Clodius, in order to secure the election of the right people; but the powers behind these urban gangsters were the great commanders of the legions in the provinces. Rome by herself, with her traditional regard for law and constitutional practice, might well have avoided tyranny; but Rome, as the head and conqueror of a great Empire, was ripe for civil war and military despotism.

The disorders which spread throughout the civilized world, the misery, the instability, the terror, gave rise to another phenomenon which was to arise in other times of trouble and to presage other tyrannies, namely to the frantic desire for and expectation of a Messianic saviour and a new Golden Age. This passionate desire to escape found classic expression in Virgil's Fourth Eclogue in which he prophesied the birth of a child who would inaugurate a new era of peace and felicity. Various suggestions have been made about the subject of this prophecy, which was naturally enough interpreted by the early Christians as a reference to the birth of their Saviour. What is certain is that the prophecy reflects a widespread longing and expectation during an interval in the civil wars before the last act which was to bring Augustus to absolute power. In his propaganda the Emperor was able to exploit this longing for peace and 'the Golden Age'. But it would be an exaggeration to say that these apocalyptic expectations played an essential part in the Emperor's seizure of power; they formed rather part of the climate of opinion suitable to tyranny.

However, the centre of apocalyptic thinking at that time was not in Rome but in Palestine, where the visions of the end of the world which appeared over the two centuries around the birth of Our Lord, ranging from the Book of Daniel (second century B.C.) to the great Christian Apocalypse of the Book of the Revelation (first century A.D.) were to have a profound effect on the ideological and social background of several future tyrannies. These visions arose in a time of troubles for Israel, when the nation was struggling against foreign conquerors and finally succumbing to them. The Book of Daniel was probably written in the heroic period of the wars of liberation of the Maccabees. The author projects back his vision to another time of troubles, the captivity in Babylon four centuries before. In some respects therefore it is a prophecy after the event and this is a characteristic of other apocalypses which are often pseudonymously attributed to historical or mythical figures of the past. They attempt to place the existing age in the pattern of history and to explain and give purpose to the sufferings of the present time. The references to history are generally couched in obscure and allegorical language, no clear distinction being made between the spiritual and physical world. In the climax, there arises some Great Beast or Anti-Christ, whose coming heralds the end of time and the advent of the Golden Age. This is initiated by a struggle between the forces of Good and the forces of Evil which is decided by the appearance of a Deliverer who will bring an age of peace and felicity to the chosen people or saints and death and damnation to the enemy.

These apocalyptic expectations arose in conditions of insecurity and desperation, foreign tyranny and the struggle against it, and the clash of cultures. They contained elements of Babylonian and Zoroastrian thought which were combined with Judaism in a revolt against the dominating Hellenistic-Roman culture. Their appeal was to the oppressed who were assured of their historic destiny, of a divinely ordained victory and of a glorious reward for their present sufferings. The obscure and mystifying language and symbolism of these apocalyptic visions was part of their attraction. Those who understood them correctly were an *élite* with a secret knowledge which gave them the key to salvation, a sense of superiority over those who appeared more prosperous and powerful, and the right to use every means to overcome their opponents; indeed to bring about the millennium any crime is justified and even becomes a virtue. While it is impossible to assess the precise importance of these apocalyptic movements, they profoundly affected the Jewish consciousness in the decades around the birth of Christ. The Dead Sea Scrolls indicate in the monastic community of Qumran the belief in an apocalyptic struggle between the Sons of Light and the Sons of Darkness. The gospels, St Paul's earlier epistles, and finally the Book of the Revelation reflect the visionary expectation of the end of things among the early Christians. Among them this expectation did not emerge in political action, although it is a plausible explanation of Judas Iscariot's betrayal that he wished Jesus to put himself at the head of a national liberation movement against the Romans and their puppets, was disappointed at his failure to do so, and hoped to force his master's hand. Be that as it may, others gave these eschatological visions a political content and in the disorders and assassinations which preceded the final revolt and the destruction of Jerusalem the Messianic expectations played a considerable part.

It cannot be said that this eschatological vision, when it first appeared, became a cause of tyranny. In so far as it was a political factor it took rather the form of a revolt against tyrannical and alien rule. But it arose from the conditions that do produce a certain type of tyranny – the total alienation of fanatical bodies of men from the society in which they live, their belief that their opponents are utterly evil and to be exterminated if they stand in the way of the divinely ordained salvation of the world, their conviction that they alone hold the key to salvation. Such men will be ready to follow any leader whom they take to be the deliverer destined to sweep away the evil and corrupt society in which they live and to make all things new. For such supremely righteous ends, all means are justified; the evils which are condemned in the enemy become virtues in the chosen people and their infallible leader.

Since such millennial fervour has been a recurring feature of ages of revolution and tyranny it may be convenient here to break chronological sequence and to trace its development and influence down to the present day. In normal and settled times it may exhibit itself in small and fanatical sects of little significance. Often it pursues a kingdom which is not of this world. That is why Marx condemned religion as 'the opium of the people' because it diverted the revolutionary longings of the oppressed and alienated towards other-worldly goals. But in times of trouble these religious fervours can become a political factor to be exploited by fanatical or unscrupulous leaders.

No one would accuse the saintly Abbot Joachim of Fiore of tyrannical or violently revolutionary intentions. Yet his prophetic system is described by Professor Norman Cohn in his fascinating study of the chiliastic movements of the Middle Ages, the *Pursuit of the Millennium*, as 'the most influential one known to Europe until the appearance of Marxism'. Joachim's prophetic vision vouchsafed at the end of the twelfth century was spread through Europe by wandering friars during the thirteenth century. It was a trinitarian doctrine which divided human history into three equal ages, the age of the Father in the Old Testament, the age of the Son from the birth of Christ to the thirteenth century, and the age of the Holy Ghost fated to begin in 1260 A.D., and to be initiated by a struggle between the Great Beast or Anti-Christ and a New Leader or Deliverer.

Abbot Joachim's prophecy fell on well-prepared soil, particularly in the Lombard plain and the cities of North Italy and of the Rhineland and Flanders. These were the 'boom' areas of the Middle Ages. The more settled times which had followed the invasions and migrations of the Dark Ages had led, on the one hand, to a rapid growth in population, which could not be contained in the rustic and peasant communities of the feudal world; on the other hand, to an increasingly flourishing trade, to the growth of banking which overcame the Church's ban on usury, and to an increasingly sophisticated urban economy. As a result, a growing landless, uprooted proletariat found itself confronted with an increasingly prosperous new class of traders, bankers and master craftsmen, whose wealth was shared by the Church. These were new inequalities and they gave rise to a new social consciousness which is perhaps most briefly summed up in the jingle associated with John Ball the leader of the English Peasants' Revolt,

> When Adam delved and Eve span
> Who was then a gentleman?

This expresses the yearning for a return to the Garden of Eden or the Golden Age in which all men were equal, and all earned their living by the sweat of their brow and all were at peace. The yearning for peace was natural since social upheaval was accompanied by war and class war, particularly in Northern Italy.

The strife and inequality were at odds with the Christian teaching of peace and the exaltation of the humble and meek. The great gap between the Church's preaching and practice naturally made the biggest impression on those who were educated in the Church but failed – whether through inadequacy or idealism – to secure a share in ecclesiastical wealth. These disgruntled and sometimes half-educated intelectuals – poor friars or failed priests – often supplied the prophets and leaders of the millennial sects which proliferated in these times. Thus the peace and penance movement known as 'the Great Hallelujah' which swept northern Italy in A.D. 1233 was led by Franciscans, Minorites and Dominicans preaching that the Golden Age of peace was at hand; as a contemporary chronicler put it: 'All were drunk with heavenly love, for they had quaffed the wine of the Spirit of God after tasting which all flesh begins to rave.' Leading great crowds of penitents, mendicant friars seized power in some cities, for example Brother Gerard in Parma and the Dominican Brother John in Verona where he deposed the nominee of the Emperor Frederick II, the monstrous Ezzelino. However the success was shortlived; four days after 400,000 North Italians had gathered round Brother John at Paquera to swear a pact of eternal peace, war broke out again and Brother John was thrown into gaol.

One cannot, of course, blame these eschatological movements which continued and reached their climax in the mass Flagellants' movement of 1269, the year for which Joachim had forecast the New Age, for the tyrannies that were to arise in Northern Italy during the next three centuries. Indeed they sometimes struggled against tyrants. However they did contribute towards the kind of situation that could be exploited by a really great despot, and such a one had indeed arisen in the shape of Frederick II Hohenstaufen. How far Frederick believed in his prophetic mission to bring about a golden age of justice and peace or how far he deliberately exploited the myth that arose around him, it is hard to say. Pope Gregory IX attacked him as the anti-Christ, the Great Beast, rising from the sea to blaspheme the Holy Name, and to trample the world to fragments and to batter down the Catholic faith; 'Behold,' he declared, 'the head and body and tail of the beast, Frederick, the so-called Emperor'. Frederick responded in the same apocalyptic tone, 'Lift up your eyes, prick up your ears, O ye children of men!' says his first manifesto. 'Mourn for the woe of the world, the discord of peoples, the exile of justice, since the abomination of Babylon goeth forth from the elders of the people.... Thou who as Shepherd of the sheep preachest poverty according to the commandments of Christ, why dost thou so diligently flee the poverty which thou commendest?' This was a popular accusation, appealing to the widespread indignation against the wealth and worldliness of the Church and the Papacy; among many of the millennial sects, as later among Protestants, the Pope came to be regarded as the whore of Babylon, the Anti-Christ and as such Frederick accused him of being 'a Prince among the Princes of Darkness'.

Frederick therefore exploited the widespread millennial longings against the Pope, with some success, it would seem, since for hundreds of years after his death the great Emperor was expected in Sicily and Italy but even more in Germany to return from the mountain fastness where he was hiding and to usher in the New Age, establishing the reign of justice, chastising the Church and leading the people of Christ into the new Jerusalem. But while exploiting these millennial longings Frederick persecuted those who shared them as heretics, thus running with the hares and hunting with the hounds, a common enough treatment of revolutionary movements by tyrants.

Again and again through the late Middle Ages in times of stress and social upheaval these religious revolutionary movements recur with their mixture of religious fervour and social revolt. There were the great Flagellant processions at the time when the Black Death swept Europe in 1348–9 naturally arousing expectations that the millennium was at hand. In the next century the Taborites – the fanatical revolutionary wing of the Hussite movement of religious reform – took control of the town of Usti in Bohemia and there set up a rule of saints with a system of primitive Communism. A century later in Thuringia, Thomas Müntzer, a learned contemporary of Luther (who attacked him with great vigour) preached the coming of the Millennium, forming a League of the Elect to initiate it and played a leading part in the great Peasants' Revolt in his own local area. A few years later in 1534 revolutionary Anabaptists seized control of the city of Münster in Westphalia. They were led by Jan Bockelsen of Leyden, who preached that the end of the world was at hand and that Münster would be saved as the New Jerusalem. Withstanding a year's siege by the Prince Bishop of Münster, John of Leyden introduced his kingdom of Saints with himself as Messiah. He rapidly proceeded from primitive communism and egalitarianism to extreme luxury at his court, which contrasted strongly with the poverty and starvation of the people, from sexual puritanism to polygamy and promiscuity, from libertarianism to the extremes of sadistic terror; he personally inflicted the death penalty for the most trivial offences. When the besieging forces recaptured Münster, John of Leyden's fate was as atrocious as his rule. He was led around in chains for public execration and finally publicly tortured to death. His main claim to fame was that he was one of the very few fanatical leaders who had the power to act out the bloodthirsty fantasies of the final struggle and to set up the 'millennial Kingdom' – the thousand-year Reich – even if it lasted for less than a year. Millennial sects again played an important part in the English Civil War. The Levellers and Ranters were descendants of these religious radical movements and the Fifth Monarchy men under General Harrison were a strong party in Cromwell's Barebones Parliament, that short-lived Rule of Saints. They believed that Cromwell's rule was the Fifth Empire prophesied in the book of Daniel, destined to succeed the Assyrian, Persian, Greek and Roman Empires and usher in the Millennium. One would scarcely expect Cromwell's pragmatical mind to be impressed by such fantasies. However he was not uninfluenced by them and was himself speaking the language of the millennialists when he said: 'We know who they are that shall war with the Lamb against his enemies; they shall be a people called and chosen and faithful. Indeed I do think somewhat is at the door. We are at the threshold...' This cloudy apocalyptic language, however, gave way to hard common sense when the extremists tried to put their visions into practice by ending the common law and substituting the code of Moses. Cromwell dissolved the Barebone's Parliament to the bitter disappointment of the sectaries, who came to regard him as the Prince of Darkness, the Anti-Christ who must be overcome before the millennium could be initiated.

This was the last time, if we exclude Brigham Young and the Mormons in the nineteenth century, that such sectaries played any significant part in the politics of the Western World. From the eighteenth century onwards fanaticism became secularized. However, significantly such cults have had a spectacular revival in the colonial and newly independent countries in our century.

Fanatical sects of this kind have developed in rich profusion and variety during the past century in many parts of the world. In the Congo the Messianic cult founded by the prophets Simon Kimbangu and André Matswa won a great following. Similar movements have developed in South Africa, in Kenya, Nyasaland and Nigeria. The Peyote cult among the North American Indians promises salvation and renewal. A wide variety of prophetic cults have developed among the Indians of Latin America. In Jamaica the Ras Tafari cult offers an earthly type of salvation in the form of a return to the promised land of Ethiopia. Among the Melanesian islanders the Cargo cults have arisen which involve a belief in the return of the dead with rich cargoes of food and goods to bring salvation and plenty. Numerous other prophetic cults, in Australia and New Zealand, in Polynesia and Indonesia, in Vietnam and Japan are described by Vittorio Lanternari in his book *The Religions of the Oppressed*.

In all their rich variety, whether they spring from Christianity, from Paganism, from Buddhism, from the Mahdist movement of Islam, or as is most usual from a combination of two or more of these, they have certain characteristics in common. They spring from a clash of cultures, the impact of Western civilization on a native society struggling to maintain or reassert its identity. The destruction of the old way of life and the mixture of fear, envy and disgust at the new, produces a sense of extreme insecurity which expresses itself in a craving for certainty, regeneration and salvation. New beliefs from the New and Old Testament are grafted on to the old culture, Christ and Jehovah take on the characteristics of the African Supreme Being or the American Indian Great Spirit. The prophets of the sects are often missionary trained (just as the prophets of the medieval cults were often priests or failed priests), but often at the same time hostile to the missionaries as bearers of alien creeds. To the sectaries these movements bring a new confidence, a sense of superiority over their oppressors, a belief in their own absolute rightness and the absolute wrongness of their opponents which is only confirmed by persecution, a conviction that has for example displayed itself in the Congo that they are immune to the white man's bullets. Before the development of fully fledged national independence movements these sects sometimes play a political role, as did the Kimbangu cult in the Congo and Hoa Hoa and Cao Dai in Indo-China and of course in a different way the Mau-Mau in Kenya. When independence comes the fanatic devotion aroused by the prophet is often transferred to the national leader, who becomes the Redeemer leading his people into the Promised Land; all opposition to him becomes deadly sin to be exterminated, all the failings of the millennial state of independence are attributed to the enemy, to the anti-Christ of neo-Colonialism. This is the psychological background for tyranny; since the new leaders very often come from similar origins to the prophets of the sects, from the minority of mission-trained new intelligentsia, they understand this psychology and often share the same fanatical convictions themselves;

thus the temptation to move through one party dictatorship to tyranny is extremely strong.

The importance of these millennial sects from the Middle Ages onwards is that they demonstrate in simple form the extreme revolutionary psychology and, as Professor Norman Cohn has pointed out, they foreshadow the mass totalitarian movements of our time. Thus leaders regard themselves as an *élite* destined to lead their people into the Millennium, whether it be Hitler's Thousand Year Reich or the Communist classless society; they are to achieve this in a bloody struggle against the enemy, the Anti-Christ, who must be exterminated by all means however atrocious, as in Hitler's Final Solution against the Jews and the Communists' class struggle against the bourgeoisie. The Leader is the sole repository of divine wisdom and inspiration, the sole interpreter of the Party line, and the sole object of a quasi-religious devotion. The followers have faith in the Leader's infallibility; they give him blind obedience. In return they have the consciousness of being the Elect who are set apart from and above other men by their esoteric knowledge and faith. This releases them from the ordinary restraints of morality; violence and deception become virtues in the good cause. The appeal is to a dispossessed and insecure urban or rural proletariat; and the leadership is provided by the priests, friars and failed priests – the equivalent of the alientated intellectuals who play a great part in the leadership of modern totalitarian parties – who make their appeal by denouncing the very real abuses of their time.

The parallel could be carried further; but it is enough to say now, that in modern secular society such quasi-religious fanaticism – or an artificially imposed and stimulated imitation of it – forms the basis of the radical type of tyranny, the kind of tyranny which tends to follow the collapse of dynasties and empires.

However, to return to our chronological sequence, under the Roman Empire (when these messianic movements first appeared) it was force or arms that settled the issue; and the Roman Empire has supplied the model for military despotisms ever since. Where power is directly dependent on military force tyranny tends to become endemic. As Machiavelli put it :

> Whereas in other principalities the ambitions of the nobles and the insolence of the people only have to be contended with, the Roman Emperors had a third difficulty in having to put up with the cruelty and avarice of their soldiers, a matter so beset with difficulties that it was the ruin of many; for it was a hard thing to give satisfaction both to soldiers and people; because the people loved peace and for this reason they loved the unaspiring prince, whilst the soldiers loved the warlike prince who was bold, cruel and rapacious, which qualities they were quite willing he should exercise, so that they could get double pay and give vent to their greed and cruelty.

The authority and prestige of an Augustus or a Hadrian might for a time keep the Legions and the Praetorian Guard under control. But even during such intervals of peace as the Antonine Age no effective tradition of subordination of the military to the civil power was established.

The despotisms of the Renaissance were also largely military in character. Their ancestor, Frederick II Hohenstaufen, was engaged in more or less continuous warfare against the Lombard states or against the Pope; he surrounded himself with a Praetorian Guard of Saracens, loyal only to his person. His method of rule was passed down through his lieutenant Ezzelino to the later Italian despots. Sometimes they were themselves *condottieri* who had usurped power; normally they employed mercenaries to maintain their rule. Indeed the continuous warfare and civil strife between the Guelphs and the Ghibellines, the Papal and Imperial parties, which embroiled state with state, and split cities and families into warring factions, was the natural soil for tyranny. These divisions were to lead in the end as in the case of the Greek city-states to domination by a foreign conqueror. Besides, the old feudal forms of society had broken down more rapidly in Italy than elsewhere in Europe. The rise of a mercantile middle class and plutocracy had brought new wealth, but also a strong contrast between the ostentatious splendour of the grandees and the general poverty of the people.

Such drastic social changes normally bring with them a general sense of insecurity and collapse of traditional moral standards such as helped usurpers to power in the previous epochs of tyranny. But in Renaissance Italy there were two special factors at work – the decay of the Church and the rediscovery of classical antiquity. Ecclesiastical abuses, the misspent wealth of the Church, the luxury and immorality of clergy and monks, the shameless sale of indulgences, the nepotism and simony of the prelates, the degradation of the Papacy to an instrument of secular power, all these features which led to the Reformation in Germany and elsewhere in Europe had a vastly different effect in Italy. The Church, in fact, and many of the Popes acted tyrannically in the sense of 'exercising arbitrary power beyond the scope permitted by the laws, customs and standards of that time and society'; and tyranny breeds tyranny. The Papacy became the object or the instrument of political struggle, squandering its spiritual authority in a fight for secular power which reached its climax nearly three centuries later under the Borgia Pope, Alexander VI. He and his terrible son Cesare Borgia even exceeded the very lax standards of their time in murder, simony and corruption, not only in putting down the petty despots of the Papal states and the Roman factions of the Orsini and Colonna which had bullied successive Popes, but also in removing anyone who might limit them in the unbridled exercise of power.

The effect on those who saw the process at close quarters can be seen from the remarks of the historian Guicciardini who wrote in 1529:

No man is more disgusted than I am with the ambition, the avarice, and the profligacy of the priests, not only because each of these vices is hateful in itself, but because each and all of them are most unbecoming in those who declare themselves to be men in special relation with God, and also because they are vices so opposed to each other that they can only co-exist in very singular natures. Nevertheless my position at the court of several Popes forced me to desire their greatness for the sake of my own interest. But, had it not been for this, I should have loved Martin Luther as myself, not in order to free myself from the laws which Christianity, as generally understood and explained, lays upon us, but in order to see this swarm of scoundrels put back into their proper place, so that they may be forced to live either without vices or without power.

It is not surprising that many, unlike Guicciardini, saw these abuses as an occasion to free themselves from the 'laws of Christianity'. An alternative system of values lay ready to hand in the newly discovered classical authors. The result of this clash of cultures was, at the highest level, the thought of humanists, at the lowest level, the crimes of the Borgias, and ultimately an entirely new conception of man and the state. The profusion of tyrannies in Renaissance Italy is the other side of the coin to the marvellous flowering of the arts and sciences. Since the traditional forms of authority, succession and the legitimation of rulers had broken down, nearly every ruler was in some sense a usurper or had to act as such. He had to live by his wits and win and exercise power by his own abilities. Governing became for the first time since the Roman Empire and the chaos which followed its collapse a career open to talents and no longer a hereditary closed shop. On all sides men were taking advantage of the collapse of standards and institutions to develop a greater and more complete individuality than was possible in the traditional and corporate framework of the feudal and ecclesiastical system of the Middle Ages. The princes were those who were able to develop their individuality in the richest – and sometimes the most atrocious – variety. In the prevailing state of anarchy and lawlessness, all restraints were thrown off and some despots became indistinguishable from bandits. Whereas in the rest of Europe, which was also passing through a revolutionary period, the tyrants tended to be hereditary rulers who, while exceeding their traditional rights and prerogatives, were still subject to some traditional restraints, at least paying lip-service to religious and moral standards, the Italian despots owed allegiance to no power in heaven or on earth. The state became the canvas on which the ruler painted his self-portrait; his subjects were the raw material on which he worked according to his individual whim; the subjects owed no allegiance or loyalty to the ruler, who maintained himself only by force and fraud and was constantly exposed to the force and fraud of others. Hobbes's state of nature – 'A perpetual struggle of all against all, and the life of man nasty, solitary, poor, brutish and short' – developed progressively from the thirteenth century onwards in Italy. This was the unpromising soil from which the modern secular state has grown.

The men of the Renaissance were no longer contented to govern and be governed in the traditional ways. The state came to be regarded as a field for experiment, as 'a work of art' as Burckhardt puts it. Machiavelli represents this view in an extreme form. In his *Prince* there is scarcely a word about the aims of government, only an empirical survey of the various means of gaining and maintaining power without regard to their moral value. He draws his examples from the ancient world and from his own time. He hoped that the House of Medici would learn from these examples; and in the experimental spirit of the age it was not an unrealistic hope.

This radical, experimental, aesthetic approach is one of the attitudes that has endeared tyrants to the intelligentsia. The despot may apply the intellectual's theories, may re-model the state, give it pattern and beauty; any traditional constitutional body of rulers is unlikely to do more than tidy up the muddle of customs and habits. Plato had perceived this eighteen centuries earlier; his *Republic* was certainly a work of art, and in his younger days he hoped that a despot might apply his theories, although he learnt better in later life. This intellectual, aesthetic approach to the state first appeared in the modern world at the time of the Italian Renaissance.

Above all the Renaissance gave man a new image of himself, no longer as a member of a divinely appointed corporate society bound by the duties of his station, but as an individual entitled to unlimited self-development untrammelled by re-

ligion or traditional social obligations, seeking only to exploit
his own abilities for his own honour and fame. There is no
need to emphasize the extraordinary achievements that resulted from this new conception of man in art and thought and
heroic virtue. But politically the results were disastrous. The
right to unlimited self-development was too often exercised
only by the ruler and his agents; the subjects became the means
of satisfying the needs of the ruler. There was nothing democratic about this Renaissance concept of man; the ruler had all
rights and powers; he owed it to his honour to treat his
subjects well; if he did not, they had no remedy except flight,
or tyrannicide; and the despot who was clever enough or
ruthless enough to avoid the plots against him was admired. In
Renaissance Italy a man might rise, by his skill as a *condottiere* or by some other means, to supreme power; but he would
be the exception to what was essentially an aristocratic concept
of rule. Ultimately this new Renaissance concept was, as it
were, institutionalized in the absolute monarchies of the sixteenth, seventeeth and eighteenth centuries, which had a
natural tendency to lapse into tyranny.

The next time that a new image or concept of man appeared
– at the time of the Enlightenment in the eighteenth century – it,
too, was to release great creative energies, but also to contribute to the political excesses of the French Revolution. Here it
is necessary to ask: why did the ideas of the *philosophes*
emerge in France and why did they have their most explosive
effects there?

France had long been subject to absolute monarchical rule,
but by the end of the eighteenth century the monarchy was
losing its grip and was even, in a somewhat half-hearted way,
trying to reform itself. However, as Tocqueville observed:
'The social order destroyed by a revolution is almost always
better than that which immediately precedes it, and experience
shows that the most dangerous moment for a bad government
is generally that in which it sets about reform.' And again:

It is not always by going from bad to worse that a society falls
into revolution. It happens most often that a people which has

supported without complaint, as if they were not felt, the most oppressive laws, violently throws them off as soon as their weight is lightened. ... Feudalism at the height of its power had not inspired Frenchman with as much hatred as it did on the eve of its disappearing. The slightest act of arbitrary power under Louis XVI seemed less easy to endure than all the despotism of Louis XIV.

Tocqueville's profound observation has been confirmed in the collapse of many an Empire and dynasty since his time; but the close analysis made by recent historians of the conditions of the French Revolution enables us perhaps to apply his maxim with more precision. It is true that in the second half of the eighteenth century economic conditions were generally improving in France, that the expanding mercantile and professional middle class was prospering, that the monarchy only rarely exercised arbitrary power and that there was certainly growing freedom of expression. On the other hand there were economic setbacks, too; the government had run deeply into debt as a result of the American War; there were recurrent grain shortages including a severe one in 1789. Further the weakening of the absolute monarchy had resulted in an increased usurpation of powers by the aristocracy, both in the revival of old feudal rights and extortions, and in the monopolizing of privileged positions to the exclusion of other classes; the Church enjoyed and abused great wealth and privileges. Thus rising expectations met with disappointing performance. There was furthermore a split in the ruling classes. When the Crown attempted to introduce long overdue taxation reforms, it was opposed by the land-owners in the Parlements and it was this division of the ruling classes that opened the door for the revolt of the third estate – the rising middle class, which was able to exploit the grievances of the petty bourgeoisie, the small tradesmen and craftsmen and proletariat of the cities – the *sans-culottes* – to its own advantage. But a revolutionary situation is not necessarily, although it is often, ripe for tyranny.

What were the conditions that led to the terror of Robespierre, which was the beginning of the new tyranny? There were three main causes, inflation, class war and war. The assignats with which the revolutionary government paid its way dwindled to about a quarter of their original value. The resulting economic chaos could only be met by increasingly severe measures. With the execution of the King the moderates who had sought some form of constitutional monarchy were squeezed out and the struggle against the aristocracy became an irreconcilable and lethal civil war. Finally foreign invasion drove the revolutionary leaders to extreme measures. Some form of dictatorship became inevitable. But these factors alone would not account for the phenomenon of the Revolution devouring its own children. The extra dimension of horror was due to the new view of man which Robespierre and Saint-Just derived from the *philosophes* of the Enlightenment, the idea of man noble, free and equal by nature but corrupted and distorted by the compulsions of society. It was only necessary to abolish the oppression of man by man, and the 'reign of virtue' would follow. When this did not happen, when black marketeers and profiteers defied the general will, when opponents disagreed with Robespierre about what was the virtuous course, these failings could not be attributed to the normal depravity and fallibility of human nature, but rather to the malevolence of men incurably corrupted by the old régime. The guillotine was the only remedy. Men must in Rousseau's ridiculous phrase, 'be forced to be free'. There could be no more apt recipe for tyranny than this attempt to have in one way what can only be had in another. Thus a brilliant paradox can become a terrible reality. But the role of ideology in tyranny deserves more detailed treatment at a later stage.

Robespierre saw the Reign of Terror as a sharp surgical operation which would bring in the Reign of Virtue. In fact operation followed operation until the patient was so weakened that he lent himself readily to the military régime of Napoleon. Robespierre and Saint-Just were themselves the victims of one of these operations. Their successors, men who had done well out of the Revolution, sought to re-establish security and to consolidate their gains. But facing risings both from the left and the right, and seeking to counteract domestic bankruptcy and inflation by foreign conquest and exploitation, they found themselves increasingly dependent on the army. The first instalment of tyranny under the Terror had removed most of the more prominent men and had made survival the main aim of the politician; thereby it spared Napoleon the necessity of blood letting which normally follows the seizure of despotic power. The Republic, weary of strife and craving peace, surrendered itself with enthusiasm to its greatest General who gave it nearly fifteen years of war. However without the impetus of revolutionary nationalism Napoleon's militaristic rule would not have been possible; in this sense Bonapartism was the first modern tyranny and the ancestor of many that were to follow.

Napoleon's rule also illustrates another of the conditions of tyranny. It grows most easily in soil prepared with the manure of absolutism. France having suffered both anarchy and terror, the liberals were able to put up only a token resistance (and to gain no popular support for it) when the First Consul reintroduced many of the characteristics of the *ancien régime*. The revolutionary decentralization of authority was rapidly replaced by centralization of the police, of justice and of administration and finance in the style of the Bourbon monarchy. Judges, mayors and above all prefects – the descendants of the Intendants or 'representatives on mission' of the monarchy – were all centrally appointed. While political prisoners were not very numerous by modern standards, they greatly outnumbered those imprisoned under Louis XVI. Bonaparte rapidly restored the hereditary principle and all the titles and trappings of a court. In particular he restored the hereditary principle in imposing members of his dynasty on conquered countries.

Tyranny, in fact, breeds tyranny. This was even more vividly illustrated in the next great revolutionary wave – in Russia in 1917. If we ask how it was that the revolutionary spring of February 1917 was nipped in the bud by the frost of October, the answer lies very deep in Russian history. By the beginning

of the twentieth century almost all the features of a classic
revolutionary situation were present in Russia. There was a
very rapid growth of population – an increase of fifty millions
in the twenty years before 1914. There was great mobility of
population and urbanization with all the insecurity that attends
its earlier stage. The urban population had increased from $3\frac{1}{2}$
million to $16\frac{1}{2}$ million in the second half of the nineteenth
century. The social upheaval that followed the abolition of
serfdom was still in progress; the benefits which the peasant
had hoped for from the emancipation had not ensued. To this
were added the hardships caused by the earliest stages of an industrial revolution, which were all the harder to bear because
they were attributed to foreign capital and management; class
bitterness was compounded by national resentment. On top of
all this came defeat in war. Plehve, the Minister of the Interior
in the early years of the century had said: 'What we need to hold
Russia back from revolution is a small victorious war.' What
Russia in fact got was humiliating defeat in the Russo-Japan-
ese war. In these circumstances the surprise is not that the
1905 rising occurred, but that it did not succeed and that
Tsarist autocracy survived for another dozen years. Indeed
with a little wisdom the revolution might have been avoided
altogether, such was the weakness of the forces supporting it.
Stolypin, the reforming minister, who probably did more for
the efficiency of Russian agriculture than anyone before or
since said: 'Give this state twenty years of quiet at home and
abroad and you will not recognize the Russia of that day.' It
was indeed one of those dangerous ages when a bad government sets out to reform itself, but the reform was half-hearted,
the right hand undoing what the left hand attempted to do.
Besides Stolypin's land reforms, industrialization proceeded
rapidly and there was a great expansion of education and
literacy. In twenty years the proportion of those at school rose
from one-fifth to one-half of the population, and the students
in universities from 15,000 to 35,000, while there were as many
as 90,000 in higher education. The universities had been
granted in 1905 an autonomy which permitted a certain free-

dom of speech and the Russian press was freer than at any time before or since. Further the Duma set up in 1905 supplied a means of enlisting the support of and giving political experience to moderate and reformist elements.

However the autocracy squandered all the benefits which it might have derived from these reforms. The Duma was constantly frustrated and rendered ineffective; the moderate reformist regional councils – the Zemstvos – were treated with suspicion and hostility; the liberals were driven into the arms of the extremists and revolutionaries; the growing class of intelligentsia was persecuted (somewhat inefficiently) and alienated until it became the classic example of a revolutionary intelligentsia. The secret police – the Okhrana – allied themselves to the most extreme right-wing reactionaries, making the Jews the scapegoats for the régime's shortcomings and persecuting them through the Black Hundreds. At the same time they infiltrated the revolutionary movements with spies and provocateurs. This reactionary policy in Russia itself was accompanied by the repression of the nationalities, the Poles and Ukrainians, in the name of Great Russian nationalism.

This was the arbitrary and traditional tyranny of the autocracy; it seems both mild and incompetent in comparison with the Bolshevik rule which was to succeed it, yet it must bear a large part of the responsibility for the rapid collapse of the Revolution into tyranny and the atrocious nature of the Communist tyranny. However it cannot be said that this stupid and reactionary rule was the precipitating cause of the revolution. But for the First World War the revolution, if it had taken place, would certainly have taken a very different form. The appalling slaughter and suffering of the war and the incompetence with which it was conducted sealed the fate of the Tsarist régime. The nature of the autocracy ensured that the moderate forces were not sufficiently numerous, vigorous or experienced to guide the revolution on a reformist path; nor could they rely on the support of the army which alone could have given them the strength to do so. The army was in dissolution and its command, even if it had given the Provisional

Government full support in 1917, could not rely on the loyalty of its troops. The split between the government and the army command, highlighted by the abortive Kornilov *coup* left no organized force capable of withstanding the Bolsheviks, the new type of disciplined conspiratorial party designed simply for the purpose of seizing power.

The condition, then, for the Bolshevik seizure of power was the total breakdown of all social institutions. The more thorough the collapse, the more likely it is that those most alienated from existing society will take over; and the greater the alienation of the rulers from existing society, the greater the necessity for tyranny. But the Bolsheviks, while rejecting Tsarist society root and branch, were the product of it. They might base themselves on the internationalist revolutionary doctrine of Marx and the traditions of the French Revolution and the Paris Commune, but they owed much in their party organization to the terrorist doctrines of Nechayev and Tkachev, which had grown up in conspiratorial opposition to Tsarist autocracy. Their party had been tempered in the struggle with the Tsarist Okhrana by which it was also deeply penetrated. The weapons of the Tsarist bureaucracy and the secret police lay to hand. The Bolsheviks picked them up to establish 'the dictatorship of the proletariat'. Lenin in his last years felt a certain uneasiness about this. Stalin, on the other hand, who had spent a lifetime in struggle against the machinery of Tsarist repression inside Russia, had no compunction in taking control of it and purging it of the inefficiency and ill-considered clemency which had allowed him to survive. In another respect too Stalin brought the revolution more in line with the new model tyranny. Lenin had been unique among modern dictators – apart from those imposed from outside – in not basing his revolution on a nationalist appeal. The Russian revolution was above all for him a means to world revolution; his appeal was to class rather than nation. Such a deviation from the norm was presumably only possible because the dissolution of Russian national society had gone so far that the aim of the great mass of the people had become survival rather than national self-respect; the slogans 'bread' and 'peace' were far more effective than any appeal to national pride. Stalin with his doctrine of 'Socialism in one country' and his appeal to patriotism in 'the great Patriotic War' returned to the nationalist norm. And subsequent Communist dictators who have come to power by their own efforts – such as Tito, Mao Tse-tung, and Castro – have relied largely on a nationalist appeal.

Indeed a sense of national humiliation is the most distinctive root of modern tyranny. Italy had won no glory in the First World War and the high expectations which attended victory were disappointed both on the national level in the peace treaties, and at the personal level. With the ending of allied help after the war, the demobilized troops faced unemployment; tens of thousands of deserters, outside the law, threatened the fabric of law and order; inflation was rampant; strike followed strike; the workers occupied the factories. For a moment, forming his Fascist party in 1919, Mussolini, in tune with his Socialist past, thought of playing the Leninist role and putting himself at the head of the revolutionary movement. But he quickly concluded that to play the nationalist card exploiting the Bolshevik threat and the weakness of the government would pay better. It did. Within three years he was in power.

Many of the traditional conditions for tyranny, therefore, existed in Italy in the early 1920s. However, there was one distinctive feature which gave the Fascist *coup* particular importance. It was the first time that a dictator had seized power in an industrialized modern state. It is true that the industrialization was still at a fairly early stage, and that Italy faced both the problems of the transition to mass urbanization and the contrast between the industrialized north and the underdeveloped south. But still it was in the industrialized north that Mussolini laid the foundations of his power. In doing so he pointed the way and set the example for the more terrible portent that was to follow in Germany, Hitler's seizure of

power in one of the most highly organized and firmly established industrial communities of the modern world.

In Germany, defeat in war, national humiliation, and a class
struggle which more than once verged on civil war, certainly
provided a familiar breeding ground for tyranny. The First
World War had demonstrated the failure of the old ruling
class, had robbed it of much of its power and self-confidence,
though not of its aspiration to rule, and had failed to supply
any solid substitute. The higher bourgeoisie was hopelessly entangled with the old ruling military caste and was in any case
mainly interested in its struggle with the working class organizations. These were divided between the Communists and the
Social Democrats, the latter being the only considerable section
of the population to show consistent loyalty to the Weimar
Republic, but a party unjustly compromised in Nationalist eyes
by its part in the surrender of 1918. The middle class had been
unable to assert itself as a political factor since the failure of
the liberal movement in Germany in 1848. In the 1920s when
it might have done so, its self-confidence and sense of security
was shattered by the great inflation. That middle section of the
population which, as Aristotle observed, has often acted as a
bulwark against tyranny, was fragmented and driven to extremes.

However, despite its inauspicious start the Weimar Republic
might still have survived had not the rising expectations and
prosperity of the later 1920s been destroyed by the Great Depression of 1929. Figures of unemployment rose from 1,320,000
in September 1929 to over six million at the beginning of 1933
when Hitler came to power and the social distress and embitter-
ment affecting the middle and lower middle classes as much as
the workers was even greater than these terrible figures indicate.
As the small men lost what little they had, the big capitalists,
the industrialists, the trusts and combines concentrated greater
power and property in their hands. Such experiences would be
enough to drive any nation to extreme measures, to dictatorship. Yet they are not sufficient to account for the monstrous
forms which the Nazi tyranny was to take.

To account for this, it is necessary to look further back in German history. Germany like Italy was a comparatively new nation. Hitler came to power only sixty-two years after the establishment of Bismarck's Reich. Germany had been unified not by any spontaneous popular uprising from below, but by conquest, diplomacy and dynastic arrangement. The resulting national morality was authoritarian, paternalistic, imposed from above on an admittedly willing people, who had not however developed by long practice the institutions and customs which make it easier for individuals and groups to act with independence, initiative and civil courage. When this imposed, externalized national morality collapsed under the impact of defeat, there remained only a chaos of conflicting standards, which, given time, tranquillity and habit, might have coalesced into a social morality with deep roots in the community. But the circumstances of the Weimar Republic did not encourage such a growth. The excesses, the cynicism, the satirical humour of Berlin in the 1920s and early 1930s would perhaps have been tolerable against a background of firmly based standards. As it was they gave rise to feelings of guilt and anxiety which opened people's ears to Hitler's appeal to *gesunde Volksempfindung*, the healthy feelings of the people, an appeal which was all the more effective because such healthy feelings scarcely existed. The room was swept and garnished for the devils of National Socialism to take possession. This perhaps helps to account for the still mysterious and admonitory portent that a highly civilized, complex and ordered society could succumb to perhaps the most nihilistic and destructive tyranny the world has ever seen.

Looking back at these conditions of tyranny as they have arisen down the ages it is easy to see that most of them exist in some form or other in one or another part of the world today. Nor is this surprising, since there are so many states in so many different stages of historical development side by side. There are new nations developing from tribalism as some of the earliest Greek tyrannies were. Many of them have institutions imposed externally with no deep roots among the people.

There is the disappointment of the exaggerated expectations raised by independence and the consequent sense of national humiliation. There is a worldwide population explosion, and mass movements of peasants into newly industrialized cities. There are the deepest contrasts of wealth and poverty both within nations and between nations, which are rendered all the more blatant by modern mass media of communication. Often a single party or the army emerges as the sole cohesive force in a society disorganized by the withdrawal of the colonial administration. There are the divisive forces inside nations and between nations seeking unity, which often seem to cry out for the dictator from within or the conqueror from without and in extreme cases lead to wars within or between the successor states of the great empires. In a world of rapid technological advance, there is chronic instability, and inflation, either creeping or galloping in many lands, leads to that constant sense of insecurity which sends men scurrying under the wings of father-figures, leaders or dictators, while the collapse of traditional moral standards and the conflict of values makes them crave the word of command.

Most nations show some of these symptoms; and some, suffering from them all, would seem to be ripe for tyranny. But the moment depends on the man. What kind of man must he be?

4. The Nurture of Tyrants

The young Hegel, returning from seeing Napoleon on the battlefield, is said to have remarked to his landlady: 'I have beheld the *Weltgeist* upon a white horse'; and indeed the great tyrant must sum up the spirit of his age, or at least some important aspects of it. Tyrants therefore will be as various in their nature as the ages in which they appear. However, as we have seen, one characteristic of every age of tyranny is a sense of insecurity. Therefore one would expect the tyrant to be at home in such an atmosphere from an early age; in many instances, this proves to be the case.

A psycho-analysis of the tyrant might often show a classic picture of revolt against the father (or absence or ineffectuality of the father) and predominant influence of the mother. To this insecure family background is added in many cases a certain social insecurity: for many of the great despots were 'men of the marches', coming from the borderland of the civilizations they were to dominate.

The great Alexander quarrelled with his father at an early age, was devoted to his mother Olympias, and when King Philip put her away in favour of another queen, mother and son were rumoured to have plotted the king's death. The fact that the young prince sprang from the alien culture of semi-barbarian Macedonia and found himself the lord of the highly civilized Greeks helps to account for the thirst for glory which led him from conquest to conquest, to deification and to an early death 'sighing for fresh worlds to conquer'.

The court of the Caesars might have been designed as a forcing house for monsters. Many of them lost their fathers in childhood, whether by murder or some other cause, and some were brought up by domineering Roman matrons who would stick at nothing to bring their sons to the purple. Gaius Caligula, the first actual lunatic to bestride the Roman Empire – although Tiberius seems to have suffered from that form of paranoia which often afflicts tryants in later life – was orphaned in childhood, saw his two brothers die young, murdered, so it was rumoured, by Tiberius and bore all this with a real or simulated indifference. Nero lost his father at the age of three, was brought up by his mother, the formidable Agrippina, for whom he was said to have nursed an illicit passion, though he later murdered her. Together with her son she was banished by her brother Caligula, later marrying her uncle the Emperor Claudius in order to secure the purple for Nero. In view of this kind of family background, no student of Freud should be surprised that – as Gibbon observes – 'Of the first fifteen Emperors, Claudius was the only one whose taste in love was entirely correct.' It is a tolerant judgement, for Claudius, as we have seen, contracted an incestuous union with his niece. Indeed some of the Emperors such as the formidably gluttonous Vitellius, who had the unenviable reputation of being a favourite at the courts of Tiberius, Caligula and Nero, presented all the symptoms which are nowadays commonly associated with an insecure and deprived childhood. It would be of little concern if this insecurity had affected merely their behaviour in bed and at table; but it had its repercussions in the court, the council chamber, the forum and the camp and sometimes shook the Empire.

Moving on to the Middle Ages, the childhood of Frederick II, *Stupor Mundi*, could not have been more insecure. His father Henry VI died when he was two years old; his mother Constance, who was suspected of poisoning her husband, died two years later. From the age of four the boy was alone, harried and persecuted by German feudal lords, finding his own education in the streets of Palermo, that city on the verge of the Europe which he was to rule, where the monuments and cultures of ancient Greece and Rome met and jostled those of Byzantium and Islam and of the Norman conquerors – an education which set him apart from the medieval world, and brought him to an early maturity. The transformation from his miserable, hunted childhood to the Imperial crown at the age of eighteen, gave him a sense of divine destiny. A similar insecurity of family background and fortune tended to be the lot of the Renaissance despots, the bastards, younger sons, wicked uncles, the sons of peasants turned *condottieri*, the bankers, all surviving by their wits in the struggle for power and yielding the stuff for romances and some of Shakespeare's plays. Those who have seen Eisenstein's great film, *Ivan the Terrible*, will remember the oppressive scenes of the orphan boy surrounded and intimidated in the narrow passages and vaulted chambers of the Kremlin by the arrogant and stupid Boyars, on whom he was to take a terrible revenge.

More modern tyrants also have sprung from a similar insecure background and have also appeared as, to some extent, 'outsiders' to those whom they were to dominate. As far as Napoleon is concerned, his family background was relatively normal. His father, able, volatile, but not a great family man, made little impression, compared with the formidable Madame Mère, the matriarch of the family. Throughout her life she spoke French with a Corsican accent, as did her great son. He, indeed, was only born a French citizen by the accident of a few weeks, the French having conquered the island shortly before his birth. By Corsican standards Napoleon was of noble birth, coming of an old Italian family. By French standards he was an outsider and upstart bent on making a career by his own precocious talents. The first Corsican to pass through the *École Militaire*, we find him a lieutenant of artillery at the age of sixteen, professing the fashionable advanced views of his time, writing a defence of Rousseau and an attack on the Church for undermining the loyalty of the people to state and nation. Already in fact he is responsive to the spirit of the age. He sketches a history of his native Corsica and in 1789 at the age of twenty he leads the revolutionary forces in the island against the Royalist Intendant. The Revolution released his brilliant and restless talents so that at the age of twenty-nine we find him in Egypt sated with glory, writing to his brother Joseph in the true romantic spirit: 'My feelings are dried up and I am bored with public display. At twenty-nine I am bored with glory and there is nothing left for me but complete egotism.'

A similar early insecurity and early maturity characterizes most of the revolutionary leaders of the twentieth century. Lenin, it is true, had a relatively secure childhood, coming of a well-to-do family of the minor aristocracy which had made its way up through the Tsarist civil service. Indeed his secure and happy childhood may account for his freedom from some of the more repugnant personal characteristics common in tyrants. He was not of pure Russian birth, being a quarter German and a quarter Kalmuk. The shock which precipitated him into revolutionary activity came at the age of seventeen when his elder brother, Alexander Ulyanov, was executed for his part in a conspiracy against the life of the Tsar. That a man of his temperament would have become a revolutionary in any case can hardly be doubted; but it is to be conjectured that this traumatic event contributed to the dogmatic and ruthless character of Lenin's revolutionism in contrast to the more romantic and idealistic approach of the National Will movement to which his brother belonged.

Lenin, indeed, was the greatest, though not the first, of a new class of professional revolutionaries. This class needs somewhat careful definition. It is not distinctive in its origin. Its members are of widely differing social status, from the aristocratic Bakunin to Stalin the son of a freed serf, from the wealthy bourgeois Engels to the peasant's son, Tito. Persons of much humbler origin than Lenin have risen to the supreme power in previous ages, such as the great Emperor Diocletian, the son of a slave, or Francesco Sforza Duke of Milan, the son of a peasant *condottiere*. However, these previous great outsiders had forced their way into the ruling class either by military prowess, administrative skill or the arts of the intriguer or courtier; they had done so in order to gain control of the existing power structure, not in order to abolish or transform it, although Diocletian did in fact transform the Roman Empire. The new class of professional revolutionaries is therefore distinguished by its methods of seeking power, its subordination of every other purpose to this purpose, and the aims for which they intend to use it.

Apart from Lenin, the four most successful members of this class in our time, Stalin, Mussolini, Hitler and Mao Tse-tung, had certain characteristics in common with each other and some previous great tyrants. All revolted against their fathers and all at an early age cut loose from their families to make their own way in conditions of some hardship.

Stalin's father, Djugashvili, after the freeing of the serfs tried to make his way as a cobbler, failed and took to drink. The pattern of Stalin's boyhood is the familiar one of revolt against the father. By the devoted efforts of his mother he was sent to the Theological Seminary at Tiflis, training for the priesthood being one of the ways in which a peasant's son might secure education and rise to a higher station in life. From the first he was a rebellious and pugnacious youth. The Tiflis seminary was a centre of the Georgian nationalist movement and the young Josef Djugashvili very soon came to play an active part in it, which got him into trouble with the authorities. He wrote romantic and patriotic verse in Georgian, and all his life spoke bad Russian with a strong Georgian accent. Like Napoleon, therefore, he was pre-eminently an outsider in the society of which he was later to become the master. From the first the Georgian tradition of the blood feud and the vendetta determined the savage temper of his will. The shooting in prison of Ketskhoveli, the Georgian revolutionary whom he most admired, probably helped to drive him unto the underground revolutionary movement, which with its conspiracies, Siberian exiles and escapes was to be his university. The dogmatic cast of his mind was already formed in the Orthodox Seminary, an upbringing which was to determine the hieratic style of many of his utterances when in power, while his revolutionary temperament was already fired in the Georgian national movement, before Marxism, narrowed and concentrated by Lenin into a technique for seizing power, gave the final direction to his activity. The Georgian nationalist became more Russian than the Russians, suppressing the independence movement in his native country.

Benito Mussolini was born four years after Stalin in the stormy province of the Romagna, home of the Borgias in the Renaissance and of revolutionaries in the late nineteenth and early twentieth centuries. He came of a family of peasant proprietors – the petty bourgeoisie which he was later to despise – his father a drunken, spendthrift, argumentative blacksmith of extreme Socialist views for which he had gone to prison, his mother, whom he loved, a gentle and religious school-mistress, who held the family together by her earnings and her character. Against this stormy background, the boy, named Benito after the Mexican revolutionary Benito Juarez, developed – aggressive, obstinate and violent, but talented and quick to learn what interested him. Expelled from two schools for stabbing fellow-pupils with whom he quarrelled, he developed chronically anti-clerical views from his hatred of the Fathers who taught him in the school at Faenza. Despite this unpromising beginning, he secured his teacher's diploma at the age of eighteen. But teaching bored him, and within a few months he was off to Switzerland, to lead the Bohemian life of the romantic revolutionary. This was the pattern of his life during his most formative years, in and out of odd jobs, in and out of prison, in and out of Switzerland and Italy, wenching, raping and picking up syphilis, arguing and brawling among the revolutionary students – Russians and others – in Lausanne and Berne.

Mussolini read voraciously and indiscriminately among the revolutionary writers of the nineteenth century – Marx, who bored him; the Russian anarchist Prince Kropotkin; Sorel, after whom he called himself an apostle of violence; the French champions of violent revolution, Babeuf and Blanqui; Nietzsche, whose picture of the superman could not but appeal to his domineering and self-dramatizing temper. From these sources and his revolutionary associates he formed the notion of a conspiratorial *élite* designed to seize power on behalf of the people. He first chose the left wing of the Italian Socialist Party for his organization, violent anti-militarism, anti-nationalism and anti-capitalism for his programme, and the Socialist newspaper *Avanti!* for his vehicle. A brilliant journalist and a forceful mob orator, he was already by 1912 a figure to be reckoned with.

Hitler by comparison was a slower starter, but this perhaps helped to give him greater staying power in the long run. The family pattern again is one of revolt against the father. Alois Hitler, born illegitimate but later legitimized under his father's name, came of Austrian peasant stock, and worked his way to a respectable position as minor official in the Imperial Customs, an unsympathetic man, three times married and the father of an illegitimate child and over fifty years old at the time of the birth of Adolf. The latter declares that he quarrelled with his father, because he was unwilling to follow in his footsteps as a civil servant but was determined to become an artist. Since the father died when the boy was fourteen, and since Adolf also quarrelled with his schoolmasters, it seems more likely that the cause was his poor performance at school.

Hitler's failure to secure a school-leaving certificate barred him from entering the School of Architecture, just as his lack of talent as a painter and draughtsman kept him out of the Academy of Fine Arts and thwarted his ambition to become an artist – except in the field of picture postcards and shop signs. Drifting listlessly from one odd job to another, sticking to nothing, totally without self-discipline, he slipped from the petty bourgeoisie into what Marx dubbed the Lumpenproletariat. He was sometimes literally in rags. The dosshouse and the Charity Hostel in Vienna were his university in the formative years from eighteen to twenty-three. He was exaggerating less than usual when he wrote in *Mein Kampf*: 'Vienna was a hard school for me, but it taught me the most profound lessons of my life.'

First he felt in his own person the desperate insecurity, the experience of slipping from a precariously held social foothold which hit a great part of the German nation when the slump of 1929 gave Hitler his chance. His life in the Vienna under-world taught him to operate under the law of the jungle in which *homo homini lupus*, and the most ruthless and un-scrupulous survived. Secondly his experience in Vienna, though what precise experience is not clear, pin-pointed for him the enemy, the Jew, on whom he was to concentrate his own pent-up frustration and hatred, as well as that of so many of his countrymen. Thirdly, the mixed nationalities of that modern Babylon kindled in him the burning pan-German nationalism which was the basis of his appeal to the German people. Finally, he studied with the keen eye of hatred the arts of mass-organization and leadership in which the Social De-mocrats of pre-war Vienna excelled.

It is perhaps stretching the definition rather far to include him in the class of professional revolutionaries, He had indeed sunk to an altogether lower stratum than the revolutionary intelligentsia with whom Lenin, Stalin and Mussolini associ-ated, and was not temperamentally capable of Lenin's deep study of revolutionary literature and technique or even of Mussolini's more superficial journalistic acquaintance with these subjects. His early years saw the formation of the pro-fessional counter-revolutionary, but the two classes had more in common than either will allow.

Hitler was in the most complete sense an outsider, *déclassé* as the petty bourgeois who had sunk into the Lumpenprole-tariat, denationalized as the Austrian who aspired to be a German and who was always to speak the language of his adopted nation with the provincial accent of the Austrian borderland. It was not until the age of twenty-three that he set foot in the country which he was to lead to ruin. Arriving in Munich he felt he had come home and within two years there came the moment when, as he recorded in *Mein Kampf*: 'I sank down upon my knees and thanked Heaven out of the fullness of my heart for the favour of having been permitted to live in such a time.' The occasion was the outbreak of the First World War and all the great European tyrants of our time had reason to echo in their own peculiar ways Hitler's prayer of thanksgiving, since it was this shattering of the old order that gave them their chance.

One could extend this list of great despots who quarrelled with their fathers and suffered a restless and insecure childhood and youth. Mao Tse-tung, for example, revolted against his father, a – by Chinese standards – fairly well-to-do peasant. Now – as those who lean to the psycho-analytical explanation of tyranny may be inclined to emphasize – there is not a single well-to-do peasant left among all the 700 million Chinese, and in Mao's final phase millions of young Red Guards, in that most patriarchal of countries, have been systematically taught to harry and bully their fathers. Indeed one of the reasons for studying the childhood of tyrants is that they are liable to repeat the excesses of youth on a vaster scale and with lethal effect in their dotage.

Despite these similarities in the early background of a fairly wide and representative sample of tyrants, it would be absurd to suggest that such a disturbed childhood is a universal feature of the species or that it leads inevitably to the despotic temperament. The sins of the sons are not necessarily to be visited on the fathers; for example the wise and virtuous Marcus Aurelius devoted great attention to the upbringing of the young Commodus, providing him with the wisest maxims and the most admirable tutors. As perhaps modern psychology might have predicted, the young prince followed rather the example and cultivated the favourites of his licentious mother and preferred the role of the Roman Hercules to that of the philosopher king, thereby plunging the Empire back into its traditional welter of tyranny after two generations of the Antonine Golden Age.

It should further be added that there is a certain form of tyranny for which a restless and disturbed youth may be a positive disqualification, namely the more conservative type of despotism which is represented, for example, in Republican Rome by the conservative and aristocratic Sulla as contrasted with Marius. The ruling classes feeling themselves threatened by the demands and disorders of the popular leaders rally round a leader of their own choice, generally a man of solid background, a Franco or a Salazar. Francisco Franco came of a solid family of naval officers which had married into the aristocracy. The family had been settled for 150 years in the isolated naval base of El Ferrol in Galicia. He conformed to the family pattern of many other dictators in having a devoted and even saintly mother and a libertine father who deserted the family and could scarcely inspire respect. In 1898, when he was six years old there took place an event which made a profound impression in the naval society in which he was brought up – the crushing defeat of the fleet and army by the U.S.A. and the loss of Cuba. It was a background of family and national humiliation which might well have produced a radical rebel, as it did in his brother Ramón Franco, who became a national hero as the first aviator to fly the South Atlantic and then a left-wing conspirator against the monarchy. However, Francisco Franco became a proud, narrow, nationalist, conservative army officer who spent most of his younger days fighting with distinction in the colonial wars of North Africa. From this outpost he watched the political confusion and degradation of his country. But, although he studied social problems quite seriously he kept as clear of politics as any ambitious army officer could.

Less attention has been paid in this study to these more conservative types of tyranny or indeed to the tyranny which often arose in established absolutism because these forms of the disease are less relevant to our restless and radical age. The nurture of despots of this more conservative type would, however, naturally be expected to differ from that of the radical type.

We cannot always say, therefore, that the child is father of the tyrant, since tyrants are made, not born. *Nemo fuit repente turpissimus* – not even Hitler was a monster from birth. He showed in his early days a certain perverted idealism, an obstinate individuality, and resilience and courage in getting to his feet again when fate and his own temperament appeared to have dealt him a knock-out blow. Again the ascetic, indefatigable and single-minded devotion of Lenin to the cause of revolution through half a generation of defeats and disappointments cannot but arouse admiration. We can understand too how Lenin, on their first meeting, came to describe Stalin as that 'wonderful Georgian', since the life of an underground revolutionary in Tsarist Russia must have required courage and resource of a rare order; unfortunately, as Stalin's case shows, the virtues of the underdog easily become the vices of the despot. And the *bravura* of Mussolini's early career, if we forget the cosh and the castor oil, still has power to charm. In fact, while all in their own way were capable of the cold calculation recommended by Machiavelli, all had from an early age something more – a sense of their own destiny which they were able to identify with some great cause.

The nascent tyrant therefore will often show remarkable virtues. It could not be otherwise since, although on the pinnacle of power he may stand alone, he will need the help of others to climb there. The aspiring despot must in fact organize his party; the organization of the party, its strength and the sources of its membership will vary according to the nature of the society which the ruler seeks to control.

5. The Preparation for Power

Polycrates of Samos, most magnificent of the Greek tyrants, seized power in the island with the help of his two brothers and fifteen hoplites. He had the essentials – a small body of civilian lieutenants, the nucleus of a party, and some organized force. The strength of the party and the degree of force required will depend on the size and the coherence of the state to be seized. The class from which the would-be ruler draws his adherents will depend on the class structure of society and the distribution of power in the state.

The earliest tyrants, hereditary monarchs, such as Pheidon of Argos in the seventh century B.C., who exceeded their legal and traditional rights, had the easiest task since many of the levers of power were already in their hands and they were in a position to recruit agents dependent on themselves to assist them against the more powerful of their vassals. As Machiavelli puts it: 'The hereditary prince has less cause and necessity to offend; hence it happens that he will be more loved; and unless extraordinary vices cause him to be hated, it is reasonable to expect that his subjects will be naturally well-disposed towards him.' Yet the transformation of feudal monarchy into absolute monarchy was the cause of great upheavals – witness the Wars of the Roses – and the King who sought to go beyond his prerogative without enlisting a sufficient support among his nobles and burghers might easily meet with defeat at the hands of his powerful vassals and the Church. These struggles, while they have contributed to the present structure of society and the state, have little direct relevance to the problem of tyranny in a post-dynastic age.

More relevant to our time are the methods employed by the

Greek tyrants of the later sixth century B.C., and particularly, since we know most about them, and since they deeply affected the views of later Greek writers on tyranny, the methods of Pisistratus. 'The half-wicked tyrant', as Aristotle calls him, is one of the great borderline cases, whose magnificent contributions to the cultural, political and economic greatness of Athens would outweigh in the eyes of many more modern historians the charges of tyranny and abuse of power brought against him by the Greek aristocratic and democratic writers of the following two centuries. He has relevance to our time because he seized power in an old-established and thriving state, in a condition of economic ferment and revolution. The reformist policies of the wise Solon – a combination of cancellation of debts, denunciation of the rich, and encouragement of the land workers to come into the city as craftsmen, had only temporarily halted the rising discontent and class-war. The two dominant parties were the men of the Plain and the men of the Shore who are probably to be identified with the old landed aristocracy and their clients on the one hand and with the rising mercantile plutocracy with the craftsmen on the other. Civil war broke out between these two factions. Pisistratus, himself an aristocrat and a wealthy mine-owner, tried to form a third party from the *diakrioi* – perhaps the men of the mountains or the mines, whom Herodotus describes as the poorest section of the population. Having previously won distinction in war Pisistratus wounded himself, feigning an attack on his person, with the result that he was voted a bodyguard of men armed with clubs. With their help he seized the Acropolis and set up a dictatorship, ruling with moderation according to the laws. But his opponents combined to drive him out. Subsequently, Pisistratus formed an alliance with the aristocratic party and returned, securing popular welcome by the simple ruse of dressing up a very tall girl called Phye as the goddess Athene and driving her into Athens in his chariot, thereby combining both a nationalist and religious appeal. Driven out again, he spent ten years in exile collecting foreign help and mercenaries to reconquer Athens, which he did without serious fighting. This time his rule was sterner and he kept the sons of some of his opponents as hostages.

Pisistratus' story foreshadows many of the means of seizing power employed by subsequent dictators – the sham attack on himself to gain public sympathy, the use of para-military forces to seize power, the nationalist propaganda appeal, the combination of support from left to right in the temporary alliance of the poor men of the mountains and the aristocrats of the plain, the enlisting of foreign aid, the use of hostages as a means of control. Finally, the stability and duration of the dictatorship which lasted Pisistratus' lifetime and half the life-time of his son and was a magnificent period in Athens' history, bears out later experience that a long and contentious preparation for power may be a factor in its durability. However, Pisistratus was spared two problems which confronted later would-be tyrants, namely control of a standing army and a democratically active and politically conscious *demos*.

It was left to Sicily – a land in which as we have seen, foreign invasion had provided a fertile soil for tyrants – to show the way in dealing with these problems in the seizure of power. The great city of Syracuse had, around the middle of the fifth century B.C. after the overthrow of the dynasty of Hieron, enjoyed a period of democracy. But towards the end of the fifth century the city was under threat from the Carthaginians. The Syracusan general Dionysius, wishing to establish his power, feigned an attack on his person, and thereby secured from the people a personal bodyguard of 600 men which he used to suppress and execute his main opponents. He also suppressed an army revolt and from then on ruled Syracuse for some thirty-eight years, using the fear of the Carthaginians to strengthen his position and to maintain his mercenary army and even apparently going to the length of provoking a new war with them. It was perhaps from Dionysius that Plato got his notion of tyranny, having visited both his court and that of his successor, Dionysius II, whom he tried in vain to convert into a constitutional monarch or philosopher-king. Plato's *Re-public* may well represent part of the advice he would have given if he could, Syracuse's loss being posterity's gain. Aristotle's idea of the tyrant as one who combined the positions of *demagogos* and *strategos* – leader of the people and leader of the army – may also be based on this greatest of the tyrants of the early fourth century, although he was doubtless able to revise his opinions at the court of Philip of Macedon, as tutor to Alexander. Indeed the career of Dionysius foreshadows, as a military despotism, the empire of Alexander and in its combination of military and political elements the Roman Empire itself.

It was the founder of that Empire, the subtle Octavian, who brought the technique of the seizure of power to its highest point of refinement in the ancient world. The ground, as we have seen, was prepared by the Civil Wars which had periodically ravaged the Roman world for half a century. Furthermore Octavian, like two of the greatest modern tyrants – Napoleon and Stalin – had a forerunner, from whose triumphs he could profit and from whose blunders he could learn. The intentions of his great uncle and adoptive father Julius Caesar during his brief period of absolute power are not clear. He was only in Rome for fifteen months during the last five or six years of his life. Although he legislated with enormous vigour during that time no clear constitutional plan emerges. Two interpretations seem possible, first that having acquired power more or less by the necessity of civil war, he was merely exercising it pragmatically without any long-term plan for the future of the Empire; secondly, that despairing of the reconstitution of the republic he was meditating the role of God-King on the Hellenistic model.

Whatever the motive, despite his much vaunted but genuine clemency and toleration of differing opinions, he did not trouble to conceal his power or his contempt for the forms of the Republic. As Gibbon puts it: 'Caesar had provoked his fate as much by the ostentation of his power as by his power itself. ... Augustus was sensible that mankind is governed by names: nor was he deceived in his expectation that the senate and people would submit to slavery provided they were respectfully assured that they still enjoyed their ancient freedom.'

This regard for the constitutional forms, for legality, combined with the shrewdest assessment of the realities of power, was Octavian's most original contribution to the technique of seizure of power. One of his first acts on coming back to Italy after Julius' murder was to seek out Cicero, the elder statesman of the Republic, whom he later managed to convince that the name of Caesar and all the command of the legions which that ensured would be put at the service of the Republic – no mean achievement for a boy of eighteen. When he came on the scene Mark Antony, on the one hand, leader of the Caesarian party and Consul, and the liberators Brutus and Cassius on the other, were poised in uneasy equilibrium, each side unwilling to raise the legions and the provinces. Antony hesitated to exploit the cult of Julius and his prestige with the people and the legions, because that way lay a renewal of the Civil War. The young Octavian had no such scruples. Using his position as Caesar's heir he rallied the support of the plebs by stimulating the cult of the divine Julius and games in his honour, and the support of the legions by liberal donations from Julius' patrimony. Without constitutional sanction or legal right, Octavian marched his legions to Rome to make himself the champion of the constitutional cause against the popular party of Antony. Cicero in his *Philippics* inveighed against Antony, hoping either to harness Octavian – 'the divine youth' as he called him – to the Republican cause or to use him and cast him aside. Never was greater eloquence deployed in a more hopeless cause, not only through the elder statesman's vanity and gullibility which Octavian skilfully exploited but also from the conviction that one of the military potentates must be allied to the Republic; he chose the wrong one. For, having secured an equal balance with his great rival, Octavian made common cause with Antony in the triumvirate for 'restoring the Republic', which it then proceeded to destroy. Among the victims of the Reign of Terror which followed was Cicero whose championship of Octavian could not outweigh the consequences of his invective against Antony. The Proscriptions broke the back of the Republican cause in Italy. Octavian was subsequently able to shift the blame for these executions on to his fellow rulers – particularly Antony during the latter's absence from Rome and after his death – but he himself was to be the main beneficiary of this slaughter of many of the notables of Rome and the confiscation of their estates. There was no question of the clemency which cost Julius his life. The dictator was avenged and the Republican party was finally shattered on the battlefield of Philippi, more by the military prowess of Antony than that of Octavian.

In two years, Octavian had made himself the equal of Antony with the help of the Republicans, and destroyed the Republican and aristocratic party with the help of Antony and the Caesarian popular party. Like other great tyrants in modern times he transcended distinctions of left and right. It took him another ten years to build himself up as the great national leader of Italy and the West against the oriental despotism of Antony and Cleopatra. In the process he used all the arts of patronage in bestowing magistracies, of bribery in the giving of donations to the legionaries and settling the veterans in colonies, of propaganda in defaming his opponents and extolling his own services. In the oath of allegiance which he secured by every form of persuasion and pressure from the entire population of Italy, he foreshadowed the plebiscites of more modern dictators. By these means he had thoroughly consolidated his power when the time came for the final reckoning with Antony at Actium.

It might have been from Augustus that Machiavelli culled the maxim that 'In usurping a state, the usurper ought to examine closely into all those injuries which it is necessary for him to inflict and to do them all at one stroke so as not to have to repeat them daily.... For injuries ought to be done all at one time, so that being tasted less they offend less; benefits ought to be given little by little, so that the flavour of them may last longer.'

The Octavian of the Proscriptions and the Civil Wars had

run through the necessary injuries, if not at one stroke – for there were a great many – at any rate early in his career. So after Actium the Augustus of the Empire could afford clemency to his opponents, illustrating another of the principles of Machiavelli that such opponents often make useful instruments, since the ruler has a hold on them. Accordingly he awarded magistracies to some of the noble champions of the Republic and followers of Antony and admitted others to the Senate, having purged it of the more disreputable figures who had been installed during the triumvirate. To this now respectable body the Prince restored – in form at any rate – its traditional powers and prerogatives only to have all that was necessary for his rule handed back to him in proper constitutional form. *Vindex libertatis*, the champion of liberty, he had banished it from the Roman State; restorer of the Republic, he had turned the Commonwealth into a permanent dictatorship in all but name, achieving the kind of semantic chaos which has become all too familiar in modern times. The former ruling class now derived its authority from the Emperor. The essential powers remained in his own hands and those of a small nucleus of ministers such as the distinguished, but low-born, general, engineer and administrator Agrippa and the wealthy Maecenas, in charge of home affairs and propaganda, men who owed all their power to the Emperor. These were the core of Augustus' party; many of the notable survivors of the civil wars and proscriptions he was able to attach to himself by family alliance and patronage.

The process of the seizure of power had taken seventeen years from 44–27 B.C. It confirms the principle that the longer and tougher the struggle for power, the greater the prospect of stability and durability for the resulting dictatorship. All political structures which can subsist independently of the ruler are destroyed; all notable men who might stand up for freedom are isolated, intimidated or dead; the ruler's own party is tempered and hardened in the fire and welded to the dictator on whom all become dependent. Augustus, having destroyed every alternative, erected a structure which was able to survive even the crimes and follies of his successors.

It was the most comprehensive and sophisticated seizure of power in history up to that time; and it was not to be matched in this respect until Napoleon's *coup d'état* of 18 Brumaire 1799, eighteen centuries later. Napoleon indeed was more fortunate than Augustus: the advance preparatory work had been done more thoroughly for him in the Jacobin Terror of 1793–4 and the counter-terror of Thermidor. This rendered it unnecessary for Napoleon to shed his countrymen's blood in civil war; and the revolutionary wars gave him the chance of gaining the military glory and control of the armies which were to be the basis of his rule.

One should perhaps examine more closely this preparatory work since the techniques of tyranny which evolved more or less spontaneously and at random after the French Revolution have provided the classic model which has been more systematically followed in revolutionary *coups d'état* since. In 1791 the Girondin Brissot had said: 'The force of reason and of facts has persuaded me that a people, which after a thousand years of slavery has achieved liberty, needs war. It needs war to consolidate its freedom. It needs war to purge away the vices of despotism. It needs war to banish from its bosom the men who might corrupt liberty.' The revolutionary war became the basis for the revolutionary terror: as Robespierre put it: 'If the basis of government in time of peace is virtue, its basis in times of revolution is both virtue and intimidation, virtue without which intimidation is disastrous, intimidation without which virtue is powerless.' The revolutionary journalist Camille Desmoulins shrewdly commented: 'Let us beware of connecting politics with moral regeneration.... Moralism is fatal to freedom.' It proved fatal to Desmoulins, who went to the guillotine with Danton when the Revolution began to swallow its children.

The march of the terror was inexorable. As the revolutionary army left Paris to meet the Prussians now on French soil, Marat, the Friend of the People and the champion of dictatorship, let loose the Paris mob to massacre the prisoners in the gaols. The murder of Marat himself precipitated the show trials of the opposition by revolutionary tribunals, as 140 years later the murder of Kirov was the prelude to Stalin's great purges. In these trials as in Stalin's, men of the right and men of the left, the Girondins and the Hébertistes, all who were suspected of opposition from whatever direction, whatever their origin – and there were more members of the middle and lower classes than aristocrats, priests and bureaucrats among them – were charged with being agents of the enemy and the *émigrés*, either directly or by association. For guilt by association played a great part in these trials as in more recent occasions of similar character. Ultimately the term 'enemy of the people' was defined so widely as to cover such offences as defeatism and spreading false rumours and any injury to the liberty, unity and defence of the Republic. A century and a half later, one of the complaints of Khrushchev against Stalin in his denunciation of him in 1956 was precisely this – that it was only necessary to call a man an 'enemy of the people' to liquidate him, a case of 'give a dog a bad name and hang him'. With these trials went, naturally, press censorship, the rapid development of a secret police system, denunciation by informers, and the suppression, under the *loi Chapelier*, of all independent associations of the workers and others on the grounds of a threat to liberty. This suppression extended eventually to the revolutionary and popular clubs, which formed the basis of the party system after the revolution, and by which the Jacobins themselves had risen to power. Nor was the terror confined to Paris, but representatives of the Committee of Public Safety ranged through the provinces, butchering the population of Lyons, conducting a bitter civil war in Britanny where the Church was strongest. There were attempts – or sham attempts – on the lives of Saint-Just and Robespierre, who at the end went in continual fear of assassination. Counter-terror followed terror. In the morning of 27 July forty-five opponents of Robespierre went to the guillotine – a fairly average number; in the following twenty-four hours, eighty-seven supporters of Robespierre followed them. If the régime following Thermidor was less violent and fanatical than the Jacobins', it was also more corrupt and unpopular, consisting as it did of men who had done well out of the revolution and the inflation. Not only had the revolution devoured its own children; it had destroyed the social order to such an extent that the army remained the only disciplined and coherent social force; and the Directoire convinced of its own unpopularity by the success of Royalists and Jacobins in elections had to call for army support against the popular assemblies.

Thus all was ready for the *coup* of 18 Brumaire. Napoleon, having the army, did not have to worry too much about a party, since the other parties had been shattered anyway. He relied for his political organization chiefly on three of those 'professional survivors' who are liable to arise in any revolution – three seminary-trained churchmen – the subtle Talleyrand, the cold ruthless policeman, butcher of Lyons, Fouché, and the doctrinaire constitution-monger, Sieyès, who was to play Cicero to Bonaparte's Octavian. The manoeuvre of Brumaire was a classic one – it might almost be said, a classical one, for Napoleon was well read in Greek and Roman history and in Plato's *Republic*.

Rumours were spread of a Jacobin rising. *Les Anciens*, the Senate of the Republic, were thereby induced to withdraw to Saint-Cloud under Army protection. Bonaparte assured them of his constitutional intentions. 'What we want,' he said, 'is a Republic founded on true liberty, social liberty and national representation; and we are going to have it. That I swear in my name and that of my comrades-in-arms.' The Assembly – the 500 – were less amenable. The passage of a day had given time for at least vocal opposition. Some people were saying that Bonaparte was a Caesar or a Cromwell and there were cries of 'down with the dictator' as he entered the Chamber. On the ground that their general was in danger from the daggers of the deputies, the guards intervened and broke up the assembly. In the evening a rump assembly under the chairmanship of Napoleon's brother Lucien named Bonaparte, Ducos and

Sieyès provisional Consuls. Sieyès set to work to produce a constitution which would secure the maximum balance and distribution of powers. All in vain; Bonaparte, while willing and anxious – for some months at any rate – to maintain the trappings of constitutional liberty, insisted as First Consul on the autocratic right of decision. 'Citizens,' he proclaimed, 'the Revolution is stabilized on the principles which began it. The Revolution is over.'

While Bonaparte's *coup* provided a model for future military despots, the French Revolution became the natural study of all future revolutionaries. Its terms – Committee of Vigilance, Committee of Public Safety, the revolutionary tribunal, enemy of the people and – as dangers to be avoided – Thermidor and Brumaire, became the technical terminology of generations of revolutionaries. Its personalities and techniques became their model. The Jacobin dictatorship foreshadowed the techniques of the dictatorship of the proletariat. the bitter, fanatical, tight-lipped intriguer Robespierre getting the better of the natural leader and demagogue Danton, just as Stalin was to get the better of Trotsky. These two French provincial lawyers of humble origin were in their own way typical of the new class from which future revolutionary parties were to be formed. But more exemplary for the revolutionaries of the nineteenth century was the pathetic figure of Babeuf who called himself 'Gracchus' after the Roman tribune of the people. The son of a poor peasant and soldier, himself an impoverished archivist, he sacrificed his family – his children dying of hunger and disease – and everything else to his own egalitarian ideal of the Revolution – a martyr whose blood was the seed of Communism. An enthusiastic supporter of Robespierre, Babeuf proposed to impose a system of primitive Communism by his dictatorial methods. A committee of insurgence based on a conspiratorial party with agents acting in all the *arrondissements* of Paris and in the army and police, would seize power in the capital and exercise it as the vanguard of the people, wiping out all opposition, until the whole would come to realize, by a process of propaganda, press control and education, that the committee was the representative of its true will. The conspiracy was a pathetic failure since the party of the vanguard thoroughly overestimated its support and misjudged the public mood. Babeuf paid with his life, but his lieutenant, the brilliant and handsome Buonarroti, an Italian of aristocratic family, who had been naturalized for his services to the Revolution, lived on in prison and in exile to tell the prophetic tale and to pass it on to a new generation of revolutionaries including Blanqui, who was to apply its lessons in the Paris Commune and in doing so to exercise an influence on the Marxist doctrine of the dictatorship of the proletariat and therefore on Lenin. The Marxists in principle rejected the idea of a conspiratorial seizure of power, since although the revolution must be violent it must also depend on the ripening of historical forces. However Engels wrote prophetically to the Russian revolutionary Vera Zasulich in 1885 that Russia was 'one of the exceptional cases where it is possible for a handful of people to make a revolution.... If ever Blanquism – the fantasy of overthrowing an entire society through the action of a small conspiracy – had a certain justification for its existance, that is certainly in Petersburg.'

The views of Babeuf and Blanqui were indeed very prevalent in Russian revolutionary circles around the time of Lenin's birth. They took a farouche form in the conspiracy of the young terrorist and murderer Nechayev, who is described in fictional form in Dostoevsky's novel, *The Possessed*. The repressive Tsarist autocracy provided the natural soil for such conspiratorial terrorism by professional revolutionaries. Nechayev managed to win the confidence of the anarchist leader Bakunin with whom he wrote in *The Catechism of a Revolutionist* that 'the revolutionist ... hates and despises the social morality of his time its motives and manifestations. Everything which promotes the revolution is moral, everything which hinders it is immoral.'

However, the Marxists including Lenin repudiated individual terrorism not on moral grounds, but as a distraction from more serious and organized revolutionary activity.

Lenin's views conformed more closely to those of Tkachev, a revolutionist who had joined Bakunin in Switzerland in 1874 after years in Tsarist prisons. Tkachev advocated an *élite* party of revolutionists in the style of Babeuf. 'A real revolution', he wrote,

can be brought about only in one way – through the seizure of power by revolutionists. In other words the immediate and most important task of the revolution must be solely the overthrow of the government and the transformation of the present conservative state into a revolutionary state. ... The revolution is brought about by the revolutionary government, which, on the one hand eradicates all the conservative reactionary elements of society, eliminating all those institutions which hinder the establishment of equality and brotherhood among men. ... Then, utilising its authority, the minority introduces new progressive and Communist ideas into life. In its work of reformation, the revolutionary minority need not rely on the active support of the people. The revolutionary role of the people ends the instant they have destroyed the institutions which oppressed them, the instant they have overthrown the tyrants and exploiters who ruled over them.

Tkachev's conclusion is that 'neither now nor in the future will the common people by its own power bring on a social revolution. We alone, the revolutionary minority, can and should do that as soon as possible.'

Therefore the idea of a party of a new type, a disciplined *élite* revolutionary party, which Lenin put forward in perhaps his most important pamphlet, *What is to be Done?*, is by no means original. What was original was the ruthless single-minded devotion with which Lenin applied the idea and carried it to its triumphant conclusion in 1917. In *What is to be Done?* Lenin argued against those Social Democrats who believed it their function to promote the economic demands of the workers (who were guilty of 'economism'), against those who simply believed in securing for the working classes what they themselves wanted (who were guilty of the crime of 'spontaneity') and against those who believed that Marxist theories should be adapted to meet the changing needs and conditions of the working-class (who were guilty of the crimes of 'freedom of criticism' and 'revisionism'). All these tendencies would lead to a bourgeois ideology among the workers and the trade unions. It was the business of the Social Democrats to spread their own ideology among them. Hence the importance of theory which could only be brought to the working class from outside by the revolutionary intelligentsia. According to their social status (Lenin pointed out) the founders of modern scientific socialism, Marx and Engels, themselves belonged to the revolutionary intelligentsia. It should be added that in Lenin this appreciation of the role of the revolutionary intelligentsia was combined with a dislike of intellectuals, whom he regarded as undisciplined, quarrelsome, lazy and unreliable.

Like some other important books *What is to be Done?* is extremely tedious, consisting as it does largely of outworn controversies expressed in the jargon of dogmatic Marxism. But it was the basis on which the Bolsheviks split from the rest of the Russian Social Democrats, 'the Mensheviks' or minority group in the Party Congress of 1903 in London. At that Congress Lenin's ruthlessness caused the most eminent Russian Marxist theorist, Plekhanov, to exclaim in admiration: 'Of such stuff are Robespierres made'; but very soon he found that his remark was all too true and Lenin all too dictatorial. At the same time Trotsky accused Lenin of being a Robespierre eager to convert the Central Committee of the Party into a Committee of Public Safety, the dictatorship of the Proletariat into dictatorship over the Proletariat, and of aspiring to set up revolutionary tribunals under which 'the leonine head of Marx would be the first to fall under the guillotine'. Trotsky himself, like an inverted Cassandra, was later to help Lenin in realizing this prophecy. Many others made similar prophecies throughout the next fourteen years; even after the seizure of power the leader of the Left-wing German Social Democrats Rosa Luxemburg in 1918 made her famous critique: 'Freedom only for the supporters of the government, only for the members of one party – however numerous they may be – is no freedom at all. Freedom is always and exclusively freedom for the one who thinks differently.' Warning of the impossibility of introducing socialism by decree or ukase Rosa Luxemburg continued:

Without general elections, without unrestricted freedom of press and assembly, without a free struggle of opinion, life dies out in every public institution, becomes a mere semblance of life, in which only the bureaucracy remains as the active element. Public life gradually falls asleep; a few dozen party leaders of inexhaustible energy and boundless experience direct and rule. Among them, in reality only a dozen outstanding heads do the leading and an elite of the working class is invited from time to time to meetings where they are to applaud the speeches of the leaders, and to approve proposed resolutions unanimously.

Rosa Luxemburg concludes that this is not the dictatorship of the proletariat but the dictatorship of a handful of politicians.

Lenin, who later himself warned against the danger of a minority dictatorship, can hardly have conceived such an outcome – yet it was inherent in his definition in the pamphlet of 1902 of the task of the Russian proletariat. 'The destruction [he wrote] of the most powerful bulwark not only of European but also (it may now be said) of Asiatic reaction would place the Russian proletariat in the vanguard of the international proletariat'. But the workers generally were not particularly interested in becoming the vanguard of anything, but rather in the eight-hour day, better wages and conditions. If they secured their desires, as the 'Economists' attempted, then according to Lenin they would succumb to bourgeois ideology. Their revolutionary role must be imposed on them by a vanguard *élite* party of the revolutionary intelligentsia and Lenin's entire activity for the next fifteen years was devoted to creating such a party, ruled from the centre, with the party line laid down by himself, with the personnel appointed by himself, with the discipline necessary to organize both conspiracy and propaganda in the Tsarist police state. Working for this he systematically quarrelled with all who disagreed with him including the most famous names of Russian Social Democracy, Martov, Axelrod, Trotsky and even eventually Plekhanov whom he deeply admired as a theorist. In such quarrels he would heap the most vitriolic abuse on the heads of his unfortunate victims, thinking up ever new labels and crimes for them. Thus descriptions such as 'Economist', 'liquidator,' 'petit bourgeois syndicalist' were applied like Homeric epithets to each adversary in turn – just as the Germans were once automatically 'revanchiste' and the Americans 'imperialists'. This style of polemic, since hard words break no bones, did little harm until the Bolsheviks seized power, when it became lethal.

Conducting this ruthless struggle to temper a party capable of seizing power, Lenin paid little attention to the question of how to use it when seized. 'On s'engage et puis on voit', he was fond of quoting from Napoleon. In the revolution of 1905, during which Lenin himself was hesitant and appeared late on the scene in St Petersburg – while Trotsky played the leading role in the Soviet – the Bolsheviks did not accomplish much except in instigating the workers of Moscow to armed insurrection, not from any hope that they could seize power, but in order to temper them into a revolutionary force. For Lenin it was a rehearsal from which he learnt much.

Ruthlessly, single-mindedly following this one objective, Lenin had no hesitation in employing intelligent scoundrels if they were useful to the party, in financing it from bank robberies and crimes, and in parting with any party member or ally who showed enough bourgeois prejudice to object. He even defended the police spy, Malinovsky, leader of the Bolshevik faction in the Duma, Central Committee member and Treasurer of Pravda, against the charges of Bolsheviks and Mensheviks alike. By 1916 the Bolsheviks had to all appearances been reduced – partly by Lenin's exclusive dogmatism – to a pitiable, isolated, exiled splinter group, with little contact with their agents in Russia, many of whom were in Siberian exile or prison. But the result was that, when, with the February 1917 Revolution, the chance came for which he had spent a lifetime preparing, Lenin had an instrument entirely subject to his imperious will. There were acute differences about tactics and timing; but always Lenin's singleminded pursuit of power –

proclaimed in the April theses when he returned to Russia – prevailed in the last resort. The singleness of mind allied to mastery of the techniques of power, contrasting with the often irresolute and ineffectual behaviour of the other parties of the left, acted as a magnet to many who had parted from Lenin in the years of factional struggle in exile – notably Trotsky.

From April to October the unlimited freedom of post-Tsarist Russia was exploited to undermine every institution that could withstand Bolshevik force – in particular the armed forces – and to deepen the already existing chaos to a point where the most resolute and highly organized minority could seize power. 'Bread, peace, land' were the slogans to attract a war-weary nation of peasants to arms. The sailors of Kronstadt and the armed workers of Petrograd supplied the necessary force until the army could be won over or disintegrated. The effective show of force attracted the necessary funds – not least from the Germans who had shown their sense of Lenin's value to their cause by letting him through from Switzerland in the famous sealed train. There has been much unnecessary fuss about this question of German subventions; the evidence in favour is abundant – some would say conclusive. The Bolsheviks naturally denied it at the time and have done so ever since. Yet it would have been entirely in accordance with Lenin's principles to accept help from any source whatever, provided it contributed to the success of the Revolution, and since the help did not divert him one inch from his purpose, but merely assisted him in doing what he was resolved to do anyway, the accusation of being a German agent falls to the ground. Such help would, of course, have been entirely in accord with the immediate interest of the German General Staff in getting Russia out of the war; and when two such notable practitioners of Realpolitik as the German General Staff and the Bolshevik leadership had such an obvious common interest, it would have been strange if they had not acted upon it. They had also a common interest in keeping it quiet, since exposure would have damaged the Bolshevik campaign to whip up popular support under the slogan, 'All power to the Soviets'. This was a cunningly chosen slogan, since it provided a cloak of revolutionary legitimacy for the attempts of Bolshevik agitators to create chaos and anarchy in preparation for a *coup*; for it was perfectly clear that the Soviets were quite incapable of exercising power.

From June onwards Lenin was probing for the revolutionary crisis. At the time of the All-Russian Congress of the Soviets in that month the Bolsheviks planned an armed march on the Provisional Government, but gave it up when the plot was exposed. They probably already had the necessary armed support in Petrograd, but to seize power while there were effective counter forces – particularly the army – in the rest of the country would have been to court disaster. For the same reason the Bolsheviks were hesitant about putting themselves at the head of the armed rising which broke out in Petrograd in July, at the time of the Provisional Government's ill-starred offensive against the Germans under General Brusilov. The Bolshevik leaders were either arrested or went into hiding. This was the last occasion when the Provisional Government could have struck down the Bolsheviks, but the parties of the left could not bring themselves to suppress another left-wing party. The parties of the right were of course ready to do so and likewise General Kornilov, who had taken over the command of the army after the collapse of the Brusilov offensive. The result was the Kornilov *coup*, the attempt to set up a military government. It failed, because the troops would not march on their comrades, nor would the railwaymen transport them. Kerensky and the left wing of the Provisional Government resisted the *coup* and were thus divorced from the right-wing parties and the army. The Bolsheviks' time had come. Not all of them perceived it. But Lenin did. He wrote from his Finnish hide-out in September: 'We could not have kept in power on 3rd and 4th July, because before the Kornilov affair the Army and the provinces could and would have marched against Petrograd. Now the picture is entirely different...' And from September on he sent a stream of letters to his comrades in Petrograd, in Moscow – one so violent that his colleagues decided to burn it, another threatening his resignation if they would not prepare for immediate insurrection, another laying down the precise tactics for the *coup* – seizure of the Central Telegraph Office, etc. The *terminus a quo* for the *coup* was set by the collapse of the Kornilov *coup*; the *terminus ad quem* by the All-Union Congress of Soviets in November which could be exploited to legitimize the seizure of power, and the November elections for a Constituent Assembly which would clearly show the Bolseviks to have only a fairly small minority of popular support. As Lenin put it to the Central Committee when he returned from hiding in Finland in October: 'To wait for the Constituent Assembly, which will surely be against us, is nonsensical because that will only make our task more difficult.'

No need to describe the details of the *coup*; it was no romantic affair of the barricades, but so carefully organized that all key points were seized within a few hours practically without bloodshed. The Central Telegraph Offices and the railway station were the first objectives – not as would now be the case the airport and the radio station, since these did not exist. But Trotsky did order the sailors of the *Aurora* to broadcast the false story that the counter-revolution had gone over to the offensive – this being the first time that the wireless was used for carrying out the ancient trick of Pisistratus and Napoleon. The Congress of Soviets, purged of all those unwilling to support the Bolsheviks, gave the Bolshevik government its sole constitutional basis. One of its first acts was to pass a decree abolishing the death penalty – an ironical prelude to what was to come.

For a generation Communists were to hold up the October Revolution as a model for others. But in fact it was a unique event in unique circumstances, which might perhaps recur in some ill-organized underdeveloped country, but one unlikely to appear in any highly developed state – except after a nuclear war. The virtual collapse of all social organization made it possible for a small highly organized conspiratorial clique to seize the government of a great state; but subsequent Communist take-overs were only possible as a result of prolonged civil war – as in China, Yugoslavia, Cuba and North Vietnam – or by alien imposition as in most of the countries of Eastern Europe. The unique conditions made it possible to neglect certain considerations which have been vitally important to other dictators, such as legitimacy, the control or neutralization of the army, the conciliation of the forces of left and right to secure a national following. This is not to underrate Lenin's achievement. Indeed his faultless technique in the seizure of power is all the more remarkable because he had no precedents to draw upon. There was plenty of ground for the myth of Lenin's infallibility subsequently built up by Stalin. But in fact the whole operation was based on the illusion that the seizure of power in Russia would spark off revolution in Germany and then in other European countries. In his singleminded concentration on the seizure of power in Russia, Lenin had entirely misjudged the international situation. As a result he was driven from one tyrannical expedient to another to consolidate and expand that power, with consequences which still operate in the Soviet system today. The means determined the end, and have done so ever since.

No one in Europe, in fact, came anywhere near following Lenin's example, apart from Béla Kun in Hungary and the Bavarian Kurt Eisner: the forces combining against them proved far too strong. The next dictator to seize power was a very different figure. Anyone meeting both Lenin and Mussolini in Switzerland in the early years of the twentieth century could have been excused for taking the Italian with his wild Bohemian habits and appearance and equally wild talk for the professional revolutionary and Lenin for a respectable bourgeois. Mussolini indeed started his political career on the extreme left of the Socialist Party, but what he derived from his early revolutionary associations was the idea of the seizure of power by an *élite* dictatorial party, rather than any fixed principles as to what to do with that power. A pacifist, he rapidly turned from neutrality to interventionism in the First

World War when he saw the chance of enlisting Italian national feeling; a socialist, he exploited the fear of Bolshevism aroused by the workers' occupation of factories after the war and sent his *squadristi* to break up strikes and socialist meetings. This move from the left was to become familiar enough later when Doriot left the Communists to form his French Popular Party while Déat left the Socialists to play the role of a rival Quisling in German-occupied France, and Sir Oswald Mosley abandoned the Labour Party to lead the British Union of Fascists; but Mussolini led the way. Such changes of coat need only be surprising to those who accept the Marxist analysis of Fascism and National Socialism as right-wing movements for the defence of monopoly capitalism. Of course Mussolini and Hitler took help from capitalists, if they could get it – as Lenin did from the millionaire Morozov – and they secured it on a large scale by posing as the defenders of capitalism against Bolshevism. But like most great tyrants they went beyond the distinction of left and right, exploiting left-wing forces against the right and right-wing forces against the left, treating all classes not in a doctrinaire manner, but in a radically opportunist spirit – as means to seize, maintain and increase their power.

Whereas Lenin thought of himself as the forerunner of a number of internationalist Communist dictators seizing power on behalf of a proletariat which has no nation, he in fact turned out to be unique in not basing himself on a nationalist appeal, and deluded in relying on internationalist support. It was Mussolini who turned out to be the portent for the future, being the first dictator to exploit the full range of modern nationalism. In doing so he showed himself far more opportunist than Lenin who had been willing to go zig-zag in matters of tactics, not of dogma. This had several important results. Whereas Lenin had spent fifteen years in forging his party, Mussolini came to power within four years of the formation of his (in 1919). Whereas Lenin had used the instrument of dogma to weld his followers into 'a party of the new type' of professional revolutionaries under military discipline, Mussolini's doctrines were of the vaguest nature and his *gerarchi* were held together by the looser ties of a common interest in power and its fruits. Lenin's party owed its conspiratorial discipline to its formation under conditions of Tsarist autocracy. The Fascists grew under no such pressure. After the party's miserable showing in the 1919 elections, the Government ordered the arrest of Mussolini on the charge of armed plotting against the state. When the offices of his newspaper *Popolo d'Italia* were searched, a whole armoury of bombs and explosives was found in Mussolini's office; they were perhaps for ornament rather than use, the proper trappings of the romantic revolutionary; and the government, as weak in the face of this threat, which it underrated, as in the face of the strikes and labour disorders, the inflation and unemployment, which were reducing Italy to anarchic chaos, set the *Duce* free. Thus the Blackshirts in their actions against the striking workers and left-wing gangs were able by terror to usurp the functions which the police should have performed legally. In the name of order they spread disorder, and in doing so gained the support not only of the extreme nationalists, who applauded d'Annunzio's piratical seizure of the Yugoslav port of Fiume, but also even of such respected citizens as the philosopher Croce and the conductor Toscanini. The Fascists, many of whom were unemployed ex-servicemen, also enjoyed the connivance of the *carabinieri* and the army.

Mussolini's seizure of power was indeed on classic lines suitable to one of the classical homes of tyranny. The *squadristi* with their coshes, knuckle-dusters and castor-oil bottles, who killed an estimated 3000 of their opponents in three years and brought the country to the brink of civil war, were the descendants of the gangs of Milo and Clodius who terrorized the electorate of Republican Rome on behalf of Pompey and Caesar. The situation was similar to that described by Plato in the *Republic* when he makes Socrates say: 'Then tyranny probably arises from no other constitution than democracy, severest and most cruel slavery following, I fancy, the extreme of liberty' – although, by the appalling standards of the modern age, Italian Fascism can hardly be described as 'severest and most cruel slavery'.

In accordance with this situation, Mussolini needed and was able to deploy the arts of the demagogue in a way in which Lenin who, paradoxically, was less dependent on mass support than the Fascist and Nazi dictators, was never required to do. Lenin was a clear, forceful and schoolmasterly speaker, leaving his audience in no doubt about what was to be done; but he was no rabble-rouser. Trotsky was a more notable orator as indeed was his opponent Kerensky, whose eloquence in the last resort availed him no more than that of Cicero. Mussolini was the first modern dictator to be a great mob orator.

His seizure of power was more a political than a military operation, more dependent on the threat of force, and the seduction and deception of potential opponents than on force itself. Hence many a tortuous manoeuvre in 1921–2: an alliance with the Socialists combined with attacks on their followers, subventions from capitalists combined with anti-capitalism, Republicanism combined with tributes to the House of Savoy. Right up to the last moment Mussolini sought a constitutional road to power and right up to the march on Rome he left both his opponents and his supporters – and maybe himself – in doubt as to his intentions. These tactics were met with a similar irresolution on the part of the Government. When it proclaimed martial law, the King refused to sign the decree. Mussolini surrounded by the police and troops in Milan, awaited anxiously the outcome of the march. He need not have worried; neither the army, nor the police were in a mood to resist. And when the King's telegram summoned him to the Palace, he tempered the revolutionary *élan* of his black shirt with the bourgeois respectability of bowler hat and spats. His comment to the King was no less curious than his costume: 'Please forgive my appearance; I come from the battlefield.'

In September 1919, a few months after Mussolini had held his meeting with a couple of hundred foundation members to form the Fascist Party, Adolf Hitler – an 'Instruction Officer' employed to maintain and report on the morale of the army in Munich – was detailed to attend a meeting of an insignificant group called the German Workers' Party. There were twenty-five or thirty people present at the meeting. This tiny group, partly because its insignificance matched Hitler's own, was the launching-pad for the 'unknown front-soldier', as he was fond of calling himself. The propellent in his rocket-flight to power was propaganda. He at once took over the propaganda of the party and, within a very short time, had proved his genius in this field. In the first year, he was to say later, he had secured sixty-four members for the Party; then it began to snowball.

It is worthwhile to analyse what is probably Hitler's most original contribution to the tyrant's art. Propaganda in one form or another of course, plays a role in every assumption of political power, whether legal or illegal. Some of the Greek tyrants, we are told, were skilled demagogues, since in the small city-state it was possible to influence the mass of the people by oratory. However when it came to seizing power in greater states where a direct appeal to the people was not possible, a different form of propaganda was necessary. In Rome Cicero's *Phillippics* against Antony were indeed propaganda of a high order, but propaganda addressed to an oligarchic *élite*; one of the most brilliant of them was not even delivered but merely circulated among the small group of influential men in Rome. The highly cultivated rhetoric of a Julius Caesar or Octavian would be chiefly reserved for the Senate or the courts; the nearest they would get to rabble-rousing oratory would perhaps be the General's address to the Legions before battle. Faction-leaders such as Milo and Clodius came nearer to the mixture of street-corner agitation and terror practised in this century by the Blackshirts and Hitler's storm troopers. But the more typical form of propaganda in Rome would have been the kind of broadsheets and lampoons against Antony's dalliance with Cleopatra which would appeal to Roman national feeling and aristocratic prejudice. The nearest approach to modern mass propaganda was perhaps the *conjuratio totae Italiae* by which Octavian secured an oath of allegiance from the whole of Italy for his struggle against Antony. When we come on to the despots of the Middle Ages and Renaissance, such propaganda efforts as the mutual anathemas of the Emperor Frederick II and the Pope were designed for an *élite* of prelates, priests and feudal lords rather than for mass consumption, since the control of the masses was by no means an important power factor. Modern mass propaganda begins with the Reformers – Hus, then Luther, while in England under the Commonwealth, the Levellers and Ranters and other sects went in for a type of popular propaganda which is the ancestor of modern democratic controversy.

Mass propaganda came into its own in the French Revolution on every level – the formal rhetoric of the National Assembly, mob oratory, the proclamations of the Committee of Public Safety, mass terror, show trials, the implacable eloquence of the public prosecutor, the spectacles of the artist David, the songs of the revolution. But it was all very unsystematic. The Marxists were later to analyse the process and to make the distinction, still maintained to this day in the Agitprop department of the Soviet Communist party, between propaganda and agitation. In this interpretation, proganda is the long-term inculcation of a system of ideas; agitation is the explanation and exploitation of particular issues which excite the masses. Lenin attached great importance and gave close attention to both processes; one of the reasons why he rejected individual terrorism was that it was detrimental to propaganda and agitation, which he regarded as the primary function of the underground Bolshevik cadres in Tsarist Russia. Of course, the conditions of underground struggle placed very severe restrictions on the Bolsheviks' propaganda operations. Nevertheless owing to their experience and study in the matter they were able to exploit the unlimited freedom of Russia in 1917 more skilfully than any other party in agitation on the factory floor and in the armed forces, in impressive demonstrations and mass meetings. Lenin was the first to recognize the importance of broadcasting as a medium of international propaganda. However, despite all this study and effort, when it came to the crunch Hitler was able to play the Communists right off the propaganda stage.

How did this come about? There were, in fact, very severe limitations on Communist propaganda efforts. They took their tune from the Soviet Communist Party which had been accustomed to operate first in the conspiratorial underground of Tsarist Russia, then for a short time in the total chaos of 1917, when there was no mass national public opinion to be swayed, and finally with a monopoly of all propaganda media and a total absence of competition. This gave the Communists' propaganda – however effective and opportunistic their agitation on particular questions might be – an élitist, authoritarian and doctrinaire character. Right up to the present day the contrast persists between, on the one hand, the interminable doctrinaire utterances of the Communist Parties, interesting, and indeed comprehensible, only to the pedants of Marxism–Leninism and to professional students of their pedantries, and infinitely tedious to the masses whose will they are supposed to represent, and on the other hand the often effective exploitation by the Communists of class and racial grievances in capitalist countries. The doctrinaire polemics between Moscow and Belgrade in 1948 and between Peking and Moscow since 1963 resemble nothing so much as the mutal anathemas against heresy interchanged by the prelates of the early Church. They fly to and fro above the uncomprehending and uninterested heads of the masses whom they are supposed to influence. They are code messages exchanged between party bureaucrats more designed for legitimation, self-justification and party discipline than for mutual persuasion. Such doctrinaire pronouncements have the disadvantage of limiting the field of possible converts, alienating possible supporters and restricting the scope of opportunistic agitation. So it was that the Marxist parties in Germany, both the Communists and the Social Democrats, while able to hold most of their working-class supporters, by their restricted class attitude alienated those among the bourgeois parties who might have made a common front with them, abandoning the nationalist appeal to the Nazis.

Hitler knew no such inhibitions. The Nazi Party had, it is true, a programme – the Twenty-five Points – and Hitler insisted that it must remain unalterable, only in order that he might ignore it. The socialistic and anti-capitalist elements in it were useful for winning mass support, but the Fuehrer never allowed them to restrict him in making a deal with the capitalists, when this was tactically desirable to gain power.

His purposes and circumstances were indeed widely different from those of Lenin. Whereas the Bolshevik leader was intent on finally smashing the already shattered state machine and army in order that a disciplined conspiratorial minority might seize power by a *coup d'état*, Hitler wanted to lay hands on a highly organized and efficient governmental and military machine in order to use it for his purposes. To this end he concentrated on propaganda, penetration of all levels of society and a constitutional take-over of power.

By far the most brilliant and penetrating passages in the turgid and unreadable prose of *Mein Kampf* are those which deal with propaganda. Hitler gave the term a very broad meaning, covering not only 'the magic power of the spoken word' – to which he himself attached the greatest importance – and the written word, but also the mass display of disciplined force, the highly organized terror which inspired in the movement confidence in its own invincibility and in its opponents a sense of their own impotence. For the masses, the objects of this propaganda, 'the great stupid flock of our sheepishly patient people', he displayed a boundless contempt, but he had an instinctive grasp of how to stir their lower depths. The principles he lays down are few and simple – no abstract ideas, an appeal to the emotions, concentration on a few basic necessities and repetition of stereotyped formulae, no objectivity but a systematically one-sided attitude to every problem, uncompromising assault on the adversary in which the bigger the lie the more likely it is to be believed, the identification of a single enemy (e.g. the Jew) whose conspiracy can be blamed for all popular grievances, however diverse. These principles must be applied with boundless determination, fanatical conviction and indomitable pugnacity, backed up by force where necessary.

Hitler professed to have learnt some of these techniques from the Austrian Social Democrats in Vienna and their opponent, the anti-Semite Lueger, some of them from the effectiveness (exaggerated in his mind, one fears) of British propaganda in the First World War. But his inspiration in his first major attempt to apply these techniques was Mussolini. The Beer Hall *putsch* of November 1923 came a year after Mussolini's march on Rome, and Munich was supposed to be the base for a similar march on Berlin. Regarded as a *coup d'état* it was a bungling and incompetent operation compared, for example, with Lenin's seizure of power. There was no attempt to occupy any of the key points, the Central Telegraph office or the Railway Station except by the soldier of fortune, Roehm, who seized the Army Headquarters. Instead Hitler attempted by the crudest of propaganda means – at the revolver point – to induce the rulers of Bavaria to join him in taking over the government of Germany. Next, using the 'big lie' technique, he proclaimed that they had joined him. They had not, in fact, done so, realizing that with the Army High Command against it the *putsch* could not possibly succeed. The only resource left to Hitler was to demonstrate that the authorities would not, when it came to the crunch, fire on him and in his demonstration in the Feldherrnhalle in Munich he exploited, for this purpose, the legendary figure of Field-Marshal Ludendorff – in principle the same sort of trick which Pisistratus had played with the simulated figure of Athene twenty-five centuries before. It failed; the police fired; Hitler fell, and although Ludendorff marched fearlessly on, the game was up.

It was a knock-down propaganda defeat, but such defeats are rarely decisive, and Hitler was able to turn his trial into a triumph. His judges permitted him to exploit the court as a propaganda forum, an opportunity which he seized with great skill and daring. The light penalty imposed – 'in a State [to quote Alan Bullock] where disloyalty to the régime was the surest recommendation to mercy' – gave Hitler time to reflect on the lessons of his failure and to prepare in, *Mein Kampf*, the ideological basis for the next attempt.

It was at this time, in 1924, that Hitler came to the conclusion that there must be no more armed risings – although the threat of a *putsch* might be useful for scaring the adversary – that the take-over of power must be constitutional – although to encourage his followers and terrorize his enemies, he announced that heads would roll after the take-over – and that the Nazi Party should be fashioned into a state within a state, ready to substitute the Third Reich for the Weimar Republic when the system had been sufficiently undermined. Hitler indeed, after the ensuing seven lean years, expressed himself thankful that the Munich *putsch* had not succeeded, since the motley Party of that time would not have been the well-tempered instrument of power which it later became. A comparison of the solidity of Nazi power, which could only be overthrown by conquest, with the flimsiness of the Fascist régime in Italy, which collapsed from its inner divisions, bears out earlier lessons that such a long period of preparation contributes to the durability of a régime.

Hitler set about building the Party with a single-minded ruthlessness which has been matched only by Lenin. Many of his techniques were similar. His principle, too, was that 'the strong is strongest alone'. Very early, like some great cuckoo in a hedge-sparrow's nest, he had ousted the petty bourgeois leaders of the tiny German Workers' Party, and, exploiting his genius as a popular orator and propagandist to win both converts and financial support, had made himself the indispensable dictator of the Party. He refused to ally himself with other parties which he could not control. Instead he surrounded himself with 'outsiders' of one sort and another who were entirely dependent on him – men from the margins like the Balts Scheubner-Richter, that most tedious and addlepated of ideologues, who was shot while marching at Hitler's side in the Munich *putsch*, Alfred Rosenberg, and Gertrud von Seidlitz, who helped to finance the Party newspaper; or like Hess who had spent most of his early life in Egypt; or scoundrels from the political underworld like the blackmailer Hermann Esser and the sadistic Jew-baiter Julius Streicher; adventurers like the homosexual soldier of fortune Roehm or Heines, and the air-ace and former drug-addict Goering. Like Lenin, Hitler believed that scoundrels could well do better service in a revolutionary party than respectable bourgeois. However he was well aware of the need for more respectable supporters, too, and exerted his considerable personal magnetism to attract them. He did not mind if his followers feuded among themselves; indeed he followed Machiavelli's advice in playing them off against each other. What he would not tolerate was any leadership independent of his own. When the Strasser brothers made common cause with the Social Democrats in demanding expropriation of the great estates of the former royal houses and by their devotion to the Socialist points in the Party programme endangered the finances of the Party, Hitler outwitted them and seduced their most able supporter, Goebbels. Otto Strasser was expelled from the Party in 1930 for taking the Socialist part of the programme seriously; Gregor Strasser, the one man who, by his organizing ability, energy and eloquence, might conceivably have challenged Hitler for the leadership of the Party, was reserved for a grimmer fate.

The years from Hitler's release from prison in 1925 down to 1929 were lean years for the Party electorally, The crisis resulting from the inflation and the French occupation of the Rhineland, which had created a revolutionary situation in 1923, had receded. There was growing prosperity and decreasing unemployment. By May 1928 in the Reichstag elections the Nazi party could gain only 810,000 votes and only 12 seats out of 491 in the Chamber.

However all this time the membership of the Party was growing and – what is more important – Hitler was building his state within a state. He reduplicated every department of government within the Party apparatus; but what really mattered was the apparatus of propaganda on the one hand, and, on the other, the apparatus of force to impress it upon the mass of the people. The soul in this propaganda body was Hitler himself, the mob orator. No one who ever heard him will doubt his genius in this field; no one merely by reading his speeches could imagine the effect. When speaking to a brief he would often start off awkwardly, fumbling for words, showing every sign of boredom. Then suddenly he would get a response from his audience; he would feel the emotion of the moment in himself, and become transformed by it. The halting stream of words would become a cataract of sound; the exact sense might be obscure, but the emotional meaning was unmistakable and it was this that gripped his audience. In time, as the technique was perfected, the process became more mechanical and automatic; a feed-back system was built in; the correct emotional responses were guaranteed by the nature of the audience; Hitler himself responded to these stimuli; the resonance between speaker and audience was established. The technique became a regular one at Nazi meetings and was of course exploited by other speakers. Goebbels in particular was a brilliant speaker, more polished than Hitler; but no one could match the Fuehrer in the apparently spontaneous display of daemonic force, above all the force of hatred of the Jews, of the Czechs or any other adversary of the moment, and in the brutal will to overcome. His was the kind of rhetoric in which words became deeds and its success depended on the machinery to transform words into deeds.

The machinery consisted above all in the storm-troopers, the brown-shirted S.A., who were permitted – with some resistance from the Social Democrats and Communists, but little restraint from the police or government – to dominate the streets and meetings of the Weimar Republic. For Hitler, the S.A. was a propaganda instrument of terror; so far from concealing this he sought publicity for the storm-troopers' terrorist activities. For some of their leaders, on the other hand, including the most famous of them, Roehm, the S.A. were a supplement or even a substitute for the army. This was precisely what Hitler did not want. His aim from the first was to co-operate with the High

Command, until he could gain control of it. He had launched the Party newspaper, *Voelkischer Beobachter*, with the help of secret army funds. He had intended to carry out the 1923 *putsch* with at least the tacit consent of the army and not against it; when he failed in this, he gave up. The loyalty of the army to the Weimar Republic was at best dubious, but during the relatively prosperous and secure years from 1924–9 there was little to test it.

The test came in 1929–33, with the economic collapse, mass unemployment, the bankruptcies and fear of bankruptcies among the middle classes and petty bourgeois; and, when it came, it revealed that, apart from the Social Democrats and their following in the trade unions, there was no considerable body of opinion loyal to the Weimar Republic. Even working-class loyalty was divided by the Communists, who acting on instructions from the Comintern and convinced that there was a revolutionary situation which would lead to the dictatorship of the proletariat, concentrated above all on attacking their rivals for the leadership of the proletariat, the Social Democrats – 'the Social Fascists', as they called them with a characteristic mixture of self-deception and mendacity.

For the rest, disloyalty began at the very top with the senile President Hindenburg and the petty intriguers who surrounded him, the devious General Schleicher, the conceited Papen, and the Field-Marshal's feeble son, Oskar von Hindenburg. The Chancellor Bruening, the conscientious and well-meaning leader of the Catholic Centre Party, was unable to secure sufficient support in the Reichstag to implement the measures necessary to restore the economy. He therefore sought emergency powers from the President, putting the fate of the Republic in Hindenburg's infirm and indecisive hands. The Weimar Constitution included practically every possible safeguard of democracy, every means of measuring the will of the people. But the people simply was not interested in freedom and in those circumstances every possible guarantee of democracy can be turned to its destruction. The long series of elections, general, presidential and provincial – there were five elections in eight months in 1932 – the constant campaigning and agitation, led to bitterness and extremism and merely contributed to the general disorder and insecurity. The mutual vituperation between the Marxist and the middle-class parties made any common front impossible; the middle-class parties were unable to unite among themselves either at the local or the national level. The capitalists, fearing a rising revolutionary tide among the workers driven to desperation by unemployment, were prepared to finance the Nazis as a reinsurance.

From 1928 to 1932 the Nazi vote rose from 2½ per cent of the poll to 37 per cent. They had become the strongest party in the Reichstag and together with the other party bent on destroying the Republic, the Communists, they formed a majority which could make any stable constitutional government impossible. What was even more serious the Nazis had infiltrated into every institution and in particular the police, the civil service, and the nationalist and militarist clubs that abounded in Germany. Even so there was still a chance for the Republic when in April 1932 Bruening and his Defence Minister General Groener, the one army leader to show consistent loyalty to the Republic, banned the S.A. But this firm measure was revoked by the intrigues of Schleicher, and the stormtroopers were free, by their terrorist activities, by their street riots with the Communists and the Social Democratic Reichsbanner, to resume their work of social disruption.

The process did not differ widely from that described in Dostoevsky's account in *The Possessed* of the activities of the Russian terrorist Nechayev and of the creation of a revolutionary situation in a small town. The Nazi process was more elaborate and organized, but the psychology was similar, this being a field in which the distinction between right and left is not very important. Mr W. S. Allen in *The Nazi Seizure of Power* has described the operation in a small Hanovarian town between 1930 and 1935, basing himself on contemporary documents and interviews with survivors. It shows Hitler's propaganda monster stretching its tentacles down to the very roots of German life, gripping the nationalist instincts of the middle class and petty bourgeoisie, the civil servants, shop-keepers and school teachers, and at the same time strangling the resistance of the working class already weakened by the unemployment and insecurity of the Depression. The certainty and confidence of the Nazis appealed to the idealism of people paralysed by insecurity and despair, while the psychological terror of the S.A. added an appeal to self-interest. The result was the atomization of society, a preparation for the tyranny which was to come. It was an extraordinary triumph for the Nazi propaganda machine; yet even a month after Hitler came to office the Nazis could win only 44 per cent of the votes cast in a general election; and if any considerable body of the Weimar establishment, the army, police and civil service had stood firm the Nazi seizure of power could have been pre-vented.

We have come a long way from Polycrates' seizure of power with the help of two brothers and fourteen hoplites to Hitler's *Machtergreifung* twenty-five centuries later with all the appar-atus of modern mass-organization, terror and propaganda. Yet despite the differences in scale certain similarities remain. Polycrates very soon killed one of the brothers who helped him to power and sent the other to be held as a prisoner in Egypt. The fate of some who have helped modern tyrants to power is not dissimilar.

6. The Consolidation of Power

When asked what he thought of Mussolini's prospects, that other great Italian gangster, Al Capone, replied: 'He'll be O.K. if he can keep the boys in line.' This is the modern equivalent, in the age of the highly organized mass party and state, of the oldest maxim of tyranny – that given by Periander the ruler of Corinth in the late seventh and early sixth century B.C. When his fellow tyrant Thrasybulus of Miletus sent to him for advice on how to rule, he took his messenger out into the fields and, without saying a word, lopped off the tallest ears of corn with his stick. The same advice was given by Frederick II Hohenstaufen to his monstrous satellite Ezzelino da Romano, and has been acted on by most other tyrants before and since.

Aristotle tells us that this same Periander of Corinth instituted most of the traditional safeguards of tyranny, although a number of them were borrowed from Persian despotism. Besides lopping off the outstanding men and destroying the proud, the ruler must guard against everything that causes the twin emotions of pride and confidence among the people. He must prohibit all associations among them such as common meals and clubs for fellowship and education and study circles and debates. He must prevent anything in fact that will enable the people to have knowledge and confidence in each other. He will keep the people always on show and hanging around his palace gates in order to make them slavish. He will send out informers, so that people may fear to speak freely. The tyrant will stir up quarrels between nobles and people and among the rich. He will not make one man great, but will exalt several in order that they may keep an eye on each other. If the ruler wishes to remove someone from power he should do so by gradual stages and not take away the whole of his authority at once. He will make his subjects poor so that they may be too busy to plot against their rulers – hence most of the great building works of tyrants. Finally he will be a maker of war in order to keep the people busy and in need of a leader. Tyranny, in fact, says Aristotle, aims at three things – first to keep the subjects humble, secondly to have them distrust each other, thirdly to render them powerless for political action.

There has been progress in the tyrant's technique since Aristotle's time, but the essentials remain similar. The basic dilemma of tyranny is how to combine that fragmentation of society, which will enable the ruler to maintain his power, with the degree of social organization which will enable him to achieve his purposes. The solution depends largely on the circumstances in which he comes to power.

The first priority obviously is to smash all the organizations of the opposition. In the case of a ruler who comes to power after a long period of civil war or disorder this work may largely be done, as we saw in the last chapter, before he has absolute control of the government. This was naturally the case with those early Greek tyrants who converted traditional kingship into absolute rule. Further the earlier wave of Greek tyrants in the sixth century B.C. did not have to contend with organized opposition parties. It was sufficient to execute or exile a few of the aristocrats and to hold hostages from their families as Pisistratus did in Athens. He rewarded his followers with the estates of those whom he exiled, bound the aristocracy to him by diplomacy and the commons by welfare measures. The rulers of the second wave of tyranny at the end of the fifth and during the fourth century B.C. had a sterner task. Arising in conditions of stasis or class-war and having to contend with parties organized on a class basis, they were correspondingly violent in their methods. For example, Agathocles of Sicily, at the beginning of the third century, went a little too far even for Machiavelli's tolerant taste, when he called together the Senate and the people and slaughtered all the richer ones on the spot.

In Rome, as we have seen, all organized opposition to Augustus had been shattered in the civil wars and proscriptions culminating in the Battle of Actium. His purpose therefore was not to smash any oppositional organization, but to bind potential opponents to himself. This he did by purging the Senate, by distributing the lands of his fallen opponents among his own supporters and among the retired legionaries, and by cautiously drawing into alliance the surviving Roman potentates and giving them offices in which they could not hope to rival him in authority or military strength or prestige. Those provinces which would confer the most military power were awarded to new men who owed their rise only to the Emperor.

Napoleon was able to follow a similar policy, since most of the killing had been done for him by the Jacobin terror and the counter-terror. The consolidation of power which followed the *coup d'état* of Brumaire between 1799 and 1804 was carried through with a minimum of bloodshed and a maximum of efficiency. Considering that it was executed concurrently with the elaboration of the Code Napoléon and the conclusion of the Concordat with the Church, the statecraft of Napoleon in this phase must be regarded as matching his military genius. The basis of this great manoeuvre was, of course, military power, and without the victory of Marengo – a close-run thing – it probably could not have been carried through.

The First Consul, after Brumaire, had absolute power and had been able to get rid of the constitutional restraints which Sieyès had sought to place on him, turning Sieyès himself and the senators into his prisoners. Marengo, the peace with Austria, the Peace of Amiens with England, put him in an unassailable position. He was able to suppress the Jacobin opposition on the left as a result of the Opéra bomb plot of December 1800 which led to over a hundred executions and deportations. The Royalist opposition on the right suffered four years later with the trial and execution of the Duc d'Enghien, which Napoleon later tried to blame on Talleyrand, but which served him as a useful deterrent against *émigré* conspiracies. He had no difficulty in dealing with a couple of military plots. He was able to reduce the Senate and legislature to a mere rubber-stamp function. Napoleon concentrated all important appointments in his own hands and supervised the setting up of a thorough police and espionage system under Fouché, reinforcing it with powers of arbitrary arrest, special tribunals and a well disciplined judiciary. The press was radically cut back and a thorough-going system of censorship imposed. The *Moniteur*, for which Napoleon himself wrote articles, laid down an official propaganda line. In a word, the foundations were laid for the first modern dictatorship. The fact that it was a popular dictatorship does not affect the fundamental principle. The two plebiscites, in which he received overwhelming popular support as First Consul for life and then as founder of an Imperial dynasty, were more genuine than subsequent similar operations. Opposition could be openly registered, but there was not much of it. The Emperor had, after all, brought peace, military glory, order and some prosperity to a distracted people. But he was not prepared to rest his power on popular support; with his contempt and fear of the mob he would probably have agreed with Machiavelli's dictum that he who builds on the people builds on mud. Indeed, the Bonapartist dictatorship differed from its successors in the avoidance of any mass movement.

Lenin, while of course he did not share Bonaparte's horror of the mob, and was indeed very well able to exploit it for his own purposes, had a very similar attitude towards dependence on the masses as a support and sanction for political action. When putting the case for the October *coup d'état* to the Bolshevik Central Committee he said: 'We cannot be guided by the mood of the masses; that is changeable and unaccountable. We must be guided by an objective analysis and estimate of the revolution.' True he went on to say: 'The masses have given their confidence to the Bolsheviks and ask from them deeds, not words' – entirely without evidence, since when the masses went to the polls three weeks after the Bolshevik seizure of power, the Bolsheviks won less than a quarter of the seats in the Constituent Assembly. This posed a problem for Lenin who had at first been opposed to any compromise with other parties. He had indeed authorized discussions with the Left Socialist Revolutionaries and the Mensheviks on the matter of a coalition, but only as a delaying tactic. Now the Socialist Revolutionaries had won a large majority in the Constituent Assembly. Therefore Lenin decided for tactical reasons to split the Party by forming a coalition with the Left Socialist Revolutionaries and three of them became ministers in the Government. By this opportunistic expedient Lenin originated what was to become a classic Communist technique in dealing with other parties – what the Hungarian dictator Rákosi was later to describe, in a grisly phrase, as 'salami tactics'. The left Socialist Revolutionaries were brought into the government, but some of the leaders of right Socialist Revolutionaries were arrested even before the Constituent Assembly met and the right-wing Kadets (Constitutional Democrats) were outlawed. Lenin at once laid it down that to take notice of any decisions of this last democratic assembly of Russia would be treason to the proletarian revolution. In any case it was not to be allowed to take any decisions. The Bolsheviks walked out of the Assembly and the sailors on guard closed the proceedings on the ground that 'the Guard was tired'. The next day a handful of sailors excluded the representatives, who tamely acquiesced. There was a peaceful demonstration against this act of repression; a few of the demonstrators were killed. In less than a year from the February Revolution, the last sparks of democracy were stamped out; the last ashes of freedom were soon to follow.

The total abolition of all the non-Bolshevik parties took four years. The first victims of the terror were the anarchists, who with their tradition of revolutionary conspiracy were regarded as rivals. Even after their round-up and the arrest of many of them in April 1918, Makhno, the famous Ukrainian anarchist peasant leader, found some still operating in Moscow when he came there to visit Lenin during the summer. Similarly, although one of the first Bolshevik decrees abolished all newspapers showing resistance or disobedience to the

Workers' and Peasants' Governments, a Kadet newspaper and a Menshevik periodical survived until the summer of 1918. It was in July 1918 that the uneasy and opportunistic coalition with the Left Socialist Revolutionaries came to an end. The Left Socialist Revolutionaries, like the Bolsheviks, were a revolutionary and conspiratorial party with a tradition of terrorist activity. They did not, however, approve of terror by the State. Although a good many of the Security Police were Socialist Revolutionaries, the party called for the abolition of the Cheka and for the cancellation of the humiliating Peace of Brest-Litovsk. In an attempt to force a breach with Germany, they assassinated Count Mirbach, the German Ambassador, and attempted to seize power in Moscow and other towns. The *coup* was ruthlessly suppressed with shootings and arrests; and an even greater wave of terror followed in August 1918, following the assassination of the head of the Leningrad Cheka Uritsky and the attempt on Lenin. This was really systematic terror; hundreds of the so-called bourgeoisie were executed in each of the major towns; there was no pretence that they had anything to do with the assassinations. This would probably have meant the end of the political parties, but for the civil war and the foreign intervention, which caused the Bolsheviks to seek what allies they could secure and induced many Mensheviks and Socialist Revolutionaries to make common cause with them in resisting a restoration of the old régime. As a result, these two political parties continued to exist for another two years in a strange half-light of legality, now holding congresses, taking part in local elections, their leaders even addressing the Supreme Soviet, now being harried, searched and arrested by the Cheka. At the All-Russian Congress of Soviets at the end of 1919 the Menshevik leader Martov, Lenin's old friend and antagonist in exile, demanded 'freedom of the Press, association and assembly ... inviolability of the person ... abolition of executions without trial, of administrative arrests and of official terror', only to be told by Lenin that this would involve going back to bourgeois democracy, and that both terror and the Cheka were absolutely indispensable.

By 1921 with the civil war and the intervention ending, the appeasement of other parties was no longer necessary, and with widespread famine and discontent – illustrated in its most extreme form in the rising of workers and sailors in Kronstadt in March – it was no longer advisable. By the summer, all political activity outside the Bolshevik party was liquidated. From that time, the political history of the Soviet Union has been centred on the struggle for the control of the Party.

It will be seen that the 'salami tactics', by which all independent parties were destroyed slice by slice, was by no means the systematic process which it was later to become in the Communist take-over in the satellite states of Eastern Europe. Indeed, it could be argued that Lenin was pushed into it by the pressure of civil war, of conspiracies, and foreign intervention; and certainly these developments did play a part in determining the method and timing of the liquidation process. But Lenin would not have defended his actions on these lines. For him the dictatorship of the proletariat meant sole and total control by the Bolshevik Party. The Left Socialist Revolutionaries might be admitted to the government as a temporary expedient, but they must be either gobbled up or liquidated – and in 1922 their leaders became the victims of the first great political trial. For Lenin, basing himself on Marx, the political parties were the representatives of given classes, to be tolerated although permitted no power, as long as this would help to gain the assistance of members of these classes, but to be liquidated when they were no longer useful. The essential question in such relationships was 'who-whom'? and Lenin, who identified himself with the vanguard of the proletariat, was determined to be 'who'.

From this philosophy the Terror followed naturally. Again, it may be argued that Lenin was pushed into it by the civil war and intervention and indeed shortly after the Revolution he said: 'We are reproached with using terror. But such terror as was used by the French revolutionaries who guillotined unarmed people we do not use and, I hope shall not use.' But within a month 'the All-Russian Extraordinary Commission' for combating counter-revolution and sabotage was set up – the Cheka for short, the ancestor of so many terrible sets of initials through the O.G.P.U., N.K.V.D. and K.G.B. to the U.D.B.A. in Yugoslavia and the A.V.O. in Hungary. Some such organization was, no doubt, necessary in conditions of civil war and foreign intervention. The question is whether Lenin restrained it or encouraged it in its excesses. In fact, he had always regarded the Terror as an essential component of the Revolution, not the isolated conspiratorial acts of terror of the People's Will and Left Socialist Revolutionaries' type, but organized mass terror by the party in power. So far from restraining it he encouraged it and his conversation and correspondence during this period is studded with such phrases as 'shoot them', 'kill them', 'put them against the wall'; one may say that this is no more than the traditionally violent tone of Marxist controversy, but when coupled with power it came to mean a great deal more than the Red Queen's 'Off with his head'. He actually rebuked those who tried to restrain the excesses of workers, which he regarded as a symptom of revolutionary ardour.

Yet Lenin was personally not an inhumane man. He often intervened to soften the rigours of the terror against individual acquaintances. But once the label bourgeois or counter-revolutionary was affixed to a person, a party or a class, they were beyond the bounds of humanity, mere objects to be removed. Such 'blindness of heart' – to use the phrase of the litany in the Book of Common Prayer – is a defect of the moral imagination not uncommon in fanatics. Even Oliver Cromwell, a man 'naturally compassionate towards objects in distress even to an effeminate measure' was able to describe the Drogheda massacre as 'a marvellous great mercy'; but his religion was less apt to expel whole classes of people from the bounds of humanity than Lenin's ideology. In the Pole Dzherzhinsky Lenin found a suitably fanatical instrument. Of course fanaticism is not the sole cause of the 'blindness of heart'. Besides the fanatics – Robespierre, Saint-Just, Lenin, Trotsky – there are the bureaucrats of terror – Fouquier-Tinville and Eich-

mann; its careerists – Fouché and Himmler; and its degener-
ates – Yezhov and perhaps Beria; and some of the most monstrous terrorists – Hitler and Stalin – combined several of these
characteristics.

Lenin shared neither Hitler's insane obsession with mass-
slaughter of the Jews, nor Stalin's sadistic delight in playing a
cat-and-mouse game with his colleagues and subordinates; and
it has been counted to him for virtue by Stalin's successors that
he refrained from 'the cult of personality' which is – being
translated into plain language – killing Party Comrades. While
always insisting that his own line should prevail, and denouncing those who disagreed with it in most unmeasured terms, he
bore no ill-will against them and, for example, after Zinoviev
and Kamenev had opposed the October Rising, they were
nevertheless retained in leading positions in the Party; and
while Lenin was actively in control there was still vigorous
debate in the Bolshevik Party organs.

However, even before Lenin had succumbed to his first
stroke, he had become involved in the problem of 'keeping the
boys in line'. He had taken action against the sailors and
workers of the Kronstadt base near Petrograd. The very class
of men who had been called the proletariat when they had
carried out the October rising were now – two and a half years
later – condemned by Lenin as petty bourgeoisie and slaughtered by Trotsky and the battalions of the Cheka in their thousands, because they demanded freedom of trade-union organization and of elections. At the same time the so-called
Workers' Opposition arose within the Party, with demands less
extreme than those of the Kronstadt rebels, but including trade
union or workers' control of industry. At the Tenth Party
Congress held under the shadow of the Kronstadt rising, Lenin
condemned all opposition – particularly the petty-bourgeois
anarcho-syndicalist Workers' opposition. He indicated that
discussion should be carried out with rifles rather than with
words, and produced a decree punishing 'fractionalism' – that
is to say any organized opposition within the Party – by expulsion from the Party. During the ensuing months three fairly

eminent members were expelled on charges of fractionalism, and at the same time – for other reasons – the first mass purge of the Party was carried out; it is fair to add that the term 'purge' had not yet acquired the lethal connotation which it was to assume under Stalin. The greater economic freedom afforded by the New Economic Policy was counterbalanced by greater political repression.

In fact, Lenin had not much more than a year between the end of the Civil War and his first stroke in which to consolidate the Revolution. During that period he had crushed all opposition outside the Party and set the precedent for the methods by which Stalin was to suppress all inner-Party opposition. He had reduced the trade unions and other mass organizations to those 'transmission belts' or 'levers of power' which were later to be manipulated by Stalin. He had further installed the latter in all the positions of power on which he was later to base his dictatorship. As Commissar for Nationalities Stalin was able to place his nominees in the outposts of Soviet power; as head of the Rabkrin – the Workers' and Peasants' Inspectorate – which Lenin set up to restrain bureaucratic corruption and inefficiency when it began to luxuriate on a Czarist scale – Stalin became the arch-bureaucrat, penetrating every corner of the ramshackle Soviet administration; it is true, as Lenin later observed, that the Inspectorate was as incompetent as the bureaucracy it was designed to control, but it enhanced the power of its chief; finally, a month before Lenin's stroke, his successor secured the position – as Secretary-General – which, contrary to anyone's expectation except his own, was to be his launching-pad to power.

Stalin was indeed the first to recognize the true nature of the bureaucratic despotism which the Revolution had created, and the means of controlling it. Lenin, a great technician of power even when incapacitated by illness, was the first to recognize what Stalin was about. It is perhaps impossible today to reconstruct those tragic last two years, and indeed the last days of despots tend to be their most obscure, overlaid as they are by the myths of their followers, successors and supplanters, by adoration and hatred. On the one hand there is Stalin's myth that he was the successor designate, Lenin's right-hand man and the true continuer of his work; the evidence to the contrary was suppressed in the Soviet Union for a whole generation until published by Khrushchev after Stalin's death. But it was published abroad by Trotsky who contended that the founding-father of the Revolution rather regarded himself as its elder son.

It is fairly certain that Lenin intended neither. In the document known as his Testament – and it is by no means clear that he intended it as a Testament – he is as censorious of Trotsky as he is of Stalin and in fact he brings out the weak points of most of the Party notables. It was only in a postscript that he showed realization that Stalin was the greater menace. He had already tried to enlist Trotsky in a campaign to reduce Stalin's power, the traditional device of the ruler recommended both by Aristotle and Machiavelli, not to raise up one great man but to play off one potentate against another. But Trotsky remained strangely blind to the threat of his dim, grey adversary, whom to the end of his life he underrated. Having failed to restore a balance which would enable him to control the camarilla of potentates, who were sharing out the power which he was no longer able to wield, Lenin perhaps attempted in his so-called Testament to pierce the fence they had thrown around him and to reach the rank and file in the Congress of Soviets or Party Congress. Vain endeavour, by the man who had already deprived the rank and file of any significant power to influence events. If this interpretation is right, then Lenin would not have been the first or last ruler, who, feeling the power slipping from his hands, attempted to determine the future course of the régime he had established.

If Lenin in his dying days was indeed attempting to re-direct his revolution in this way, he failed – and inevitably failed – owing to his own past actions which could only lead to the kind of tyranny which such observers as Rosa Luxemburg, Plekhanov and Martov prophesied. Lenin in his brief tenure of power stands in somewhat the same relation to Stalin as Julius

Caesar did to Augustus, except that one must add that Lenin points far more unambiguously towards Stalin than Julius does towards Augustus.

It was left to Stalin to consolidate both his own power and the Soviet revolution. He justified every step along the path with a quotation or a precedent from Lenin; his 'Problems of Leninism' is not so much a distortion of the master's work as an abstraction of those parts of it which could help in the exercise and expansion of power – similar, in fact, to Lenin's own treatment of Marx and Engels. The terms for the ensuing struggle had been fixed by Lenin and Stalin himself. Lenin had determined that it would have to take place within the Party itself and that it would have to be waged between individuals and not by organized groups, since that would have involved the crime of 'fractionalism'. This meant that as long as Lenin was in power there could be no organized opposition to him. But when he became incapacitated Stalin was able not only to worm himself into a position of overwhelming strength, but also, unnoticed by his rivals, entirely to change the character of the Party and therefore the nature of the battlefield.

This helps to account for the puzzling fact that Trotsky, by far the most brilliant revolutionist surviving, and several other scarcely less formidable figures, were ousted by the obscure Stalin with such apparent ease. Explaining the phenomenon of Stalin's success Louis Fischer in his biography of Lenin aptly quotes Thucydides on the condition of stasis: 'Inferior minds were as a rule more successful; aware of their defects and of the intelligence of their opponents to whom they felt themselves inferior in debate ... they struck boldly and at once. Their enemies despised them and were confident of detecting their plots and thought it needless to effect by violence what they would achieve by their brains and so were taken off guard and destroyed.' Indeed Trotsky in all his brilliant writings after his defeat never seems to have understood quite what had hit him, until the ice-axe of Stalin's assassin settled the matter once and for all in Mexico.

So it happened that while Stalin's rivals were cavorting about the October tilting-yard in their revolutionary armour, breaking their dialectical lances on each other and wielding their ideological battle-axes, Stalin himself was at work, mole-like, in the cellarage sapping and mining and building his labyrinth of Party and police organization. In 1926, when the process was already far advanced, Kamenev remarked to Trotsky: 'It will be enough for you and Zinoviev to appear together on the platform in order to win back the whole Party.' A vain hope! Stalin had already by this time packed the Party with his agents; he had all the manoeuvres of his rivals under surveillance by the secret police; he had induced Trotsky to abandon his one power base in the Ministry of Defence; he had ousted Zinoviev from the Party Secretaryship in Leningrad on which his influence in the Party was founded and was about to remove him from the Chairmanship of the Comintern, through which he might enlist the support of the international communist movement. The rest followed inevitably – expulsion from the Politbureau, the futile, because too belated, attempt to gain support outside the Party in the army and among the masses, expulsion from the Party, exile for Trotsky and humiliating recantation for Zinoviev and Kamenev.

It was a masterpiece of the tyrannical art which deserves closer study. No one at the time of Lenin's death could have predicted such an outcome. At that time the Soviet Union was ruled by the triumvirate Zinoviev, Kamenev and Stalin, of whom Stalin was the most obscure. His more spectacular colleagues saw as their chief rival the brilliant, controversial figure of Trotsky. The ideological issue between the triumvirate and Trotsky was 'Socialism in one country' versus 'Permanent Revolution'. The issue was not in itself an urgent or vital one; Trotsky, of course, believed in continuing to build socialism in the Soviet Union even if the international revolution was delayed, but he did not believe that the process could be completed without the international revolution; Stalin also professed to believe in promoting the international revolution, but maintained that the process of building socialism in the Soviet Union could be completed even if revolution in the advanced capitalist countries did not materialize. This difference of emphasis was, however, the ideal issue for Stalin's purposes. It enabled him to represent Trotsky as an adventurist ready to put the revolution at risk by Bonapartist excesses, one without faith in Russia's own efforts; on this issue Stalin, the home-bred 'national' Communist was also able to put at a disadvantage his own allies Zinoviev and Kamenev, who owed their prominence in part to their fame in the international Communist movement and who, in any dispute on loyalty to Leninist principles, were in a weak position because of their disagreement with Lenin about the October rising; last, but not least, 'Socialism in one country' was the ideal slogan for the Party officials on whom Stalin based his power, hard-faced men who were beginning to do well out of the revolution, who wanted no adventures, but the assurance that they could get on with the job in peace and security, whatever might happen in the outside world. Not surprisingly Trotsky was defeated; his only possible recourse would have been to rely on the army, but that would have been to expose himself to the charge of Bonapartism, the bogey of all true Communists. Instead he chose to fight within the Party, but he was fighting for control of the October Party of conspiratorial intellectuals, a party which had ceased to exist, giving way to Stalin's bureaucracy of apparatchiks.

With Trotsky defeated, the triumvirate rapidly fell apart and a new struggle for power developed. Zinoviev and Kamenev were now the tallest ears of corn which must be removed. Occasion was not lacking. The next great controversy concerned the very real problem of whether to continue and even expand Lenin's New Economic Policy of giving the peasants freedom to farm their land and market their goods and of allowing some private enterprise. Bukharin, the most brilliant of the younger generation of ideologists, argued that the control of the commanding heights of the economy would guarantee socialism; therefore the more efficient peasants and entrepreneurs could be allowed to provide what the people needed and industrialization could continue at a steady pace; in this he was supported by the Premier Rykov and the chief of the trade unions Tomsky – and by Stalin. Against this right-wing group was ranged the left-wing opposition, Zinoviev and Kamenev, who eventually achieved an uneasy *rapprochement* with their old enemy Trotsky. They argued that this course would put the economy at the mercy of a new bourgeoisie in the shape of the rich peasants, who would be able to withhold their grain; there should therefore be a start of collectivization and rapid industrialization. We have already seen how Stalin crushed this left-wing opposition. Having done so, he immediately turned on the right wing which had supported him in this struggle and was easily able to overcome Bukharin, Rykov and Tomsky with even less resistance.

He was the master now and he at once swung round and made the policy of the left wing his own, carrying out the mass industrialization and collectivization which he had previously denounced, in a far more impetuous and ruthless manner than Trotsky and Zinoviev had ever advocated. It will be necessary to deal in another chapter with this decisive and unparalleled exercise of totalitarian power. Suffice it to say here that it was in fact a prime example of tyranny, in Pascal's sense of 'seeking to have in one way what can only be had in another'.

On this matter, however, history has perhaps been too hard on Stalin and too kind to Lenin. Trotsky accused Stalin of perverting the Revolution; and Stalin's heirs coined the curious phrase 'cult of personality' to thrust upon him the blame for the horrors and excesses of the last twenty years of his reign. But it must be said in extenuation – if it is an extenuation – that Stalin identified himself with the Revolution as much as Lenin did; therefore the extension of his personal power was completely equated with the extension of the Revolution; and it was Lenin who, by forcing the hand of history and by cutting out the stage of spontaneous development through bourgeois democracy, which in the more orthodox Marxist view should precede the proletarian *coup d'état*, had put the Revolution on the power lines along which Stalin now gave it a fearful second impetus. Whether Lenin, realizing the atrocious implications of this second revolution would have turned back and continued to develop the New Economic Policy – thus proving himself a Tito before his time – is more than doubtful; for he was never a man to shrink from the most extreme logic of his actions and convictions; nor is it the general experience that dictators tend to change such basic characteristics in advancing age; rather they are apt to carica- ture their younger selves. Certainly Lenin's personality was very different from that of Stalin; he would never, so to speak, have put himself in the Mausoleum, for he abhorred such hierophantic nonsense, in that respect having far less contact with Russia's peasant masses than Stalin. Further Lenin's terror was impersonal, clinical, in the style of Robespierre rather than Ivan the Terrible, while Stalin's was applied with a certain sadistic relish; but it is doubtful whether to the victims this distinction of style and atmosphere would have made much difference.

In any case, whatever Lenin himself would have done, had he survived, he had left behind him a system in which the most ruthless, suspicious and vindictive contender for power was liable to win. Stalin when he celebrated his triumph in complet- ing the collectivization and the first five-year plan at the seven- teenth Bolshevik Party Congress in 1934 – the so-called Con- gress of Victors – had much to be suspicious about. The mas- sacres, the deportations, the purges had left a bitter legacy of hatred and discontent – a discontent which had penetrated right into Stalin's own household, when in 1932 his wife had committed suicide, leaving behind a letter of reproach, both personal and political. Moreover the opponents who might exploit this situation had been scotched not killed. It is true that Trotsky, the serpent, had been expelled from the Soviet Garden of Eden, but he continued to infiltrate his venom from abroad, and Stalin, who was well aware of the revolutionary effects of Lenin's similar activities from abroad, was little inclined to underrate the danger. In dealing with these opponents, Stalin had followed Aristotle's precept to tyrants in removing them by gradual stages, not depriving them of all their authority at one blow. They had been expelled from the Party and readmitted, exiled and recalled, denounced and humiliated by their recantations. However they still existed, admittedly under the eye of the tyrant and his agents, but some of them in positions of influence. Finally with the rise of Hitler the international situation had become menacing. Here then were all the ingredients of a conspiracy; and even if it did not exist in fact – and no convincing evidence to that effect has ever been produced – the conspiracy or the compulsion to anticipate it certainly existed in the tyrant's suspicious mind.

The incident which precipitated the atrocious sequence of events that was to follow remains shrouded in mystery. In December 1934 a young Komsomolist called Nikolaevsky penetrated, unchecked by the Security Guards, into the Smolny Institute and shot Kirov, the Leningrad Party secretary, one of the ablest of the younger generation of Bolsheviks and thought of by some as a possible successor to Stalin. There was something very curious about the whole affair, as Khruschchev admitted when, in a de-Stalinizing phase, he ordered an inquiry into it. It is not known whether the inquiry took place; certainly the results have not been published.

If, as seems probable, it was not a straightforward assassination by a disgruntled or unbalanced person, there are two other fairly plausible explanations. First, it may have been engineered by Stalin himself in order to kill two birds with one stone – to get rid of Kirov and to give an excuse for the great purges that were to follow. Nikolaevsky in fact may have played the role which the half-witted arsonist Van der Lubbe played the year before in setting fire to the Reichstag and giving Hitler the pretext for destroying the opposition; it would not have been the only trick that Stalin learned from the Fuehrer. He may well also have wished to destroy Kirov, whom he had installed as the Bolshevik leader in Leningrad, but who had become, perhaps under the influence of the rather independent-minded Leningrad Communists, the leader of the liberalizing trend in the Party.

An alternative possibility is that Stalin himself was at that time inclining towards the liberal wing of the Party and that the Secret police, fearing a threat to their empire, themselves engineered the assassination in order to poison the tyrant's suspicious mind. Svetlana Alliluyeva attributes the murder to Beria, who as secret police chief in Georgia had fallen foul of Kirov, and who at that time was working his way into Stalin's confidence.

The true story of Kirov's murder may never be known. But whatever the explanation, it started a new and original chapter in the annals of tyranny. There is no precise parallel to the great Stalinist purges although there are some partial precedents. The atmosphere in some ways resembles that surrounding Ivan the Terrible's struggle with the Boyars, with the N.K.V.D. playing the role of the Oprichnina, the gang of thugs whom Ivan put above the law to kill and rob and strike terror into all potential opponents. There are resemblances also to the French Reign of Terror, except that what happened in the heat of Revolution and foreign invasion is scarcely comparable with this cold-blooded bureaucratic campaign of mass murder. Machiavelli's description of Cesare Borgia's rise to power affords a precedent for some of the techniques used. Borgia seized Romagna by defeating the great family of the Colonna with the help of their bitter rivals the Orsini and then turned and destroyed the Orsini, just as Stalin destroyed the Bolshevik left wing with the help of the right and then turned on the right wing. Cesare first dispossessed the noble families and then exterminated them just as Stalin ousted the Bolshevik notables from power and office, then had them tried and executed. Cesare packed the College of Cardinals with his agents just as Stalin treated the Central Committee; but of course Stalin had more time and went further and proceeded to liquidate most of the Central Committee, too. Borgia put in Ramiro de Lorqua to carry out his reign of terror and then, thrusting the blame for the severity upon him, had him executed and left his body lying beside the block and bloody knife in the piazza at Cesena. 'The barbarity of this spectacle', comments Machiavelli, 'caused the people to be at once satisfied and dismayed'. Similarly Stalin executed the two successive N.K.V.D. chiefs Yagoda and the monstrous Yezhov who were his agents in the purge.

However Stalin's purge was unique in three respects: in its magnitude, ubiquity and comprehensive scale; in the fact that there was no evidence that its victims were or were likely to become a threat to the tyrant's power; and in the fantastic confessions by which the victims embraced their executioner and destroyed their own reputation. Although the means by which these were extracted are by now fairly well known, they continue to give the whole episode an extra dimension of the macabre and the mysterious. Other revolutions have devoured their own children; it was reserved to Stalin to make them vomit in public first.

These purges marked the completion of Stalin's consolidation of power. But they clearly went a great deal further than was necessary for this purpose and determined the character of the whole Stalin epoch. The attempt to separate the purges, under the title of 'the cult of personality', from the formidable achievements of the tyrant fails to take into account the essential part they played in his whole system of totalitarian rule, which will be dealt with later.

While we are better informed about Hitler's tyranny than any other owing to the capture of documents and the testimony of its agents, the moment of its birth is still shrouded in some mystery. When Hitler became Reichschancellor on 30 January 1933, at the bidding of President von Hindenburg by strictly constitutional methods, the Nazis were in a minority in a government in which most of the more important posts were held by the parties of the right, who, with the wily Franz von Papen as Vice-Chancellor and Prime Minister of Prussia, thought they could harness the Nazi beast. The problem was to make Hitler dictator, by constitutional methods, and to do it quickly, in order not to lose the impetus of the movement. The day after Hitler became Chancellor, Goebbels recorded in his diary: 'In a conference with the Fuehrer we lay down the line for the fight against the Red Terror. For the moment we shall abstain from direct counter-measures. The Bolshevik attempt at revolution must first burst into flame. At the proper moment we shall strike.' The trouble was that the Bolshevik revolution showed no sign at all of bursting into flame. The Communists were still mainly concerned with disputing the leadership of the working-class with the Social Democrats and the Social Democrats were defeated and dispirited. Did the Nazis, therefore, themselves start the fire? On the night of 27 February the Reichstag building burst into flames and the Dutchman Marinus van der Lubbe, a pyromaniac of feeble mind and left-wing views, was caught on the premises; he always contended that he did the deed single-handed and recent researches give support to his statement. The Nazis of course at once proclaimed that it was a Communist plot; but at the Leipzig Fire Trial – an object lesson in how not to arrange a show trial – the German Communist leader Torgler and the Bulgarian Comintern agent Dimitrov were easily able to refute the charge. The world believed that it was a put-up job by the Nazis, and Goering, who was then chief of the Prussian Police, boasted in private of having organized it, although denying it at the Nuremberg trial. All one can say is that, if it really was a coincidence, Providence, *die Vorsehung*, to which Hitler so often appealed, was working overtime.

The very next day Hitler got President Hindenburg to sign an emergency decree cancelling all the safeguards of the Wiemar Republic and giving himself and Goering, who had already packed the Prussian police with S.A. and S.S. men, full powers to terrorize the opposition. Hitler had already outwitted his right-wing partners in the Government into accepting new elections on 5 March. Now, with the organs of government publicity in their hands, with the Red Terror as their slogan, with the S.A. and S.S. and police terrorizing their opponents, with the money streaming in from industrialists anxious to climb on the band-waggon, the Nazis mounted their

last election campaign. The highest support they had ever
achieved in a genuinely free election was 37 per cent in July
1932; now in this last half-free election, despite prodigious
efforts, they only succeeded in raising their vote to 44 per cent
– a disappointing result, but sufficient for their purpose. With
the right-wing Nationalists – and even without them if the
Communists were to be proscribed, as they would be – the
Nazis had a majority. But to sweep aside the Weimar constitution through the Enabling Law, which was to be the constitutional foundation of Hitler's dictatorship, required a two thirds
majority. Hitler prepared carefully. In an impressive ceremony
at the historic Garrison Church in Potsdam he paid his allegiance to the aged Hindenburg, thus identifying his movement
with the ancient glories of Prussia. When the day came for the
Reichstag to meet in the Kroll Opera House S.S. men surrounded the building, baying their slogans and S.A. men
crowded the lobbies to show who was master. The Catholic
Centre Party allowed itself to be deceived by the assurance that
all measures under the act would be approved by President
Hindenburg. Although many of the Communists and some of
the Social Democrats were already in gaol, the latter alone of
the parties maintained their loyalty to the Weimar Republic to
the end and voted against the Nazi take-over. At this late
stage, even if the democratic parties had shown some degree of
unity and resolution, they could probably not have stopped the
Nazis; but they might have forced them to an illegal seizure of
power, and this would have affected the great issue of the
allegiance of the armed forces. As it was Hitler came to power
with the connivance of the representatives of the majority of
the people and the active support of a very large minority.

Here perhaps it would be in order to say a word about the
relationship between tyranny and majority rule. It is sometimes assumed that one who rules with the support of the
majority cannot be a tyrant; yet both Napoleon and Hitler, two
of the greatest tyrants of all time, may well have had majority
support through a great part of their reigns. Napoleon in many
of his most aggressive campaigns, probably had majority sup-

port among the French, but his actions, according to our definition, were none the less tyrannical for that. Hitler, for all we know, might have had at least the tacit support of the majority of the German people in his campaign against the Jews; his action was none the less tyrannical for that. Let us assume – *per impossible*, one would hope – that a democratically elected Prime Minister were to start on a similar campaign, he would be acting tyrannically; the probable result would be that he would be opposed by a majority so vehemently that he would have to take tyrannical measures to suppress it and thereby cease to depend on the popular vote and thus become an absolute tyrant. A tyrant, then, may in many of his measures have popular support, but in general his power will not depend on it.

Hitler had secured absolute power by constitutional means. He now set out to establish an arbitrary rule which would be dependent neither on the constitution nor on popular vote. although he wished to be in a position to manipulate the popular vote for tactical purposes, if desirable. The process was politely known as *Gleichschaltung* – co-ordination – and it comprised most of the devices of tyranny as outlined by Aristotle, now applied systematically on a mass scale. It was all the easier because many of the hitherto autonomous bodies which made up German society had been largely infiltrated or subverted by the Nazis before they came to power, so that any opponents of the régime were already paralysed by that mutual distrust which the tyrant aims at creating.

The Nazis abetted by Papen had already seized the government of Prussia and Goering had used its police as an instrument of power. Now the other state governments were taken over by Nazi *Reichsstatthalter*, including that of Bavaria from which Hitler had launched his first bid for power. He was determined that no one else should do likewise. Within a year the provincial governments and parliaments had been abolished.

The parties succumbed even more rapidly; for Hitler's salami chopper operated more rapidly than Lenin's. The Communists had already been proscribed in March. In May, Goering seized the Social Democrats' headquarters and a month later the party was dissolved. The Catholic Centre and People's parties quickly took the cue and dissolved themselves. The National party soon received its just reward for helping Hitler to power. The police and S.A. seized its party headquarters throughout the country and the obtuse Hugenberg, its leader, resigned from the Government and dissolved his party. On 14 July the Nazis proclaimed themselves the sole political party of Germany.

On May Day the trade unions joined with the Nazis in unprecedented mass demonstrations. The next day their headquarters and funds were seized and their leaders flung into concentration camps. The Labour Front was set up under the drunken Dr Ley; party labour trustees were installed, collective bargaining abolished and strikes banned.

Meanwhile all over the country the brown-shirted S.A. ran riot. They had already undermined the fabric of law and order; now they had all the forces of law and order behind them. The Jews, of course, were the natural object of their excesses. Some thousands of them were robbed, beaten or murdered. Their shops were stoned and subjected to a national boycott. They were expelled from the civil service, the universities, the professions. It was a foretaste of more terrible things to come. All over the country there was a paying off of old scores as the Party comrades moved into the position they had long coveted and prepared for.

For example, in the small Hanover town described by W. S. Allen in *The Nazi Seizure of Power*, there was a purge at all levels of the administration. Police, gasmen, night-watchmen who had not gone along with the Nazis were ousted. There were arrests – of Communists of course – although there were very few of them in this little town – of Social Democrats when arms were alleged to have been found in the quarters of their mass movement, the *Reichsbanner*. Publicity was given to the terror, to the arrests and house-searches: there were pictures in the press of the first concentration camp at Dachau.

Rumours were circulated about the efficiency of the Gestapo and its informers; there were said to be five Gestapo officers in the town although in fact there was only one. There were rumours of a Nazi black list (which may or may not have existed) just as there were when Britain faced invasion in 1940. The arrests, dismissals and boycotts produced a feeling of impotence and mutual distrust. All communal life among the working class was destroyed with the Social Democratic Party and the trade unions. The one class and organization which had been loyal to the Weimar Republic to the end found itself unable to put up any resistance; it had entirely misapprehended the nature of the Nazi menace by conceiving the movement as an agency of the capitalists capable of a *putsch*, like the Kapp *Putsch* which the trade unions had defeated by a general strike, but not as a radical mass movement capable of penetrating every corner of German national life. Weakened and dispirited by unemployment, there was no decisive point at which they could rally to resist this '*coup d'état* by instalments'. Still less was any resistance to be expected from the rather numerous clubs and sports clubs in the town; with their nationalistic and militaristic leanings they had no strong loyalty to oppose the Nazis. The church, Lutheran and strongly nationalist in that area, gave vocal support to the new masters, although the Nazi-controlled German Christians made little headway. In this rather middle-class town with its high ratio of civil servants and professional men, proud of their *Kultur*, there was no protest when some 500 books – a quarter of the town library – were burnt by the S.A.

Thus the people were rapidly reduced to that 'lonely crowd' of isolated and distrustful individuals which the tyrant can most easily control. However it would be wrong to depict this first year of the Nazi take-over entirely in these negative terms. By August, unemployment had been done away with in this small town – some of it, to be sure, by compulsory labour – and this gratified not only the unemployed, but also the middle classes who had seen in their existence the threat of red revolution. The young were mobilized in the *Arbeitsdienst* and the *Hitler-*

jugend and given a sense of purpose – however perverted – which had been lacking in the despair and disillusion of the Depression. In organizations like the *Winterhilfe* the party mobilized people's charitable idealistic impulses. Thus, while few outside the S.A. and the nationalistic lunatic fringe can have felt in 1933 'Bliss was it in that dawn to be alive', it was certainly exciting for the young and many of their elders were able to convince themselves that they were jumping on the band-waggon from the best possible motives. In the little town described by Mr Allen there were 100 Nazi Party members in January 1933, 400 by February, and, after the Nazi victory in the March election, there came the flood of the so-called *Maerzgefallene,* so that by May 1200 or 20 per cent of the town's population had joined the Party. When in October 1933 the plebiscite on Germany's departure from the League of Nations and the Disarmament Commission brought the Government a 96 per cent vote, the result represented far more popular support than most totalitarian plebiscites.

For years, Hitler had laboured – and had been allowed – to create a state within a state. This had now paid off in the smooth seizure of power at every level of national life. However two problems remained which every tyrant must face before his position is really consolidated – that of 'keeping the boys in line' and the control of the armed forces; and one factor made it particularly vital to solve both problems rapidly – the great age and declining health of President von Hindenburg.

The old Field-Marshal had done Hitler an indispensable service in permitting him to come to power constitutionally and casting a cloak of respectability over his gangster-like activities. Now Hitler was intent on securing the succession as Head of State and thereby the allegiance of the armed forces. For this he needed the support of Hindenburg, who was known to favour the restoration of the Hohenzollerns, and also of the army leaders. Both were becoming increasingly nervous about the excesses of the S.A., who were demanding a second revolution, and about the efforts of their leader Roehm to secure the

Gleichschaltung of the armed forces with the S.A. The disreputable and immoral behaviour of the S.A. leaders was an additional offence to the code of the Prussian officer caste. As far as the Fuehrer himself was concerned, the Brown Shirts had performed their function. He no longer needed gangs of bravoes to destroy the fabric of law and order now that the apparatus of the state was in his hands. A terrorist corps of *élite* troops was a different matter, but this Himmler was already building up in the shape of the black-shirted S.S.

Hitler at first tried to win over Roehm by persuasion and to appease him by bringing him into the Cabinet. He was one of his oldest Party comrades and had done more than anyone else to bring him to power. The effort was unsuccessful. Roehm went on agitating for the second revolution, and this was all the more disturbing because the prize of the succession was almost within Hitler's grasp. By May 1934 the leaders of the armed forces had agreed to endorse Hitler as the successor and this should clinch the matter, if nothing were to intervene to swing Hindenburg and the generals the other way in the meanwhile. But the ancient Field-Marshal was at last receiving some inkling from his entourage of the kind of monster he had raised up; and relying on Presidential support, the Vice-Chancellor Franz von Papen, who by his intrigues had secured a respectable road to power for the monster, now issued a warning that it should not behave so monstrously. Papen's speech in mid-June 1934 – the last public utterance critical of the Nazis in Germany – at Marburg would have been a courageous act if he had stood to it. Instead in the ensuing purge those who had composed it for him were murdered, while he continued to serve as the pliant instrument of the tyrant who now had an additional hold on him. However for the moment his protest was to be taken seriously because it was backed by the threat of the Minister of Defence, General von Blomberg, that unless the tension was relaxed the President would impose martial law and put the army in control.

Hitler, who would still probably have preferred to settle the matter by conciliation, was being pushed towards drastic

action, particularly as rumours of *putsches* and purges were
thickening in Berlin. It is probable that Roehm was indeed
seeking to force the Fuehrer's hand towards a more radical
policy and a fusion of the S.A. and the army; he may have
entered into conversations with the irrepressible intriguer
Schleicher, who wished to stage a come-back, and with the
radical Nazi leader, Gregor Strasser. His rivals Himmler, the
chief of the S.S. – still officially Roehm's subordinate – and
Goering, who had built up his own personal police, may indeed
have convinced Hitler that he was going so far as to plan a
putsch. But the unpreparedness of the alleged conspirators on
30 June makes it certain that they were not.

Hitler vacillated up to the last moment, and then acted with
characteristic ruthlessness and treachery. The victims of the
'Night of the Long Knives' were certainly more than the 71
officially announced; they may have amounted to the Nuremberg trial estimate of 1,000. We shall probably never know,
since the records have disappeared. They included besides the
principal S.A. leaders, Roehm, Heines and Ernst, Schleicher
whose intrigues had paved the way to power for the Nazis,
Gregor Strasser who might at one time have rivalled Hitler for
the leadership, and some minor agents who knew too much.
The slaughter bore out Machiavelli's dictum that 'He who is
the cause of another coming to power is ruined; because that
predominancy has been brought about either by astuteness or
else by force, and both are distrusted by him who has been
raised to power.'

Hitler may not have planned such drastic action in advance,
but he certainly derived the greatest possible advantage from it.
Inveighing against the *putsch*, which after the event he can
scarcely have believed in, an alleged plot with the French,
which he certainly never took seriously, and the immorality
and perversion of some of his victims, which had never
worried him while they could be of use to him, he secured the
applause of the army leaders, who thus made themselves the
accomplices of his crimes and later, after Hindenburg's death,
their oath of allegiance which was to make them his accom-

plices in far worse crimes. He had forged for himself a Praetorian Guard in the shape of Himmler's S.S. which had proved
that it would stick at nothing. It is perhaps not surprising that
after such a salutary act of terror Hitler was elected Head of
State, as Fuehrer and Reichschancellor, by 90 per cent of the
voters. Flushed with confidence the Fuehrer was able to pro-
claim: 'In the next thousand years, there will be no other
revolution in Germany.' In fact, ten years passed before there
was any serious internal threat to his power.

Such then is the consolidation of power. It is a double process comprising, on the negative side, the completion of the
fragmentation of the old society which has already been
started before the seizure of power and also the destruction of
those organizations and people which were necessary for the
demolition of the old society, but which might menace the
ruler's retention of power; on the positive side, the substitution
of those instruments or levers of power which will enable the
ruler to carry out his purposes – the bureaucracy, the security
police, the military and para-military forces, the propaganda
machine, the controlled trade unions or Labour Front and
so on. Aristotle perhaps lays too much stress, even for his own
time, on the negative side. It is true that the ruler must destroy
pride and mutual trust among the people, but most of the great
tyrants have succeeded in generating at any rate at the beginning of their rule a new sense of collective pride in military
exploits, in the sense of superiority which comes with feeling
oneself part of the vanguard of the proletariat or the master
race, in the revolution or the nation with which the leader
identifies himself.

Aristotle speaks of the tyrant as keeping his subjects always
on show and hanging around his palace gates in order to keep
them slavish. The modern tyrant's equivalent is something far
more positive, namely to have them all on parade and demonstrating in favour of whatever his wish of the moment, to have
them applauding and marching for him in order that he may
convince the outside world, his own people and indeed himself
that he truly represents the people.

It is true, as Aristotle said, that the tyrant will want to keep his subjects busy and dependent on himself and that this may involve keeping them poor. For example Stalin's mass collectivization certainly made the peasants poor, but the purpose was to gain control of the wealth which they produced to secure the rapid industrialization of the country. This industrialization in its turn was designed not primarily to increase the well-being of the Soviet people – not at any rate the existing generation – but the power of the ruler. There has been, indeed, for the past fifty years a built-in dogma of Communism, although it has already changed in Yugoslavia and is changing elsewhere, that investment in heavy industry must exceed investment in light or consumer industry. This means essentially that defence industry and those commanding heights which enable the ruler to control the whole economy must be given priority over those branches of production which would benefit the ordinary consumers. There are obviously times when such a decison on priorities is in the national interest – for example, during the period the U.S.S.R. was threatened with Nazi aggression. But the dogma has often been applied regardless of such considerations to build up the power of the ruler. Similarly, it is certainly true that Hitler increased Germany's wealth and benefited many of the six millions, who had wasted away in unemployment in the last years of the Weimar Republic, by putting them to productive work; but the work, although it may have contributed immediately to their own well-being, was essentially designed for the purposes of the ruler. The purposes of the tyrant when he has achieved his power and how he sets about realizing them are our next concern.

7. The Exercise of Power

'The subjects, under God, draw breath only by the force of the illustrious Caesar'; thus at the beginning of the thirteenth century Frederick II Hohenstaufen enunciated the principle of totalitarianism. 'The earth obeyeth us and the sea doeth homage, and all that we desire cometh forthwith to pass'; thus he foreshadowed the boasts of Stalin about changing the face of nature and the omnipotence attributed to the thought of Chairman Mao.

There is no more improbable episode in history than Frederick's attempt to impose totalitarian rule on the centrifugal society of the Middle Ages. That he failed in the straggling Holy Roman Empire is less remarkable than that he came so near to succeeding in his own Kingdom of Sicily. The means by which he achieved this have already been indicated (see Chapter 2). In the Middle Ages he was an entirely original figure, but he himself regarded the totalitarian rule to which he aspired as typical of the great rulers of the past. He compared himself to Caesar Augustus as the *Imperator Invictus*, the *Felix Victor ac Triumphator*, the *Rex Justus*, to Julius Caesar in his clemency (a quality for which he himself was not remarkable), to Alexander the Great in his uniting of the Kingdoms of the East and West. He studied at first hand the methods of oriental monarchy and was much attracted by them, as later Napoleon was. In a letter to the Nicaean Emperor Vatatses he complained about disaffected subjects and turbulent and deceitful priests, writing: 'But such things happen more easily in our Western lands. O happy Asia! O happy rulers of the Orient! who fear neither the dagger of the rebel, nor the superstitions invented by the priest!'

The same comparison is made by Gibbon, in a contrary spirit, when he contrasts the sufferings of the Romans under the cruel, bestial and profligate successors of Augustus with the conditions of the subjects of Oriental despots.

'When Persia was governed by the descendents of Sefi, a race of princes whose wanton cruelty often stained their divan, their table and their bed with the blood of their favourites, there is a saying recorded of a young nobleman, that he never departed from the Sultan's presence without satisfying himself whether his head was still on his shoulders.' Here we might interrupt Gibbon to recall that, according to Khrushchev, Stalin's ministers when leaving his presence in his latter years experienced much the same sentiments. Rustan, however, was used to it. In Gibbon's words:

Yet the fatal sword, suspended above him by a single thread, seems not to have disturbed the slumbers or interrupted the tranquillity of the Persian. The monarch's frown, he well knew, could level him with the dust; but the stroke of lightning or apoplexy might be equally fatal. ... His name, his wealth, his honour, were the gift of a master, who might, without injustice, resume what he had bestowed. ... The history of the East informed him that such had ever been the condition of mankind. The Koran, and the interpreters of the divine book, inculcated to him that the Sultan was the descendant of the prophet and the vice-gerent of heaven; that patience was the first virtue of a Mussulman, and unlimited obedience the great duty of a subject.

The minds of the Romans [continued Gibbon] were very differently prepared for slavery. Oppressed beneath the weight of their own corruption and of military violence, they for a long while preserved the sentiments, or at least the ideas of their free-born ancestors. The education of Helvidius and Thrasea, of Tacitus and Pliny, was the same as that of Cato or Cicero. From Grecian philosophy they had imbibed the justest and most liberal notions of the dignity of human nature and the origin of civil society. The history of their own country had taught them to revere a free, a virtuous and a victorious commonwealth, to abhor the successful crimes of Caesar and Augustus, and inwardly to despise those tyrants whom they adored with the most abject flattery.

Owing to these attitudes, many generations were to pass before any Roman Emperor could imitate the oriental forms of totalitarian tyranny, although some of them would have liked to have done so – the crazy Caligula, for example, who is said to have exclaimed: 'Would that the Roman people had all one throat in order that I might cut it.'

It is easy for modern man to forget that the totalitarian civilization of the great river valleys of the Middle East has proved the most stable and durable the world has ever seen. It has been suggested that these mass civilizations came into being as a result of the exploitation of the floods of the Nile and Euphrates and could only survive by collective discipline in controlling these floods; hence their totalitarian character. However that may be, although the later Greeks despised these orientals as barbarians, their age-old cultures were bound to impress the early Greeks as they emerged from tribalism into self-conscious statehood. Possibly the earliest of tyrannies arose in Lydia on the border of one of these oriental empires; and, as we have already seen, the early Greek tyrants had special connections with Egypt and Persia. These Oriental influences have made repeated contributions to the development of totalitarian rule in the West.

Besides these oriental connections, there was an indigenous totalitarian element in the Greek city state which was by no means confined to the tyrannies. Sparta was the most totalitarian of the Greek states, and yet for the longest period immune from one-man tyranny. The Spartans present the picture of a master-race, dominating a far more numerous subject-race of Helots through arbitrary secret police action by the *krupteia* and deprived of all rights and a race of *perioikoi* who were permitted certain rights in order to carry on the economic life of the country. South Africa presents a modern parallel of a white minority tyrannizing over an African majority which is in large measure outside the law; and there is danger of Rhodesia going in the same direction. As the fear of the subject-race increases, these collective tyrannies tend to become more totalitarian and arbitrary in their control of all independent institutions, such as, in South Africa, the press and the courts of justice. South Africa, admittedly, has a long way to go before it becomes a totalitarian state on the Spartan model and there are a number of factors which militate against it – wealth for example. The disciplined Spartan system of government broke down badly under the impact of the new wealth resulting from the defeat of the Athenian Empire in the Peloponnesian War; similarly the affluent society of South Africa seems ill-adapted for totalitarian discipline. In general however the pressure of an alien subject-race tends to consolidate a collective tyranny, the master-race being conscious that, if they do not hang together, they will hang separately. Only when factional strife breaks out among the rulers is there need for a one-man tyranny.

The Spartan model inspired Plato when he drew up his blueprint for a non-tyrannical totalitarian state in the *Republic*. In addition he is said to have travelled in Egypt and to have been impressed by that hierarchical despotism. He had also studied at first hand one of the greatest of the Sicilian tyrants, Dionysius of Syracuse. The Sicilian tyrants foreshadowed in a remarkable way many of the devices of modern totalitarianism. They are given credit for introducing a rudimentary secret police in the shape of *otakoustai* (or police spies) and *potagogides* (or female *provocateuses*). They were also the first to imitate the oriental habit of mass transfers of population.

In the early years of the fifth century Gelon, the military dictator who defeated the Carthaginian invaders, transferred the populations of the cities of Camarina and Gela and sold the inhabitants of Sicilian Megara into slavery; his successor Hieron, who repulsed the invasion of the Etruscans, treated the population of Naxos and Catane likewise. That later Sicilian tyrant Frederick Hohenstaufen, having defeated the Saracens in Sicily, transferred them *en masse* to the city of Lucera in Southern Italy, where they became his most loyal subjects and formed his Praetorian Guard. Stalin's mass transfers of population, equally carried out under the pressure or in the aftermath of war, were on an incomparably larger scale, and Hitler's transfers of slave labour and the Jews during the war were still more massive, the resulting genocide of the Jews being the supreme example of modern totalitarian tyranny. However the principle was the same as that applied by earlier tyrants, just as Dionysius of Syracuse by imposing confiscatory taxation on the farmers and thus driving them to slaughter their cattle foreshadowed Stalin's mass collectivization and, by sending his opponents to the stone quarries, anticipated the forced labour of Hitler's camps and the mines of Karaganda.

Totalitarianism, therefore, is not a unique feature of our age. Many tyrants have aspired to total control, some few have come near to achieving it; none have managed to be so totally totalitarian in their rule as Hitler and Stalin or, as one would have said up to the middle of 1966, Mao Tse-tung. The degree of control must depend on the nature and size of the society on which the tyrant imposes himself, his purposes and the instruments which he has for carrying them out.

The Greek tyrants were in a specially strong position because of the small size of the units of government. The free-born subjects of each city might number thousands or tens of thousands; the slaves might be more numerous, but the ruler had no need to worry about them. Such a small citizen body could be controlled without any elaborate bureaucracy or armed forces. A fairly small band of mercenaries might be enough. On the other hand, the tyrant had great external difficulties to cope with, because of the numerous small states with their lively political life. His opponents, like those of Latin-American dictators now, could often find refuge in near-by cities and work up a faction there. Partly for this reason, the Greek tyrannies tended to be short-lived.

Alexander's Empire and its successors, like the Roman Empire, suffered from the opposite difficulty in securing total control over their subjects. They were too big. Alexander and his successors might introduce many of the features of oriental despotism. The courtiers, generals and potentates might become subject to an increasingly arbitrary rule; and when later this happened in the Roman Empire which covered most of the then known civilized world, there would be no place of refuge for the victim. On the other hand, for those who did not come within the immediate ambience of the ruler there was a very great measure of freedom under the law. The great Roman colonies and Greek cities preserved some of the advantages of the city-state; and ever more numerous Roman citizens enjoyed rights which were often conscientiously safeguarded by Roman magistrates. The career of St Paul shows how wide a field of activity was open to the enterprising citizen, even if his numerous scourgings, imprisonments and final execution illustrate the hazards of exploiting these opportunities. If in its early years the Roman Empire had been a totalitarian state, Christianity would never have been able to take root and spread throughout the known world. By the time a great Emperor tried to establish total control, it was too late to prevent the growth of the religion.

The Roman Empire had known tyranny in most of its forms: the capricious madness of Caligula, the sadistic licence of Nero, the brutal stupidity of Commodus, the unlimited rapacity and cruelty of Caracalla, 'the common enemy of mankind', the voracious savagery of Maximian. But it was left to a monarch who was, by these standards, enlightened, moderate and sagacious to impose on the Empire the form, though not the substance of totalitarian rule under which it eventually collapsed, becoming an easy prey to the barbarian. The tyrants of Rome had long since debased the majesty of the Senate, obliterated those deceptive images of Republican liberty and responsibility, which Augustus had been at such pains to preserve, had placed the Empire in pawn to the Praetorian Guard and devastated great provinces by their exactions, oppression and civil wars. But their excesses were arbitrary, sporadic and unsystematic. It was the achievement of Diocletian and his successors in the fourth century to build a new Imperial court on the oriental model, based on a bureaucracy entirely dependent on the Emperor and the great officers nominated by him, to reinforce it with the rudimentary apparatus of a police state in the shape of the *'Curiosi'* or masters of the post spread through the empire, to finance it by a system of taxation which was eventually to cripple all initiative, and to regulate – unsuccessfully – everything down to the price of the smallest commodities, to tie the peasant to his land and the craftsman to his trade in a hereditary hierarchical system and finally to proceed to a systematic attempt to extirpate Christianity as the one body of opinion owing an allegiance beyond the reach of the imperial power.

It was natural that an Emperor intent on establishing a totalitarian power should wish to destroy an organization which, while politically innocuous, yet was not in all respects subject to the imperial will, which did not 'draw breath only by the force of the illustrious Caesar'. His problems in doing so were very like those of the Soviet Government in our time. A cautious monarch, he had no wish to promote disorder in the Empire which he had recently pacified and aggrandized by a victory over the Persians. But he was on the point of retirement, an aging man in a hurry, who wished to round off his reconstruction of the Empire before handing over to his successor. The latter was the savage and fanatical Galerius who pressed him on to extreme measures, and may even have incensed his mind against the Christians, by the fairly typical tyrant's trick of setting the imperial palace on fire and blaming the intended victims for it. Whatever the cause, Diocletian's persecution was more ruthless, universal and efficient than any that preceded it. The number of the martyrs was no doubt exaggerated by later devotees, and was, as Gibbon observes, very much less than those massacres which Christians were to become accustomed to inflicting on each other in the name of their faith. However, they were attended by all the circumstances of totalitarian terror to which we have become accustomed in our times, torture, brain-washing, the closing down and destruction of churches, the burning of books. By this time many leading men in the Empire were attached to the Church and they now faced the choice of renouncing their faith or their career – a familiar dilemma in Communist countries nowadays. Many of the faithful proved infirm, many of the clergy subservient to the despot; and this was to lead to a controversy, somewhat similar to that which has recently threatened schism in the Russian Orthodox Church, as to the lengths to which the Church should go in submission to the secular power, the Donatists maintaining that the hands which had abandoned the holy books and objects to Diocletian's agents were not worthy to administer the sacraments. The Soviet Christians might derive some dubious comfort from the fact that within a generation of this nadir of persecution the ancient church was transported to the apex of power and prosperity by the conversion of Constantine. Less consoling, however, might be the reflection that they live under a system which is the lineal descendant of that originated by Diocletian and consolidated by Constantine. The Christian Emperors developed the totalitarian style originated by Diocletian and very soon abandoned the generally tolerant attitude which had allowed their own religion to spread throughout the Empire. They used their power to such effect that between the fourth century, when the Christians were a small minority, and the sixth nearly the whole population of the Empire was converted – the kind of mass conversion which Mao Tse-tung is now aiming at in China.

Diocletian may indeed be seen as the direct ancestor of the modern totalitarian system in its eastern form, albeit a very remote one. It is true that even before his death, while he was in retirement, the new Empire broke up in renewed civil war, and that the seeds of division were already there in his system. However, that system in its essence was taken over by the great Constantine and, handed down through the eastern Empire, was to have a profound influence on the Tsarist autocracy, which in its turn, as we have seen, determined many of the forms and methods of Soviet communism.

Whether the great architect of this system should be included among the tyrants is a matter for doubt. Perhaps he may be included with Augustus, among the great border-line cases. Gibbon compares him somewhat adversely with the founder of the Empire, writing: 'Like the modesty affected by

Augustus, the state maintained by Diocletian was a theatrical representation; but it must be confessed that, of the two comedies, the former was of a much more liberal and manly character than the latter. It was the aim of the one to disguise, and the object of the other to display, the unbounded power which the emperors possessed over the Roman world.' Yet, while in the time of Augustus the shoots of republican liberty were still alive, although sadly mangled, by the time Diocletian came on the scene they had been trampled underfoot by generations of despots. Augustus, in fact, had a choice as to the form the Empire should take; Diocletian had very little choice at all as to how it should be preserved. In his persecution of the Christians, he perhaps exercised arbitrary power beyond the scope permitted by the standards of the Empire which, apart from some excesses, favoured religious tolerance; and his attempt to exercise detailed control over the lives of his subjects went beyond the laws and customs of the Empire up to his time. But these measures were not embarked upon with a view to increasing or maintaining his personal power, since he shortly retired to build his great palace and gardens on the shores of the Adriatic in Split and to cultivate his cabbages.

Diocletian showed himself well aware of the dangers of the system he had set up. 'How often', he is quoted as saying, 'is it the interest of four or five ministers to combine together to deceive their sovereign! Secluded from mankind by his exalted dignity, the truth is concealed from his knowledge; he can see only with their eyes, he hears nothing but their misrepresentations. He confers the most important offices upon vice and weakness and disgraces the most virtuous and deserving among his subjects. By such infamous arts the best and wisest princes are sold to the venal corruption of their courtiers.' And of course many of Diocletian's successors were neither good nor wise.

The majestic remnants of the great Emperor's palace of retirement still stand in the Yugoslav seaside town of Split. Within them there have been built down the ages, like a honeycomb in the corpse of a lion, a whole city, a Christian cathedral, Venetian palazzi, the tenements of the poor and – the latest addition – a modern café of chrome and concrete and glass. In it there hangs beside the massive pillars of Diocletian a portrait of President Tito. The juxtaposition is not inept. For the latest of the great Illyrian dictators had built up one of the most recent totalitarian states – on the Stalinist model which, as we have seen, had descended from the line of Diocletian – only to demolish it cautiously stone by stone, as it became evident that the pattern was inadequate to the needs of the modern world. The reluctant 'de-totalitarianizer' – if one may coin such a word – has something in common with the reluctant totalitarian.

It is a natural trick of historical perspective that modern totalitarian dictatorship should seem, to the age which has observed it at such close quarters, an entirely new and distinctive form of government. That the system has a number of distinctive features is indisputable. At a conference held at the American Academy of Arts and Sciences in Boston at the time of Stalin's death in 1953, Mr Carl Friedrich defined these distinctive characteristics as (1) An official ideology ... covering all vital aspects of man's existence ... focused in terms of chiliastic claims as to the 'perfect' final society of mankind; (2) A single mass party consisting ... of men and women passionately and unquestioningly dedicated to the ideology ... organized in strictly hierarchical oligarchical manner, usually under a single leader; (3) A technologically conditioned near-complete monopoly ... of all means of effective armed combat; (4) A similarly technologically conditioned near-complete monopoly of control (in the same hands) of all means of effective mass communication; (5) A system of terroristic police control ... directed against demonstrable 'enemies' of the régime ... [and] against arbitrarily selected classes of the population ... systematically exploiting scientific psychology.

Mr Friedrich argues that although one or other of these characteristics may have been present in earlier despotism they have never before all been present in combination. They are only possible in a state of advanced technology combined with widespread literacy and he adds as preconditions 'democratic' antecedents and the predilection of Christianity for convictional certainty.

If we take the Nazi and Soviet régimes as norms to which modern totalitarian dictatorships aspire, then this will serve well as a description of their distinctive characteristics. But the two régimes have in fact proved to be the exception rather than the rule among modern dictatorships; where their forms have been imitated by others, it has often been with quite different content; and indeed the significance of these forms has varied widely with the passage of time both in the U.S.S.R. and in Nazi Germany. For example, up to mid-1966 at any rate, when the great proletarian Cultural Revolution broke out the two most totally totalitarian societies in the world appeared to be little Albania and vast China. Both systems were established in conditions of not very advanced technology and with a low literacy rate (as indeed the Soviet system was); nor were there, in either case, any very pronounced democratic antecedents, while in China there was no extensive Christian background, and in Albania the background was as much Islamic as Christian. While there was a common ideology, the parties were different in their natures and functions, the Albanian Communist Party centring on a small coterie of leading families, the Chinese Communist Party sharing, as the Great Cultural Revolution was to show, the leading role with the People's Liberation Army. Even in the Soviet Union itself during the fifty years of Soviet rule, the party has changed its role from the conspiratorial revolutionary party of Lenin to the bureaucratic party of Stalin, which was itself terrorized by the secret police; then to the dominant party of Khrushchev and his successors. The role of ideology, and its claim to regulate all aspects of the individual's life, while it is certainly a distinctive feature of modern totalitarianism has varied greatly from country to country and from time to time. In Stalin's time ideology was merely the instrument of the tyrant's power. Under his successors, the ideologue Suslov became a person of importance. Hitler's handling of his own

ideology was cavalier, and he treated his own chief ideologue
Rosenberg with benevolent contempt.

When examined more closely, these distinctive features of
totalitarianism present themselves as variants, arising from
modern conditions, of traditional means by which despots have
in the past seized and maintained power. Ideology, which will
be dealt with in more detail in a later chapter, is a more precise
and self-conscious version of the mystique that has commonly
attended great rulers. The disciplined single party is the
modern bureaucratic highly organized equivalent of the faction which has always been necessary to help the tyrant to
power and sometimes to keep him there. A near monopoly of
control of all means of armed combat has always been the
essential for any tyrant, and the lack of it one of the principal
causes of his downfall; but this theme needs separate treatment. Mr Friedrich's fourth condition of modern totalitarianism – a near monopoly of all means of mass communication –
is certainly distinctive since the technological means did not
exist under previous tyrannies, except of course where there
was the means of direct communication with the small population of the city-state; such control of the means of mass
communication is necessary for the inculcation of an ideology.
The fifth condition – a system of terroristic police control
directed against both demonstrable enemies of the régime and
arbitrarily selected classes of the population – is a systematic
development of something as old as tyranny itself. It has
developed with the progress of civic organization, of technological means of detection, and perhaps of scientific psychology as a means of pressure on the victims. The latter is
possibly the most dubious form of progress. Ancient vigilantes
and inquisitors seem to have shown by instinct a very fair
grasp of the principles which Pavlov laboriously demonstrated
in his experiments with dogs and which later inquisitors have
applied in order to brainwash their human victims. Our
generation has been justly astounded by the spectacle of some
of the most famous leaders of the Communist world recanting
views which in many cases they never held and confessing to

crimes which they never committed. Yet the means of producing these results do not seem to have differed substantially from the traditional methods of isolation, impotence, sleeplessness and privation, the interchange of terror and hope, pain and relief. Nor were the successes of these methods in the modern ideological war so very different from the recantations and confessions which proliferated in the theological war which raged round the Arian heresy in the fourth century A.D. A candid old Bolshevik, if any had survived and had been in a position to speak out, might have said with Bishop Hilary of Poitiers: 'We repent of what we have done, we defend those who repent, we anathematize those whom we defended. We condemn either the doctrine of others in ourselves, or our own in that of others; and, reciprocally tearing one another to pieces, we have been the cause of each others' ruin.' However, unlike the old Bolsheviks, most of the episcopal contestants in this theological controversy survived into old age, including Athanasius the main opponent of the Emperor Constantius; the monks of the Thebaid enabled the Archbishop to evade Imperial control, something which would certainly not be possible under modern totalitarian dictatorship.

Time has, therefore, seen progress in tyranny as in other forms of government. One may say that it is the natural tendency of the tyrant to seek to extend his power either extensively or intensively, either by subjugating fresh subjects or by intensifying his controls over existing ones. What differentiates some modern tyrants from their predecessors is their ability, and, in some cases, their need to exercise more intensive power over more extensive areas and populations; the ability varies with the degree of social and technological development; the necessity of control varies both with the social conditions and with the purposes of the tyrant.

Between the age of the Greek city-state and the nineteenth century – and with the exception of some of the city-states of the Renaissance, it was not normally necessary for the tyrant to exercise any very detailed control over the majority of his subjects. Most of them were tied to the land with little freedom of movement or action; but they had a limited, though real, autonomy, which was more in danger from the local feudal lord than from the King, who might indeed be the protector of the peasants against local tyrannies and had in any case little to fear from them; for while there have been many peasants' rebellions in history, none of them has been successful. A medieval tyrant, therefore, would only need to exercise arbitrary control over a minority of powerful ministers, vassals, soldiers and prelates. However with the growing complexity of society and the diversification of the economy, with the growth of the new urban bourgeois and craftsmen classes, the field of control was extended as were its instruments. Many of these means were evolved in the Italian city-states of the Renaissance. The despots of Ferrara in the fifteenth century introduced travel documents and the system of registration for travellers, the basis of the totalitarian control of movement. The oligarchy of Venice with its wide trading interests and the bankers of the Florentine Republic laid the foundations of statistical method and of the taxation and financial system which is indispensable to the modern state.

These methods were applied on a larger scale by the monarchs who transformed feudalism into absolutism. The exactions of a Louis XI in France or Henry VII in Britain or Henry VIII's dissolution of the monasteries might well be rated as tyrannical actions, since they certainly went beyond the customs and standards of their time. It is tempting, indeed, to equate the new absolutism with the first wave of ancient Greek tyranny which arose from kings exceeding their traditional rights and prerogatives. The differences are at least twofold; the old order had for some time been breaking down in an anarchy of petty tyrannies, which made a more centralized form of rule imperative; and the King was able to carry over enough of the legitimacy and popular allegiance from the old régime to establish the legitimacy of the new. With time, this absolutism came to be regarded by the most articulate section of the population as the quintessence of tyranny; and that there certainly were tyrannical elements in the absolute monarchies, that is to say abuses of power that exceed the traditional limits of their age, is indisputable. There were the special tribunals such as the Star Chamber in Britain, which enabled the monarch to by-pass the independent courts of justice and to deprive the subjects of the traditional safeguards of law. In France the *lettre de cachet* system exposed any opponent of the King's agents to arbitrary arrest. With the centralization of the administration under the Bourbons, more and more cases were regulated by the decree of the monarch, and taken out of the hands of the ordinary courts. The traditional rights by which the various classes would have been able to resist the encroachments of the monarch were steadily eroded. Parliaments and assemblies fell into atrophy. The regional and local systems of administration which flourished under the feudal system were replaced by a centralized bureaucracy. Officials became increasingly dependent on the central authority; and the formerly independent offices of local government became atrophied and merely ornamental.

In a word, the absolute monarchs evolved much of the machinery of totalitarian rule, and, on occasions, such as Peter the Great's immense effort to modernize and westernize Russian society and in Frederick the Great's development of Prussian militarism, they exercised something very like totalitarian power. The indefatigable Frederick indeed intervened personally in every aspect of the administration and, in Macaulay's view: 'This well-meant meddling probably did far more harm than all the explosions of his evil passions during the whole of his long reign. We could make shift to live under a debauchee or a tyrant; but to be ruled by a busybody is more than human nature can bear.'

But, in general, despite occasional half-hearted attempts at reform, the autocrats were content to govern and change nothing or very little. In this they could rely on the traditional loyalty and allegiance of most of their subjects over whom they had no need to exercise detailed control. Thus, in their hey-day, the absolutist monarchs of the eighteenth century were self-confident enough, despite censorship and restriction of the press, to permit a reasonable freedom of speculation. As Frederick the Great put it: 'My people and I have come to an agreement which satisfies us both. They are to say what they please, and I am to do what I please.' Under a modern totalitarian dictatorship the ideas of the Encyclopaedists which helped to spark off the French Revolution would never have seen the light of day. Not until the Revolution could the absolute monarch seriously fear that mere ideas could shake his unassailable position. In consequence hereditary kings were less liable than usurpers to that persecution mania which helps to drive the ruler down the steep slope of totalitarian control.

The absolute monarchy, therefore, prepared much of the machinery for totalitarian rule without actually exercising it. As de Tocqueville points out: 'Requisitioning, compulsory sales of foodstuffs, and the fixing of maximum prices – all are practices which had their precedents under the old order ... the old order provided the Revolution with many of its methods; all the Revolution added to these was a savagery peculiar to itself.' And he shows how Napoleon hunted among the wreckage of the old order for those institutions, customs and prejudices which tended to keep men separate and thus make them easy to rule. 'Thus there arose, within a nation that had but recently laid low its monarchy, a central authority with powers wider, stricter and more absolute than those which any French king had ever wielded.' Although there were fewer political executions and imprisonments than under subsequent dictators there were a great many more than under the kings. There were more informers, a more systematic secret-police machine, greater control by the indefatigable dictator over the minor details of social life to which Napoleon devoted his infinite capacity for taking pains. The thorough-going control of the Press and censorship had such an effect that Benjamin Haydon found when he visited Paris in 1814, 'popular hatred and dread of the English ... extraordinary ignorance of the French people as to their own political position and that of other nations'.

Nevertheless by the standards of subsequent tyranny Napoleon's rule can scarcely be described as totalitarian. The great war-lord was so busily occupied in extending his rule that he was not able to govern so intensively as he would doubtless have done if his energies had been confined within the borders of France. War, provided it is reasonably successful, has a great advantage for the ruler. It enables him to hold the loyalty and devotion of the most active part of his people while controlling them by military discipline rather than by police methods. It provides a common good and a common external object of hatred and fear which – since *salus populi suprema lex* – affords a justification for all the excesses of the tyrant. Discontent becomes unpatriotic, and police persecution by agents and informers a patriotic duty. This great theme of the tyrant and war needs separate treatment; enough to say here that war produces a sort of natural totalitarianism, putting the ruler – even the great legislator, Napoleon – above the law and enabling him to take, without difficulty, measures which would in peacetime be resented and resisted by the subject. While victory attends his standards, the ruler has no need to demonstrate the totality of his control.

War, in fact, solved for Napoleon, the first modern tyrant, the distinctive problem of modern tyranny, namely that of moving masses of men in a highly organized society to positive action. Subsequent tyrants have found it necessary to simulate the conditions of war even in peacetime; and this rather than any specific form of organization is the distinguishing feature of modern totalitarianism.

Napoleon, then, had sufficient control for his purposes, at any rate so long as he was winning battles. His purposes did not include changing human nature. He had seen the Reign of Virtue turn into a Reign of Terror; and he hated and feared Jacobin enthusiasm. He set the old Jacobin Fouché as a watchdog over his fellows. But Fouché in the end betrayed him, as did his other most able minister, Talleyrand. Otherwise, in later years, he had surrounded himself with mediocrities, and even over these Napoleon never established a totalitarian control, making them altogether dependent on himself.

In him, it is said, nepotism was next to egotism, and this gave members of his family, and by extension some of his marshals, a certain independence. Nor, in countries other than France, could he establish absolute domination in defiance of the force of nationalism.

However, over France he established the most total control that had ever been exercised over a great nation up to this time. And the absolute monarchies, which re-established themselves after his fall, learnt from Napoleon's techniques and in doing so helped to lay the groundwork of modern totalitarian rule. The absolute monarchs of the nineteenth century, shaken by the assault of the Revolution and Bonaparte, lacking both the self-confidence of their eighteenth-century forebears and the unquestioning reverence of their subjects, forfeited many of the advantages of the hereditary dynasty and took on many of the negative characteristics of the usurping tyrant, without his positive appeal to the romantic revolutionary intelligentsia. Metternich's secret police was not more numerous nor more oppressive than Fouché's, yet it incurred far more odium among the intelligentsia, who set the tone of international opinion. But it was in Russia that the administrative foundations of a totalitarian society were most thoroughly laid. Tsarist Russia in its latter days cauld not itself be described as a totalitarian state; indeed it was less so than the model established by Peter the Great two centuries before. But to the heirarchical bureaucracy, which the great autocrat had established, was added the Okhrana, the all-pervasive secret police, which grew in power as the autocracy declined in security and self-confidence under the impact of revolutionary conspiracies. The bureaucracy and the secret police were the two great legacies of Tsarism which made Soviet totalitarian rule possible.

The Communists, as poachers turned gamekeepers, exploited these instruments ruthlessly and systematically. They were determined to allow none of those loopholes that had permitted their own rise to power. Thus after the Kronstadt rising in 1921 the trade unions were reduced to the position of transmission belts or levers of Party control – an expression which Stalin particularly fancied. The peasants, after their brief interlude of comparative freedom under the last of the Tsars and under Lenin's New Economic Policy, were again reduced to serfdom by the mass collectivization. Ideologically, this has been justified as a step towards Communism and the abolition of the inequalities of bourgeois society; economically, as the means of producing the surplus value for the rapid industrialization of the U.S.S.R., by which alone it was possible to withstand the Nazi onslaught. Whatever one may make of such justifications, it is certain that politically it was the greatest demonstration of totalitarian power ever seen up to that time. Stalin told Winston Churchill that the four years of the collectivization were for him a more terrible struggle than the war itself and that they involved millions of peasants. The number of dead, which certainly ran into millions, has never been established; the number of deported must have been of the order of ten million. The process was called by one of those bureaucratic euphemisms, by which the modern age likes to veil its massacres, 'the liquidation of the kulaks'. Technically a kulak was a wealthy peasant employing hired labour; actually he was anyone who resisted the collectivization.

This 'second revolution' was the decisive act of Stalin's reign, making mass terror the distinguishing feature of Soviet social life for the better part of a generation. The labour-camps had indeed been initiated under Lenin for the re-education of his opponents. But it was the collectivization which made them a distinctive branch of the Soviet economy, and the Security forces an essential part of the economic administration, demanding a yearly *corvée* far more terrible than that which helped to provoke the French Revolution. For a whole generation these immense forced-labour gangs were the reality behind those posters of happy, smiling workers on vast construction sites – the face which the U.S.S.R. presented to the world. These tens of millions of forced labourers were the prisoners of a real act of war, planned with military and bureaucratic thoroughness. The enemy was analysed and categorized under such bureaucratic phrases as 'the kulak Aktiv', and broken down into those who were to be arrested, those who were to be deported and those who were to be resettled. But in the heat of battle these fine bureaucratic distinctions were ignored. The greater the solidarity of the village, the more indiscriminate the action. Indeed after a year or two it became so indiscriminate that Stalin had to call for a slowing down in order to avoid chaos, just as later in China Mao Tse-tung and Lin Piao were to call a pause in the 'Great Cultural Revolution' of 1966–7 when it threatened to destroy the Chinese economy and ruin the coming harvest. Despite the slowing-down, the process was carried through to the bitter end in the great famine of 1932; result – damage to Soviet agriculture from which it has not yet recovered, a massacre of half the Soviet livestock population which has only just been made good a generation later; but the objective was achieved: the peasantry was reduced to a docile passive mass, deeply resentful but capable only of dumb, negative resistance, otherwise totally under central, party control.

The vast operation left behind the fratricidal passions of a civil war. Those who had carried it through were bound together by complicity in a common crime, but divided by universal suspicion. Nobody could trust anybody; above all, Stalin, the man who had risen to the top precisely because of the surly, suspicious nature which Lenin had censured, would trust no one, not even his own wife.

This, as we have seen, was the psychological background to the great purges. We have already examined these purges in so far as they were the means by which Stalin consolidated his power and eliminated all rivals. But they were much more than this, and went much further than was necessary for this purpose. The precise nature of the dictator's purposes and motives was masked by his devious and inscrutable character, and may not have been known even to himself; for it often happens that the greater the power, the greater the self-deception. But in the light of his whole career and the admittedly incomplete evidence that has come to light since his death, it is at least possible to dismiss certain explanations as inadequate.

It has been suggested that Stalin saw war with Nazi Germany coming and, recalling how Tsarism had succumbed and the Bolsheviks themselves had been able to seize power, was determined to eliminate any such possibility in advance. He had perhaps visions of the Zinovievs, Kamenevs and Bukharins, conspiring to overthrow him, of Trotsky – backed by German money and power – returning to Leningrad in a sealed train. The confessions put in the mouth of the victims, of conspiracies with the Germans, the Japanese, the British and with Trotsky were, on this explanation, projections of the tyrant's own feverish fears. The might-have-been, just because it might be, became fact in the trials. By the same logic the purge was bound to extend to Marshal Tukhachevsky, the most eminent and popular of the generals; indeed as the commander of a disaffected peasant army, he was in an ideal position to conspire and was therefore assumed to have done so.

That the fear of war, and the desire to avoid it, entered into all Stalin's calculations at this time, need not be doubted. But it is not a sufficient explanation of either the pre-war or the post-war purges. Indeed, when war appeared imminent at the end of 1938 and beginning of 1939 Stalin very prudently brought the purges to a halt; and the great man must surely have been shrewd enough – and sufficiently apprised by the O.G.P.U. of the state of popular opinion – to know that the best preparation for war would have been the surreptitious liquidation of potential traitors, combined with the widest possible appeal to national feeling. Instead Stalin had given maximum publicity to the treason trials as a means of nation-wide terror. Exemplary terror indeed means that injustice must not only be done but seen to be done. Those outside the Party had no remedy or appeal, and Party members were expelled in large numbers on such vague charges as 'not inspiring political trust and betraying the interests of the party'. In a secret letter which was circulated in the name of the Central Committee in July 1936 it was stated: 'The inalienable quality of every Bolshevik, under present conditions, should be the ability to recognize an enemy of the Party, however well he may be masked.' In other words – 'denounce or be denounced'. So well did the Central Committee act on its own instructions that the majority of its members were dead or in concentration camps within a couple of years. This policy of atomizing the nation by mutual suspicion was the worst possible preparation for a war. In the event the disaffection caused by the collectivization and terror enabled the Germans to recruit hundreds of thousands of Ukranian and Russian defectors in the Vlassov army; such disaffection might well have had a decisive effect on the course of the war, if the Germans had not been prevented from exploiting it by an even more insane tyranny.

The war that Stalin was waging was of a different character – a war for the minds of men. The coincidence in time of the purges with the publication of the 'most democratic constitution in the world' and the *Short History of the Communist Party of the USSR (Bolsheviks)*, which was the basis for Stalin's own apotheosis, edited and partly written by himself, was no accident. It was an act of social engineering on the greatest scale, a continuance to its logical conclusions of Lenin's attempt to force the hand of history, to create truth by force. It is often said that the confessions of the accused were so ridiculous that no one could possibly believe them, and that the accused may have been willing to make them because they knew that they would not be believed. However Stalin thought otherwise; as a good Marxist-Leninist he was convinced that men's beliefs are socially conditioned, that truth is what is to the advantage of the Communist Party, and that he himself as the bearer of the Communist Party line was the judge of what was the truth, The Revolution had failed to bring for any class the kind of liberation and other advantages which the Communists had promised; indeed in the period of collectivization and mass industrialization it had brought hardships which had not been matched under the Tsars. If all those sufficiently independent of mind to point out that the Emperor's new clothes did not exist should condemn themselves as 'enemies of the people' and if the people were to vote unanimously that the new clothes were the best in the world, would it not be the same as if the new clothes did, in fact exist? Stalin was creating an immense Potemkin villlage. But there is no need to suppose that he thought of himself as doing anything particularly unusual in this respect. Not only was Russia the country of the Potemkin village, but also his dogma told him that this was what the capitalist world, of which he had very little direct experience, was doing all the time. All their talk of democratic freedom and of the increasing prosperity of the working-class was, as he well knew from Marx and Lenin, a mere sham and a mask for bourgeois exploitation. And if the picture of Soviet society which he sought to impose both on the outside world by a monopoly of all sources of information, and on his own people both by this monopoly and by force, was for the present a false one – or at any rate exaggerated – why worry? It would soon be true, if he continued to apply the doctrines of Marx and Lenin; and this kind of proleptic truth is what the Soviet official aesthetic doctrine of Socialist Realism in the arts is about. It is perhaps idle to ask how much Stalin believed in the picture himself. His conversations with Churchill, with Tito and with Djilas show an extraordinary combination of cynical realism with total illusion in regard to the outside world; and even in the Soviet Union, according to Khrushchev's account, he was increasingly reluctant to confront the reality which he had created. For example, during the latter years of his life he never went near a collective farm.

Stalin tried, in fact, to project on the world and on his own people, by force and fraud, and by all the technical and organizational machinery of the modern state, his own fantasy world. The use of force and fraud shows that he had a shrewd sense of reality; but the Marxist dialectical method which enables one to believe in contradictory propositions is an incentive to wishful thinking, to that 'double-think' which was brought to its highest level in the Stalinist era.

This interpretation is speculative like any other, but it seems to account for most of the known facts. Above all it accounts for Soviet relations with the Western world during and after the war. During the war the great dictator kept contacts between the Soviet people and the Western allies down to a minimum; for example he put his veto on B.B.C. broadcasts in Russian at that time and allied sailors in Murmansk were kept within carefully prescribed limits.

It is still a matter of controversy whether any different behaviour by the allies after the war would have changed Stalin's attitude. It appears doubtful; for it was not in Stalin's nature to rely on the good feeling roused by comradeship in war. He did not rely on it among his own people; the eye-opening effect on them of comparing even the conditions of war-devastated Eastern Europe with their own plight had been disastrous; their behaviour under German occupation had in many cases been dubious. Therefore many returning prisoners found themselves moving directly from Hitler's P.O.W. and concentration camps to Stalin's labour camps; and the rest were subjected to severe re-indoctrination courses. Such tribes as the Chechens and Inghush in the Caucasus and the Crimean Tartars, accused of collaboration with the Germans, were transported *en masse* to Central Asia by the odious Security Police General Serov, as were millions of the population of the newly-conquered Baltic States and Western Ukraine.

The war, in fact, had for a moment lifted the lid from the cauldron of Soviet life; Stalin hurriedly put it back again. Granted the marriage between Stalin's paranoiac personality and the paranoiac ideology of Communism, what followed has a certain lunatic logic. The terrible losses, devastations and sufferings of war had caused the U.S.S.R. to fall even further behind in its economic race to catch up with the advanced capitalist countries; and more Soviet people were conscious of the gap. It was also a security gap. The Soviet Union had been able at immense cost to prove itself a match for one of the most highly industrialized powers in the world. Now the U.S.A. had atomic weapons; the race was on again, since, despite the wartime alliance, struggle and perhaps war with the capitalist states was assumed to be inevitable. Stalin did not feel safe while there were any spontaneous forces within his Empire which he did not totally control; this applied, even before the end of the war, to the east European states liberated by the Red Army.

Tyranny, however, begins at home; and the Communist domination of Eastern Europe was above all a safeguard and a means to the completion of the totalitarian domination of the Soviet Union itself. This involved absolute isolation from foreign influences. It is sometimes argued that the Cold War would not have taken place if President Roosevelt's policy of conciliation of Stalin had been continued, if for example at the end of the war President Truman had not put an abrupt end to Lend-Lease aid. This would indeed have made some difference. As long as Stalin could carry out his plans for total domination with the connivance of the Western powers he was willing to allow his people strictly rationed and controlled contacts with them. The magazine *British Ally* continued to be published in Moscow for a couple of years in a very limited edition; and the U.S. Russian broadcasts and those of the B.B.C. which started in 1946 continued unjammed until 1949. But during 1947–8 Stalin was building up an unparalleled network of jamming transmitters – over 2,000, it has been estimated – throughout the length and breadth of the Soviet Union, large long-range ones for the wide open spaces and smaller and more numerous short-range ones to deal with the city audiences. This was the climax of the greatest effort ever made up to that date to isolate and brainwash an entire nation, although it has, perhaps, been exceeded by Peking since. The aim was 'a new creature' – 'the new Soviet Man'.

It was at this time, when Stalin was trying to impose his totalitarian rule on a whole empire stretching from Vladivostock to Valona, that George Orwell wrote his *1984* – the most disturbing of evil visions of the future – of *kakotopias*, as they may be called. It was extrapolated from the trends in Stalin's Soviet Union in 1948, based on the assumption that the techniques which were being applied then would be perfected with all the ingenuity of rapidly advancing science and that in the struggle between the two blocs the Western world would catch the totalitarian infection and become the thing which it hated. It was a convincing enough forecast at the time when Stalin was attempting to extend his empire by the Berlin blockade, when his chief ideologist Zhdanov was disciplining the writers, musicians and artists and directing the historians to remake or obliterate the past, when the most brilliant of the younger Party leaders, Voznessensky, could disappear suddenly and without trace because of some obscure economic disagreement or power struggle. The quarrel with Marshal Tito was at its height and the degrading ritual of treason trial and forced confession was being repeated in the satellite states against anyone who might be tempted to imitate Tito's independence, like Rajk in Hungary and Kostov in Bulgaria. In the Soviet Union the rather sporadic anti-Semitism which had appeared during the purges of the thirties was now being applied systematically, partly, no doubt, because, with the emergence of an independent Israel, the Jews had an external point of reference which aroused fears of conspiracy in the suspicious mind of the tyrant. It was in fact the height of what Pasternak described as 'the inhuman reign of the lie' which meant that 'you should hate what you love and love what you abhor'. Small wonder that it inspired Orwell's vision of a completely brainwashed society. It was the peak of totalitarian tyranny, which afterwards went downhill; but Orwell was not to know that.

The other great totalitarian dictator, Hitler, did not exercise such total power over his own people as Stalin did, and this for the simple reason that it would not have suited his purpose to do so. Whereas Stalin's struggle was to transform an already existing empire and to change the nature of its people, Hitler aimed at making the Germans what, by nature and destiny, they really – in his view – were, the master-race which should dominate Europe, then the world. This involved war; and Hitler's first aim was to secure as much power over the German nation as was necessary to wage war. This was indeed considerable, but it had its limits; as we have seen, Stalin's extension of his power through the collectivization and the great purges actually went so far as to reduce Soviet warlike efficiency by shaking the loyalty of both the peasantry and the army. Hitler on the other hand dropped the radical anti-trust and anti-capitalist elements in the Nazi programme, because the big industrialists could best help him to prepare his war machine. Since the process was useful to the Fuehrer and profitable to the industrialists, there was no need to exercise tyrannical control over them. The same was true of the peasantry and of the big landowners; the policy of autarky necessary for war was also profitable for them, and the 'blood and soil' philosophy of Walter Darré boosted their self-esteem, whereas Marxism-Leninism can scarcely conceal its authors' contempt for the peasantry. Similarly with regard to the army, at first it was enough for Hitler to have the overall loyalty of the existing officer corps, which shared his aims sufficiently to make it a reliable instrument of aggrandizement.

In these respects therefore Hitler's rule was less totalitarian than that of Stalin; most German citizens during most of his reign had a larger area of private life. But here it is worth remembering that Hitler ruled just about half as long as Stalin, if we count Stalin's reign as starting in 1928 with the beginning of collectivization, and that over five years of Hitler's were spent in war and only four of Stalin's twenty-five. During his much shorter tyranny Hitler perfected means of totalitarian control parallel in every respect with those evolved by Stalin for conditioning the subject from the cradle to the grave. Indeed Hitler first exploited to the full the modern totalitarian plebiscite both as a means of demonstrating his popular support, of indoctrinating the people and of testing his control over them. Stalin very soon followed his example by incorporating such elections in the 1936 Constitution, by bringing the plebiscitary art to new heights and by setting new standards of psephological arithmetic. The *Hitlerjugend* vied with and perhaps surpassed the Pioneers and Komsomols in disciplining children and splitting families by making them spy and inform on their parents. If the Party was less disciplined and purged than Stalin's it was because, enjoying in the rich land of

Germany more of the fruits of power, it was held together by a more material interest. The instruments necessary to control both party and people were fully forged, The Gestapo was perhaps less ubiquitous and numerous than the O.G.P.U. or N.K.V.D., but certainly not less efficient and cruel. Himmler's S.S. *élite* was possibly a more terrible force than General Serov's security divisions, although we know less about the latter. The *Arbeitsfront* guaranteed a no less total control of the workers than the Soviet trade unions. In terms of forced labour, Stalin used many more millions of his own people, while Hitler during the war exploited millions of foreign workers. As far as concentration camps are concerned, the Bolsheviks, well aware of this inefficiency of the Tsarist system of exile to Siberia, led the way, but the Nazis were soon to outstrip them in ruthless exploitation of the system. Many accounts show the callous negligence and disregard of human life in the Soviet camps, the cruel work on starvation rations in Arctic cold, the brutal and unjust rule of the criminal trusties who were set in charge of the 'politicals'. Many died of cold and hunger on the endless cattle-truck journeys to Siberia and Contral Asia, and many more when they arrived. However, the systematic and organized horror of Hitler's extermination camps had no match under Stalin; here was no Soviet Auschwitz, nor even a Belsen. The O.G.P.U. were quite capable of mass slaughter – witness the Katyn massacre of Polish prisoners-of-war which only became known because there were people in the outside world who had a special interest in finding out; there may have been other such massacres; but if there had been systematic extermination on the Hitlerite scale, reports would have reached the outside world. If it is true that Hitler's totalitarianism did not have time to develop to its true stature, the organized, cold-blooded, bureaucratic cruelty and depravity of the concentration camps, and above all the genocide of six million Jews foreshadowed its logical fulfilment.

The Jews, as 'a peculiar people', a nation within a nation, have always been a natural butt for persecution. Even before the spread of Christianity their fanatical exclusiveness proved too much for the easy-going tolerance of all religions which was one of the principal virtues of the Roman world. As they spread through that world, setting up their synagogues in the great cities, we hear of outbursts of mob violence against them as early as the first century B.C. Under the Empire they shared waves of persecution with the Christians, though the latter as a proselytizing creed got the worst of it. When Christianity became the official creed, the Jews were progressively deprived of all right. They could not hold any official position or practice the law; they could not make wills or receive inheritances; the compulsory baptisms which were to disgrace later Christendom had their origin under the Emperor Heraclius. The stories of human sacrifice and child murder which had formerly inflamed pagan mobs against the Christians were now turned against the Jews. In the Middle Ages religious prejudice and superstition led to the massacres by the Crusaders and by the peasantry who blamed the Black Death on Jewish witchcraft. In Spain compulsory conversions had as their sequel the mass burnings by the Inquisition. Persecution forced the Jews in upon themselves. Confined to ghettoes, excluded from many occupations, insecurity and ostracism drove them to become ruthless and avaricious usurers and traders. This heaped fuel on the fire of hatred and prejudice particularly among the peasant communities of Russia and Eastern Europe where the majority of the Jews were concentrated. Under the last of the Tsars, himself an anti-Semite, the reactionary forces sought to divert the discontent of the popular masses by the pogroms of the Black Hundreds. To the old slanders of human sacrifices was added the new forgery of the Protocols of the Elders of Sion, professing to set out a conspiracy for Jewish world rule.

Such were the traditions and emotions which Hitler imbibed in the peasant community near the Bohemian frontier where he was brought up and in the underworld of Vienna where Jews of many nations rubbed shoulders with newly uprooted peasants who had lost their land to the usurers. The exploitation of these prejudices which were shared openly or secretly by so many of his German and Austrian compatriots was the

supreme manifestation of Hitler's evil genius. Under previous
tyrants the Jews had often fared not badly. Many monarchs
had found them useful for raising money – which had added
to their unpopularity among the subjects. Julius Caesar had
accorded the Jewish nation special rights which were confirmed by Augustus. Frederick II Hohenstaufen, whose mother
came from a family of converted Jews, learnt tolerance from
the Saracens (from whom he also imported the yellow badge of
Judaism). Jewish scholars attended his court and studied with
their Muslim and Christian colleagues at Naples University
and he attempted to dispel the popular superstitions about
Jewish ritual murder. The Jacobins even during the Reign of
Terror established equal rights for Jews and Napoleon carried
on the tradition.

For Hitler, however, the Jew had the advantage of being the
natural scapegoat for popular discontent, bearing a traditional
fictitious burden of guilt for every national disaster, the conspiratorial enemy against whom national hatred and fear could
be concentrated, the means, too, of making most of the nation
the accomplices of his crimes and of other crimes to come. For
the relapse into childish and tribal hatred and fear of those
who are different is the beginning of all nationalist crimes. In
Germany the assimilation of the Jews had gone as far as anywhere in the world. Wherever they had risen to positions of
power and influence they aroused jealousy as much by their
virtues as their vices. If Hitler had proceeded at once to the
monstrous climax of the *Endloesung*, he could scarcely have
carried the nation with him. But the demoralization was
gradual and progressive. It began with the boycott of shops, the
take-over of businesses, the expulsion from the professions
which made hundreds of thousands of Germans beneficiaries
and accomplices. The 'respectable' repressed anti-Semitism of
the middle classes was harnessed to the obscene sadistic Jew-
baiting of Streicher's Stuermer. So it was that when Goebbels
and Himmler's Gestapo lieutenant Heydrich, representative of
the up-and-coming generation of the master-race, planned the
nation-wide pogrom of November 1938, they were able to re-

present it as a spontaneous outburst of public opinion. Everyone knew that it was not, and many Germans were disgusted. But there was no organized protest, not even by the Churches, which surely would have rallied against such crimes if anybody other than the Jews had been the victims. Only the insurance companies, who had to pay for the damage, complained. The number of deaths, which ran perhaps into hundreds, was insignificant compared with what was to come. The murderers got off with minor punishments or none; only the rapists were punished for their breach of the Nazi racial laws against so-called *Rassenschande*. Thus the essential principle of totalitarian tyranny was established. An entire category of human beings was turned into things – objects to be disposed of at will. An entire organization, ministers, officials, policemen, gangsters, had been set up to carry out the task thoroughly, efficiently and with enthusiasm. The framework for the 'final solution' had been established not under the pressure of war, civil war, revolution or famine, but in peacetime, prosperity and cold blood. The instrument was sharpened by war; the field of operation was extended; the scum of some of the conquered nations were recruited as auxiliaries in the final mass slaughter of millions. The instrument could be and was used against other objects, besides the Jews, in the occupied countries. It could be used for the inhuman and sadistic experiments of the concentration camps and foreshadowed, in case of victory, a system in which both the operatives of the master-race and their victims would become cogs in a dehumanized infernal machine.

Other tyrants have been as mad and cruel as Hitler, and as paranoiac as Stalin. But they have generally acted through a comparatively small number of agents whose loyalty was secured either by personal devotion, or fear, or by bribery, or a combination of all these; and in so far as they have acted on masses it has been through military discipline. It has been the achievement of the tyrants of our time to create great bureaucratic machines to give body to their manias. Such an achievement is only possible at a high stage of civilization, and, as we

have seen, some modern totalitarian states such as China and
Albania still fall short of the full development of the system.
This requires an advanced technology not only in terms of the
weapons that enable the few to terrorize the many, but also in
terms of the communication media that are necessary to in-
doctrinate them and the means of rapid transport which can
knit vast masses into an organic whole. Perhaps even more vital
are the forms of organization, the bureaucracy and secret
police inherited from the era of absolutism and developed on
an unprecedented scale, and the institutions of democracy
such as trade unions and elections, stood on their head and
made to serve the control of the people by the government or
ruling party which is the essence of totalitarian democracy;
and finally the economic interdependence of the masses in
modern industrial organization. All these resources are employed in unison in a real or imagined state of war against an
internal and external enemy defined by class or race.

Such is the body of modern totalitarianism. The will is that
of the ruler and a small group about him; but it can only be
enforced by the active and willing participation of a vast
number of agents, which can only be secured in a certain
climate of opinion. To define this would bring us close to the
soul of this modern Leviathan.

8. The Tyrant, the Intellectuals and Ideology

Dionysius I of Syracuse was no mean tragedian, winning a number of prizes at the festivals. Like other artist tyrants, such as Nero, he was jealous of rivals and vain of his works; so that when the poet Philoxenos refused to praise them he was sent to the quarries only to be brought back again to hear another of his royal patron's tragedies. When asked what he thought of it, Philoxenos beckoned to his guard and said: 'Back to the quarries!'

The behaviour of this early Pasternak was not typical of the relationship between the tyrant and the poet in the ancient world. Generally the tyrants sought and often found and sometimes deserved fame at their hands. Gelon, another Sicilian tyrant, was the patron of Pindar, and Pisistratus as the founder of the Dionysian festival prepared the way for the Athenian tragedians and, by his recension of Homer, left humanity for ever in his debt. The tyrants knew that their fame depended on the poets and writers and these were, during the ruler's lifetime, generally ready to play their part. After their death this might change, as the harsh treatment of tyrants by Herodotus and Plato and Aristotle showed.

The writers of the ancient world, in fact, were expected to glorify their masters, but not to contribute to an ideology justifying their actions and stimulating active support in their subjects. If Maecenas had accused Virgil of 'bourgeois pessimism' when he wrote *sunt lacrimae rerum*, the *Aeneid* would never have been written. Although the epic obviously served the interests of the Emperor Augustus and the new Roman Empire, it was a spontaneous glorification of the greatness of Rome; and the values immortalized in it were traditional

Roman virtues – of the kind certainly which Augustus wished to promote and to pose as representing – but also of the kind which any Roman poet would be glad to sing. Augustus was creating something new, even a new Roman man, but he wanted to do it by stealth under the mantle of custom and tradition. Accordingly Maecenas was no Goebbels or Zhdanov, but a cultivated Roman aristocratic patron who served the interests of the ruler in the most enlightened way; and, if Ovid was sent to bewail his lot on the Rumanian coast of the Black Sea, it was rather because of his relations with the Emperor's granddaughter than because he espoused the cause of Republican liberty. That was a cause which the writers came to appreciate more as its reality receded into the past. The tyrant Nero drove the poet Lucan to suicide, not so much on account of his tedious epic praising Caesar's opponent Pompey, as because he took part in a conspiracy to restore the republic; Lucan's uncle Seneca, the tragedian and philosopher and Nero's tutor, suffered a similar fate for seeking to restrain and advise his monstrous pupil; the witty companion of Nero's debauches, the dissolute satirist Petronius was likewise compelled to open his veins.

Nero, however, was an exception even among tyrants. In general, the relationship between ruler and writer has been a mutually profitable one, if often uncomfortable. The writer needed patronage and the tyrant was the supreme patron; the ruler needed fame and the poet and historian could give it him. This thirst for fame was even more highly developed in Renaissance Italy and the writers and artists were in a strong position for satisfying it, because the multiplicity of despots gave them a choice of patrons who competed for their services. They have adorned the age with a splendour which mantles even its atrocious crimes. In doing so they established for the intellectual and artist a new status which was not quite lost in the age of absolutism. Frederick the Great courted Voltaire as much as the latter flattered him; although the affair ended in disaster, owing to the vanity of Voltaire and the brutality of

Frederick, it was the writer, the forerunner of the new class of the intelligentsia, who had the last word.

It was the rise of this new class that transformed the relationship between the tyrant and the intellectual. Philosophers from Plato's time onwards have tried to influence the rulers. Tyrants – almost by definition – are those with whom they have failed. The Greek Sophists, as we have seen, helped to create the climate of nihilism in which the second wave of tyranny swept over Greece. Plato was swept along by this wave. His uncle Critias was one of the leaders of the Thirty Tyrants whose brief but brutal rule proved disastrous to Athens at the end of the Peloponnesian war. His attempt to educate the younger Dionysius of Syracuse ended in fiasco; and while several of his pupils became tyrants, none seems to have acted on his principles. That has commonly been the fate of wise men who have attempted to educate rulers. Aristotle's teachings seem to have left little imprint on the brilliant mind of Alexander the Great, while the Stoic principles of Seneca had as little effect on the vicious young Nero as had the Stoic tutors chosen by the virtuous Marcus Aurelius for his brutish son, Commodus.

The failure of rulers to become philosophers or of philosophers to become rulers should be a warning against overrating the importance of ideologies. However, it is natural, since each age takes from the treasure-house of Plato what speaks to its condition, that we should see in him the forerunner of our modern ideologues. Indeed he has many characteristics in common with them. Coming on the scene when the Hellenic world was in the throes of war and revolution, and when traditional values were succumbing to the nihilistic thinking which often attends such upheavals, he set out to provide a complete guide to history, to human nature and a blueprint for the ideal state to be deduced from it. In order to create this ideal state and new man it would be necessary to start with a clean canvas, to re-educate the children in an entirely new environment and to get rid of any adults who might interfere with the process. The re-education would be carried out through a complete monopoly of all the means of information and a total control of all the arts by the guardians or philosopher-kings, who would reconcile their brain-washed citizens to their rule by a Great Lie, a sort of racial myth, dividing the three classes in the city into nobler and baser metals. This brief and crude account of Plato's magnificent structure brings out some of those points which it has in common with modern totalitarian ideology and practice, whether based on race or class. However there are big differences. Plato never regarded his Republic as a historic inevitability; indeed with his pessimistic view of human history, he thought that a very special effort would be necessary to bring it into being and maintain it. Furthermore, later ideologies took on the character of secular religions, requiring a quasi-religious devotion to a class, a race or a person. Plato's Republic on the other hand was more in the nature of a theocracy; the Guardians were entitled to rule only because of their contemplation of the Form of the Good, which is a supernatural rather than a secular concept, related much more to Christian notions of the will of God, the *Logos*, the Holy Spirit, of the natural law and *Civitas Dei*. These supernatural aspects of Plato's thought have deeply affected subsequent religious thinking, while the political proposals of the *Republic*, which appear as a desperate attempt to preserve, in the city-state, an obsolescent unit of government, have had little bearing on the actions of later rulers. The courts of the Renaissance princes were influenced by Platonism rather as an aesthetic and metaphysical doctrine than as a guide to political action.

The political theory in the *Republic* which has had the longest life has been that which Socrates set out to refute, Thrasymachus' doctrine that 'Justice is the advantage of the stronger.' This, however, can hardly be called an ideology, being a principle which many rulers have acted upon but few have openly professed. Indeed, Machiavelli himself, in *The Prince*, did not openly espouse this principle, but, by concentrating on the means of gaining and maintaining power and ignoring the ends for which it should be used and the effect which the means have upon these ends, he defined the basis of modern 'realpolitik'. His principle was 'He who neglects what is done for what ought to be done, sooner effects his ruin than his preservation.' Note that this does not equate what is done with what ought to be done; those who acted on Machiavelli's advice often did make the equation or, at least, used what ought to be done as a mask for what they were going to do. Thus Frederick the Great embarked on a long perfidious career of treaty-breaking by publishing his *Anti-Machiavel*, a pious denunciation of the cynicism of the great Florentine, who would have thoroughly approved of such a procedure.

It is of the nature of an ideology to explain what ought to be done as well as what is and to deduce one from the other. This Thomas Hobbes tried to do, in describing 'the generation of that great Leviathan or rather (to speak more reverently) of that Mortall God, to which we owe under the Immortall God our peace and our defence'. Just as Machiavelli wrote his *Prince* to show the ruler how to survive and prosper in the snake-pit of Renaissance Italy, Hobbes wrote against the background of the English Civil War and the horrors of the Thirty Years War in Europe. Although it was not necessary to Hobbes' doctrine that his 'state of nature' should ever have existed – that war of 'every man against every man' with 'no Arts, no Letters, no Society; and which is worst of all, continuall feare, and danger of violent death; and the life of man, solitary, poore, brutish and short' – yet the condition of Europe in his day certainly gave him more than an inkling of what it would be like. From this the timorous Hobbes very naturally deduced that the first need and duty of man in society was self-preservation. It was easy, too, to take the next step and argue that for this end the individual should surrender all power to the Sovereign, whether a single ruler or an assembly. But, as a matter of fact, there was an age in which Hobbes's determinist view that man necessarily seeks his own self-preservation seemed less plausible than the first half of the seventeenth century when people were fanatically killing each other for a great variety of beliefs, both religious and political.

It is not therefore perhaps surprising that Hobbes's doctrine, although it has many of the characters of an ideology, was not adopted as such by anybody. His *Leviathan* pleased neither the Royalists nor the Commonwealth, and he was in some trouble with both. In that age of religion the time was not ripe for secular ideologies.

However, although the implications of Hobbes's thought were revolutionary, he was the reverse of a revolutionary in his temperament. He might, indeed, well have agreed with Shakespeare when (in *Troilus and Cressida*) he makes Ulysses say:

> Take but degree away, untune that string,
> And, hark, what discord follows! ...
>
> . . . .
>
> Then every thing includes itself in power,
> Power into will, will into appetite;
> And appetite, an universal wolf,
> So doubly seconded with will and power,
> Must make perforce an universal prey,
> And last eat up himself.

This cautious, conservative approach with its respect for established institutions and its fear of the Hobbesian 'state of nature' was perhaps Shakespeare's own. At any rate it was a fairly generally accepted attitude right down to the Romantic Revolution, when the Encyclopaedists and the men of the Enlightenment, Rousseau above all, took it and stood it on its head.

'Man is born free; but everywhere he is in chains.' With these splendid, though manifestly untrue, and possibly nonsensical, words, Rousseau launched a new political epoch which may be called 'the age of ideology'. At any time up to the late eighteenth century Rousseau's myth of the noble savage corrupted by arts, sciences and institutions would have met with the response 'Savage – yes; noble – no!' However, coming when it did, it fell on receptive ears. It was an age of optimism in which the infinite human potentialities revealed by the writers, artists and scientists of the Renaissance seemed ripe for the harvest. The only obstacles, so it seemed, were a monarchy, that had outlived its usefulness and a Church, that most signally failed to practise what it preached. Remove these, and the millennium would be at hand. The class that would hear this message was now for the first time emerging. Voltaire, Diderot, d'Alembert, Helvétius, above all Rousseau were the prophets of the reign of virtue which was to come, of the French Revolution and of the far more wide-ranging revolution in thinking and living which has certainly not yet played itself out.

This is not the place to discuss the explosive effects of the Romantic Revolution, its immense and beneficent liberating influence on thought, feeling and manners, the enormous creative and destructive forces which it helped to unleash, nor the complex question of how far its prophets were its authors or how far merely the mouthpieces of deeper forces and causes. Here we are only concerned to trace the intellectual lineage of the ideologies and ideologists which have been the distinguishing features of some modern tyrannies and which have helped some recent tyrants to move men to commit mass crimes. While this concern will involve a study of the negative effects of the life and teaching of the Encyclopaedists and men of the Enlightenment and their successors, it need neither involve saddling them with a moral responsibility for events which they could not possibly foresee, nor devaluing their genius and often heroic originality of thought and feeling.

The men of the Enlightenment were the forerunners of the alienated intelligentsia, the most distinctive class of this revolutionary age. Such a class is liable to arise wherever highly educated and intelligent men are denied any socially constructive outlet for their talents. This class first developed in France because the high civilization of the *ancien régime* educated – largely in its Catholic seminaries – a brilliant array of talent which it alternately flattered and censored, patronized and (fairly mildly) persecuted, but did not employ for any practical purpose. Montesquieu, the father of the great French school of political and sociological thought, was as down-to-earth and practical as England's John Locke. But he could not have the same sense of expressing and influencing the thought of an expanding and self-confident ruling class. Not only was Locke practically engaged in government; his works were part of the controversy which was revolutionizing political life in Britain. The same could not be said of the French *philosophes*. Largely excluded from the practical conduct of affairs, they tended to despise existing institutions and those who tried to make them work and those who did well out of them. Many of them, brought up in Catholic seminaries, were anti-clerical and some atheistic and anti-Christian. Seeing the corruption of the *ancien régime*, they rejected its religious and moral standards as hypocritical and restrictive. Largely under the influence of Rousseau, they substituted the cult of Roman Republican and Spartan virtue on the one hand and extreme emotion and sensibility on the other. Rousseau himself realized the need to supply an institutional framework instead of the one which he despised and his *Social Contract* was the attempt to supply this need. He based his structure on an abstraction, the General Will, something separated from the individual wills of the citizens, to which the partial wills of individuals and groups must be subordinated. When the corrupting influences of existing institutions and customs were removed, people would recognize their true common interests and live according to their natural virtue.

Rousseau's philosophy provided the basis for an ideology, with the notion that human nature could be transformed by a revolution in institutions; but it was not yet an ideology in the full modern sense, that is to say a guide to action in every sphere of life and a secular religion. It was the leaders of the Revolution who developed his philosophy in this direction; one thinks particularly of Robespierre and Saint-Just, but many of the other revolutionary leaders, their opponents, held similar ideas and might have acted similarly, if they had had the power. The essence of this first ideological tyranny was the belief that in the cause of the reign of virtue all means were justified to those who personified virtue against those who opposed it. The latter put themselves beyond the pale of humanity. Thus hundreds could be brought to the guillotine by Saint-Just, a passionate opponent of the death penalty. Robespierre's aim, 'the peaceful enjoyment of liberty and equality and the reign of eternal justice' was held to justify the suppression of every liberty and mass trials in which all opponents of every complexion were put in the dock together as 'enemies of the people', in which suspicion and 'guilt by association' was the guarantee of the guillotine. Robespierre and Saint-Just felt fully justified in committing all the crimes which they imputed to their wicked adversaries and conversely they accused the latter of the very actions they themselves perpetrated.

There is no need to doubt that Robespierre and Saint-Just were genuinely convinced of their own virtue and incorruptibility and they seem to have had a paranoiac sense of the conspiratorial malevolence of all who opposed them. What is more remarkable is that, in their very short tenure of power, they were able to inspire similar convictions in a sufficient number of followers to carry the Terror through most of France, to execute the massacres and atrocities of Lyons and Nantes, Marseilles and Toulon, to wage the crusading war of the Vendée. They were helped, of course, by the *élan* of the Revolution, which had released new talents frustrated under the old régime, and by the fact that their republican Rousseauist philosophy was widely shared among the new class of the intelligentsia. As a British historian of the Revolution puts it: 'It was in the Oratorian colleges that Fouché and others of his stamp acquired that union of republican politics with a monkish austerity and the ruthlessness of the Inquisition which marked the character of the most successful terrorists.' Genuine idealism and a quasi-religious revolutionary fervour combined to cast a veil of respectability over the crimes of the Reign of Terror, to give a sufficient group of leaders a sense of total superiority over all their victims and to enable them to communicate this sense of virtue to a mass of people so as to justify all excesses.

This first ideological tyranny, therefore, developed unsystematically, and in the hard school of practice, revolution and war, many of the characteristics which were to be more systematically applied by later ideologists. In the first place there was a philosophy which challenged all accepted values and institutions and promised millennial bliss through their destruction. This philosophy was in fact a complex and profound one, but from it the ideologues abstracted certain simple ideals of universal appeal and application. In a final struggle to realize these Messianic ideals to make all things new, to recall humanity to its natural virtue, every possible means was justified including those crimes which the ideologues most vigorously condemned in the old régime. All who opposed or were associated by class or otherwise with opponents were classified as enemies of the people, engaged in a conspiracy with foreign powers against the Revolution. Labels were attached to them – such words as anti-social and reactionary were coined in this mint – which put them beyond the pale of humanity and justice. The ideals inspired religious fanaticism among the Jacobin leaders and their followers, which they tried to spread more widely by a proliferation of new names and symbols. Finally, like subsequent ideologies, that of the Jacobins proved itself to be fully effective only so long as it was identified with the will of one man or a very small group, who were infallibly right however often they might change the line. The successors in the Directoire might profess many of the ideals of the Jacobins; but it was the fanatical will and personality of Robespierre, his self-identification with the cause of virtue that sanctified the guillotine and gave the revolutionary ideology its distinctive character.

Napoleon abandoned the revolutionary ideology as far as France was concerned, proclaiming that the revolution was over, although he benefited from its appeal abroad to reconcile sections of foreign opinion to his conquests and to undermine foreign dynasties. It was this betrayal of the ideology which made of Bonapartism the great bogey of subsequent revolutionaries. The Emperor kept a close control over everything published, with the usual stultifying results. 'People complain that we have no literature', he said. 'It is the fault of the Home

Minister.... He ought to get some decent stuff written.' He even anticipated future dictators by instructing the Minister of the Interior and the Chief of Police to supervise historians. However there was little intellectual opposition to him, apart from that of Madame de Staël and her circle. He put the intelligentsia to work, providing them with a career open to talents. In this respect Napoleon compared favourably with both his predecessors and successors, which taken together with the very magnitude of his achievements helps to explain why his reign contributed a new element to ideological thinking – namely the cult of the hero. Napoleon was himself a son of Rousseau and the Romantic movement; the young Napoleon depicted at the Bridge of Lodi was a suitable cult image for the young Romantics of the nineteenth century; his greatness added glamour to the combination of extreme emotionalism, idealism and unbridled egotism reflected by Stendhal in the heroes of the *Chartreuse de Parme* and *Le Rouge et Le Noir*, by Pushkin – with some repugnance – in *The Queen of Spades*, by Lermontov in *A Hero of our Time*, and by Dostoyevsky in *Crime and Punishment*.

The reaction which set in after the defeat of Napoleon helps to explain the extreme attitudes of the nineteenth-century intelligentsia and the revolt against all established standards. Instead of the adventure and opportunity of the Napoleonic generation, effete dynasts were – shakily – back at the apex of an out-of-date aristocratic structure, hallowed by a Church hierarchy which tended to treat all efforts to improve the lot of the people and to liberate them from foreign rulers as the work of the devil. Under this rigid creaking structure the young man of talent felt himself trapped, without means of advancement, unless he had the resources to enrich himself like the bourgeois, whom he at once envied and despised for their narrow and philistine outlook. It was from this background of an alienated, anti-clerical, anti-bourgeois intelligentsia that the great ideologues emerged, and it was to this class that they in the first place appealed. Behind those burly bushy-bearded ancients with their vast volumes of dogma and rhetoric and scientific and sociological analysis, there is a lonely, frustrated, idealistic romantic revolutionary crying to get out. From Hegel to Hitler, from Marx to Mao, for all their talk of historical processes and scientific laws of society, this subjective romantic egotism has played a vital role.

For the purposes of this study we can isolate from the rich treasury of the Romantic movement four trends which have contributed to the ideology of modern dictatorship. The first is anarchism directly descended from Rousseau's conception of the noble savage, of the man who is born free, of the essential goodness of human nature when liberated from the tyranny of the state, government and institutions, including private property. Its contribution to modern tyranny has been mainly by contrast. The notion that the mere destruction of oppressive institutions could bring about the millennium led naturally to a belief in the efficacy of acts of terrorism and assassination, particularly, though not exclusively, in countries such as Russia and Spain where there was no hope of advancement by constitutional reform. The main effect, particularly in Russia, was to intensify the oppression of the autocracy. But the anarchists supplied much of the idealism of the revolutionary movement, many of its most fascinating characters, such as the indomitable Bakunin and the saintly Kropotkin, and even more of its martyrs, since they were liable to be slaughtered and imprisoned by both sides indiscriminately in any civil war. They bequeathed to the Marxists the somewhat vague notion of the withering away of the state, which has nowhere been put into practice. But anarchism still has a natural appeal to the young in modern, complicated and tightly organized societies.

The second trend in the Romantic movement which has contributed to modern ideologies is the reverse of the first, namely the belief in the value of the dark and power-striving side of human nature, and in the need to liberate it. This trend first impressed itself on the imagination of Europe in the shape of Byron's satanic and melancholy self-portrait repeated in so many forms in his poems, the hero whose very fascination consists in being set apart from humanity and in destroying others. This cult figure was the prototype of the alienated intellectual; and it is worth pausing here to ask why one of the greatest prophets of this cult was more honoured in the mainland of Europe than in his own country. Britain contributed as much intellectually and poetically to the Romantic movement as any other country. David Hume – with his 'Reason is and ought only to be the slave of the passions' – was the first philosopher to arrive at that extreme scepticism with regard to all accepted beliefs and values which was the intellectual basis of the Romantic sensibility. Even prior to Byron, England pioneered the development of the Romantic novel; she produced one of the greatest religious prophets of the movement in William Blake; and several of its finest poets in Keats, Shelley, Wordsworth and Tennyson. Yet, despite this enormous literary influence, the social impact of the ideas of the Romantics has been much less in Britain than in France, Germany or Russia. What is the reason? If we can find the answer to this question, we may perhaps discover why Britain has so far been comparatively immune to the attractions of ideology. While in Europe many of the ideas of the Romantics were evolved before the French Revolution, their social impact was most pronounced in the period of turbulence, of *Sturm und Drang* which, following that great upheaval, was spread throughout the mainland by the Napoleonic wars. But these impulses stopped at the Channel.

Thus Britain reacted to the Romantic revolution, rather as David Hume tells us he did to his own revolutionary and subversive ideas:

Most fortunately it happens that, since reason is incapable of dispelling these clouds, Nature herself suffices to that purpose, and cures me of this philosophical melancholy and delirium, either by relaxing this bent of mind, or by some avocation, and lively impression of my senses, which obliterate all these chimeras. I dine, I play a game of backgammon, I converse and am merry with my friends; and when, after three or four hours' amusement, I would return to these speculations, they appear so cold, and strained, and ridiculous, that I cannot find it in my heart to enter into them any further.

The relaxed attitude of the Augustan age and his own easy temperament led Hume to make a serviceable definition of the distinctian between ideology and philosophy:

As superstition arises naturally and easily from the popular opinions of mankind, it seizes more strongly upon the mind, and is often able to disturb us in the conduct of our lives and actions. Philosophy on the other hand, if just, can present us only with mild and moderate sentiments; and if false and extravagant, its opinions are merely the object of a cold and general speculation and seldom go as far as to interrupt the course of our natural propensities. The Cynics are an extraordinary instance of philosophers, who, from reasonings purely philosophical, ran into as great extravagances of conduct as any monk or dervise that ever was in the world. Generally speaking, errors in religion are dangerous; those in philosophy only ridiculous.

It is the essence of ideology that it harnesses to a philosophy the passions commonly attached to religion or superstition; and the majority of Hume's countrymen, spared by the Channel the upheavals of revolution and invasion, found no difficulty in subsequently emulating his detachment.

How long this happy immunity to ideological passion will last, at a time when our dramatists sit in Diogenes' tub, reading de Sade or Nietzsche, when the fashionable outsiders practise the extravagances of the Cynics, and when every youth is a budding Lord Byron or Beau Brummell, remains to be seen. At a time when the Romantic revolution seemed played out as an intellectual force, it has become a mass movement, the implications of which have still to be worked out. But 170 years ago, with the revolutionary wars raging across the Channel, Jane Austen was able to poke fun at the excesses of the romantic novelists, while maintaining the values of the Augustan age. Even Byron seems at times to have regarded the excesses of the romantic image which he projected on the world with the detached irony of his *Don Juan*. In England then, romanticism was a literary cult, but only for a very few a new way of life.

Not so in Europe, torn by war and revolution. The Byronic pose became a serious model for generations of young intellectuals; and another more sinister influence began to make itself felt – that of the Marquis de Sade. His influence was not immediate and spectacular like that of Byron, but insidious and progressive. The 'Divine Marquis' differed from the 'wicked Lord' not only in the pornographic character of his works and their literary inferiority, but also in the fact that whereas Byron broadly accepted the standards of his age and revelled in defying them, de Sade professed at any rate to reverse them. In his inept and self-contradictory philosophizing, which is treated today with an undeserved respect, de Sade argues that there is a God, but that he has created the world for evil, that his essence is evil, that virtue is stupid and boring inactivity, whereas vice is delightful activity, that crime, sublime, happy and fortunate, always triumphs over sickly, sad and miserable virtue. Doubtless these moralizings (or immoralizings) would have fallen into a well-deserved oblivion, but for the attraction of the practices to which the Marquis gave his name, an attraction which is in part due to the acceptance of conventional morality combined with an exciting sense of daring and guilt in defying it. Politically, whereas Byron set the example of a romantic and idealistic nationalism, de Sade released from imprisonment for his sexual crimes by the Revolution made a certain contribution to the cult of Terror. His influence, at first esoteric and confined to the 'curiosa' sections of libraries, became such by the middle of the nineteenth century, that the critic Sainte-Beuve classified him with Byron as the chief influence on the modern writers of that time. We are concerned here not with the literary and moral consequences of the Marquis de Sade, but with his cult as a symptom of a growing admiration of power and violence in politics. We find Flaubert following him in his enthusiasm for the sadistic and perverted crimes of Nero, writing with some exaggeration: 'Les imaginations de dix grands poètes ne créeraient pas quelque chose qui vaudrait cinq minutes de la vie de Néron. . . . Le monde étant à un seul homme comme un esclave, il pouvait le torturer pour son plaisir, et il fut torturé en effet jusqu'à la dernière fibre.' Nero, in Flaubert's view, was 'l'homme culminant du monde antique'.

However it was through Nietzsche that this aesthetic cult of violence and power made its chief social and political impact. 'Caesar Borgia as Pope; that was the conception of the Renaissance, its ideal symbol', he wrote, and this was his own ideal, too. This prophet of the Superman may indeed be acquitted of the worst vulgarities of his followers. He strongly condemned German nationalism and racism. His 'homeless' alienated supermen were good Europeans; as he puts it, 'We are not nearly "German" enough to advocate nationalism and race-hatred, or to take delight in the national heart-itch and blood poisoning, on account of which the nations of Europe are at present hounded off and secluded from one another as if by quarantines. . . . We homeless ones are too diverse and mixed in race and descent as "modern men" and are consequently little tempted to participate in the falsified racial self-admiration and lewdness which at present display themselves in Germany . . .' Nietzsche in fact condemned the racism and anti-Semitism and the fanatical devotion to an ideological system which were to characterize National Socialism. However, this does not prevent him from being the principal intellectual ancestor of Hitler's moral nihilism. 'What is good?' asks Nietzsche:

All that enhances the feeling of power, the Will to Power, and power itself in man. What is bad? All that proceeds from weakness. What is happiness? The feeling that power is increasing – and resistance has been overcome. Not contentment, but more power; not peace at any price but war; not virtue, but efficiency (virtue in the Renaissance sense, Virtu, free from all moralic acid). The weak and the botched shall perish; first principle of our humanity. And they ought even to be helped to perish. What is more harmful than vice? Practical sympathy with all the botched and the weak – Christianity.

Thus Thrasymachus' blunt statement in the *Republic*, that 'Justice is the advantage of the stronger', is raised to the level of an ideal, a counter-religion to Christianity. For Nietzsche the supermen, the homeless ones, the children of the future 'do not by any means think it desirable that the kingdom of righteousness and peace should be established on earth (because under any circumstance it would be the kingdom of the profoundest mediocrity and Chinaism); we rejoice in all men who like ourselves love danger, war and adventure, who do not make compromises, nor let themselves be captured, conciliated and stunted; we count ourselves among the conquerors; we ponder over the need of a new order of things, even of a new slavery – for every strengthening and elevation of the type "man" also involves a new form of slavery.'

Nietzsche, in fact, was the first to think through to its logical conclusion the proposition that 'God is dead' – the 'transvaluation of all values', the humbug and Tartufferie of all conventional humanitarian creeds, particularly the slave morality of Christianity, the spiritualizing and intensification of cruelty as the basis of all higher culture, the glorification of the darker Dionysian side of human nature, the wild beast within, and of the conqueror, the Teutonic blond beast without, the cult of the superman. Nietzsche's prophetic psychological insights, the attempt to *épater les bourgeois* by his attack on the hypocritical stuffy moral values of the late nineteenth century, the brilliance of his style – all these naturally recommended him to the next generation of the intelligentsia. George Bernard Shaw managed, by an extraordinary contortion which even Nietzsche would have found paradoxical, to combine the cult of the superman with Fabian socialism. His approach to politics was essentially aesthetic; hence his admiration for the dictators Lenin and Stalin, and up to a point Hitler and Mussolini who attempted to impose an ordered pattern on the unruly mass of humanity, which he contrasted with the bumbling ineffectiveness of Western parliamentary democracy. When it came to paying taxes, the Nietzsche in G.B.S. triumphed over the Karl Marx and Beatrice Webb; but the tax-collector brings out the would-be superman in everyone.

This Nietzschean worship of power caused G.B.S. to admire dictatorship from afar, with the result that he and some other intellectuals who thought like him helped to promote tolerance or ignorance of the dictators' crimes in the outside world. In the dictatorial countries themselves the same cult of power and violence positively encouraged these crimes. The outstanding example is the Italian poet d'Annunzio, the son of an Abruzzi peasant, who cultivated an aristocratic dandyism and the poetry of emotionalism and violence, and put his theories into practice by his piratical grab at the Yugoslav port of Rijeka (Fiume) in 1919. He became the leading intellectual prophet of Fascism. The *Duce* also pictured himself as the Nietzschean superman, and all the little *Duces* followed his example. However it was above all in Nazi Germany that the Nietzsche cult raised its most lethal harvest. Hitler himself venerated Nietzsche – although his style might have been improved if he had read him a little more – and found a prophetic message in such passages as 'A daring and ruler race is building itself up.... The aim should be to prepare a transvaluation of values for a particularly strong kind of man, most highly gifted in intellect and will. This man and the élite around him will become the "lords of the earth".' The Nazi intelligentsia, Dietrich Eckhardt and Goebbels and the like, were deeply imbued with such ideas; and, if one were looking for the prophet of the concentration camps, of Dachau, Auschwitz and Belsen, one need scarcely look beyond Zarathrustra crying to Life: 'To the rhythm of my whip shalt thou dance and cry. I forget not my whip? Not I.'

Certainly Nietzsche would not have recognized in the ranting Hitler and his book-burning, Jew-baiting, storm-troopers the fulfilment of his prophecies. But megalomaniac fantasies inevitably become vulgarized in the age of mass movement. At a time when the cult of de Sade and Nietzsche is widespread in the modern theatre and is promoted largely by the champions of those progressive causes which Nietzsche most despised, it is well to recall the lethal consequences which such ideas have in the past produced when they became sufficiently widely diffused in society.

We have examined two of the trends ensuing on the Enlightenment and the Romantic revolution, the collapse of the old order of morals and ideas – the anarchists who held that, with the destruction of institutions, men by their innate goodness would lead a happy, virtuous and peaceful life, and the Nietzscheans who said that: 'God is dead; therefore a new race of Supermen will triumph by the power of violence.' These are, so to speak, the uncles of the modern ideologies. Let us look now at the fathers of these ideologies, the men who said: 'God is dead! Long live God,' who tried to replace the traditional notion of a God-given system of values by an earthly God – an all-embracing secular system.

The first great system-builder of modern times was Hegel. Educated under the influence of Rousseau and the impact of the French Revolution, his principal creative thinking was done during the Napoleonic wars; he was at Jena at the time of the battle and his brother was killed in the wars; then came his years of glory as professor at Berlin University under the post-Napoleonic Prussian monarchy. Against this background of disorder and insecurity, his ambition to re-establish a stable system of values is an understandable one. Rousseau's conception of the General Will was clearly too vague to form the basis of such a system of values. Hegel sought a new basis in the State, in which he saw actually existing, realized moral life, the Divine Idea as it exists on earth, the Universal which knows what it wills and is consciousness and thought. Just as, for the Christian, freedom consists in doing the will of God, so for Hegel freedom consisted in doing the will of the state. For Hegel that meant in ideal form the will of the monarch.

Thus freedom becomes submission to the ruler. In this sense the History of the World is the development of the idea of Freedom, the realization of Spirit which is the justification of God in History. Without the authority of the state, the nation or people is a mere rabble; with the state, which is the basis of Art, Law, Morals, Religion and Science, the Nation may become the expression of the World Spirit, the absolute Will against which other national wills have no rights. This will is expressed by the Great Man, who tells the time what it wills, who expresses its inner Spirit and Essence, and who carries it out. These are the Heroes, the World-historical men, the Alexanders, Caesars and Napoleons, whose deeds and words are the best of their time. Such great figures are justified in trampling down many an innocent flower and crushing many an object, even great and sacred interests, in their path. Eras of peace and happiness are times of stagnation; it is action and struggle and war which has value.

This is a very brief and inadequate account of the political thought of Hegel which merely highlights those parts of it which made it the ancestor of modern ideology. In the first place there is the modern animism or pathetic fallacy which treats abstractions and institutions as if they have a life of their own. Hobbes had spoken of that 'great Leviathan, that Mortal God', the state, not as the object of a mystical idolatry, but merely as a practical necessity for self-preservation. Hegel gives the State life, will and thought, makes it the source of all values, and bids us fall down and worship it as the will of God and historical inevitability, particularly when it is embodied in the Hero or Great Man. In addition the obscurity of his style combined with his dialectical method of argument made for that kind of semantic confusion in which words can mean the opposite of what they are commonly supposed to and can thus give the propagandist the best of both worlds, blessing submissiveness to the ruler with the emotional overtones of the idea of freedom. The obscurity of style, combined with the assurance of scientific validity, gave the adepts of Hegelianism the sense of superiority which comes from possession of an esoteric doctrine accessible only to an *élite*. This was compounded by the conviction of having on their side the *Weltgeist* or History, which would give inevitable victory to those exercising power in the name of the State.

The Hegelian idolatry of abstractions could be and was transferred by his successors to other concepts, by Marx to the proletariat and to the Aryan race by Houston Stewart Chamberlain, the half-crazy but brilliant Englishman who won the ear of the last Kaiser and who gave his blessing in old age to Hitler. But the object of Hegel's own idolatry was the Prussian state, an idolatry which was carried to extreme lengths by the historian Treitschke, who saw martial glory as the basis of all political virtues and held that since power is the essence of the State, war is a necessity to it. The idolatry of the great man is exemplified by the treatment of Julius Caesar by the German historian Mommsen: 'He remained a democrat even when monarch.... Democracy only attained its fulfilment by means of that monarchy.... What was pulled down for the sake of the new building, was merely the secondary nationalities which had long since been marked out for destruction by the levelling hand of civilization. Caesar, when he came forward as a destroyer, only carried out the pronounced verdict of historical development.' To come across such stuff in so fine a historian as Mommsen, is to realize how widespread was the worship of the Hero and History in German academic circles after Hegel, an idolatry which would justify every crime by *raison d'état*.

It is tempting to see in him the originator of the idea of modern nationalist dictatorship; however philosophers are not so influential as that. Hegel had seen the armies of the first nationalist dictator sweep across Europe; he had observed the forces of nationalism which had risen in reaction against Napoleon's domination. He both admired and feared the revolutionary strength of these forces, and produced a philosophy to justify the taming and exploitation of them by the stupid and reactionary monarch under whom he served. He rationalized and justified and even deified the existing state of affairs; while not claiming to be a prophet, he did point the way towards nationalist dictatorship and his philosophy helped to promote among the intelligentsia a morality conducive to the totalitarian state. In the course of the ensuing century this morality spread from the *élite* to the masses, who were already receptive to it as a result of a tradition of submissiveness. Hegel's secular religion only needed a devil to animate it; and this Hitler supplied in the shape of the Jews and Communists.

The next great system-builder, Karl Marx, was more explicit about his prophetic function. 'The philosophers', he said, 'have only interpreted the world in various ways; the point is to change it.' He did change it.

No thinker has been more effective than Marx in this

department of the prophetic function; in its other main department, that of prediction, in which he claimed to reach scientific conclusions by scientific methods, he proved remarkably
unsuccessful. The contrast between practical success and pre-
dictive failure indicates that he asked the right questions, but
came up with the wrong answers. This points to a distinction
that must be made in considering Marx, the distinction between brilliant and original thinker, the great researcher and
scholar, on the one hand, and the fanatical prophet of Revolution. One of his few English admirers, H. M. Hyndman, the
founder of the Social Democratic Federation, describes him
in later life. 'The contrast between his manner and utterance
when thus deeply stirred by anger, and his attitude when giving
his views on the events of the period, was very marked. He
turned from the role of prophet and violent denunciator to
that of calm philosopher without any apparent effort ...'
Marx had plenty to be angry about. His exposure of the
abominable cruelties of mid-nineteenth-century capitalism, his
stoical endurance of extreme poverty and suffering for his
family when his brilliant abilities could have assured him comfort, these are features without which he could scarcely have
become the founder of a great movement. However, these
noble characteristics were counterbalanced by others less admirable, which were to leave an equally enduring mark on the
movement. He became increasingly domineering, quarrelsome
and intolerant of all opposition, convinced of his own infallibility and regarding all criticism as the result of conspiracy
against him. He reached a new level of vituperation in dealing
with his opponents and former allies, a style which was inherited by his successors, particularly Lenin and which was to
become lethal when the latter came to power.

These personal characteristics not only affected the ideology
which was founded on his philosophy, making it a suitable
vehicle for tyranny, but also the philosophy itself. This philosophy was on the face of it descended from the rationalism of
the Enlightenment rather than from Rousseau and the
Romantics. While Marx in his early student days might have

been taken for a typical young Romantic of the 1830s, writing rather bad poetry and playing a leading part among the young Hegelians, he very soon put all this behind him, despising the emotionalism of his Romantic contemporaries, rejecting the subjectivist and idealist characteristics of the Hegelian philosophy and applying Hegel's dialectic to the analysis and exposition of objective social processes rather than to the action of the 'World Spirit'. Much of his later life was spent in bitter feud with the Romantic revolutionaries, particularly with their greatest hero, the anarchist Bakunin, but also to a lesser degree with the German Socialist leader Ferdinand Lassalle, whose flamboyant and emotional personality he found repugnant.

For himself he professed to study the objective laws of social development, and by his theories on the effects of the means of production and the social relations which arise from them on the whole of man's consciousness, he has profoundly influenced most subsequent thinkers, and may claim the title of the father of modern sociology. The solidity of this scientific sociological achievement has a great deal to do with the subsequent success of the ideology founded on it. His theories gave his followers a short-cut explanation of all social and historical questions which could be applied without the need of detailed study and which was held to lead to scientifically certain conclusions and predictions. This characteristic, against which Marx himself warned when he called for the detailed study of each question on its merits, has made Marxism the opium of the intellectuals. Busy men, scientists, writers, artists, specialists of various sorts, with little time for study of social problems are provided with a ready-made guide to action and argument. They know all the answers in advance, have no difficulty in selecting the facts to fit them, and are able to discount their opponents' arguments as being the result of class prejudice. This certainly gives the Marxist the same gratifying sense of superiority and fanatical self-confidence in action which characterized the adepts of millennial religious sects; the prophetic and visionary aspects of Marx's teaching give the adept the assurance of being one of the exclusive elect predestined to salvation.

The inconsequence of the great leap from Marx's shrewd, if one-sided, analysis of history and nineteenth-century society in terms of classes and their relations to the means of production, to the classless society to be brought about by the dictatorship of the proletariat has often been demonstrated. It was an act of faith arising from a narrow analysis of the basis of political power in terms of the ownership of property. The cool, disciplined, rational sociologist, with his contempt for Romantic idealism, gave way at this point to the prophet with fanatical faith in the efficacy of revolution, burning hatred of the exploiting bourgeoisie and idealization of the oppressed proletariat. This force of emotion was the dynamic behind the transition from what is to what ought to be, from sociological analysis to revolutionary agitation. It gave the Marxist ideology its power to arouse a quasi-religious devotion.

Marx himself would doubtless have repudiated any such religious influences. His father, a mild son of the Enlightenment, had left the Jewish religion for the Lutheran Church. Karl Marx, however, rejected both the religion of his forefathers and his father's religion of adoption. This rejection helps to explain a great deal. The international character of Marxism, its systematic undervaluation of the factor of nationality certainly had some connection with Marx's vigorous repudiation of his own race and national religion. The rejection of the two Messianic creeds in which he was brought up must also have had something to do with the unconscious Messianism of his own teaching. Bertrand Russell (*History of Western Philosophy*) produces the following equation:

Yahweh = Dialectical Materialism
The Messiah = Marx
The Elect = the Proletariat
The Church = the Communist Party
The Second Coming = the Revolution
Hell = the punishment of Capitalists
The Millennium = the Communist Commonwealth

Both Marx and Lenin would have indignantly torn to pieces such a glossary. Yet in their exclusiveness, their indignant denunciation of all opponents, their fanatical claims to be the sole orthodox interpreters of the true faith they showed all the characteristics of sectarian leaders – Lenin, indeed, more than Marx, who in later life maintained that, whatever he was, he was not a Marxist while Lenin constantly insisted on the importance of theory, by which he meant the importance of everyone agreeing with him. The quasi-religious character of the ideology became even more evident when it was transplanted to Holy Russia, the land of millennial sects, with the Orthodox seminarist Stalin as its high priest. Marx came to be treated as John the Baptist to Lenin's Messiah. Trotsky became the Devil. His followers, the heretics, were pursued with more vindictive fury than the infidels, the mere bourgeois who could not help their benighted state.

In addition, Karl Marx bequeathed to the ideology which bears his name, a distinctive style and tone. What Pascal said of the length of Cleopatra's nose and its influence on history may truly be referred to the state of Marx's liver: if it had been healthier the course of world history might well have been different. The pathological suspicion of conspiracy and persecution, the constant anger and the indignant and vitriolic denunciation of opponents, was passed from Marx to Lenin who lacked the wide-ranging intelligence of the founding father of the movement, and from Lenin to Stalin who narrowed and sharpened the ideology into an instrument for maintaining his own power and destroying his adversaries. These bellicose characteristics, inherited from the polemics of nineteenth-century *émigrés*, have become, as a matter of principle, part of the public persona of Marxist-Leninist leaders. Marx himself, while raging against the world, remained devoted to his noble wife and suffering family; the relationship of Lenin and Krupskaya was a model of steady affection; Stalin at the height of the great purges was a most affectionate father, writing delightful letters to his daughter Svetlana. But they all regarded *odium ideologicum* as a sacred duty; and this when spread through great parties and great nations was held to justify every crime. The 'cult of personality', so far from being an accidental blemish on Marxist-Leninist ideology, is an essential part of its development, and the ideology tends to lose its character when it is not the character of one man.

We are now in a position to describe the essential characteristics of a fully developed modern ideology. It must claim scientific authority which gives the believer a conviction of having the exclusive key to all knowledge; it must promise a millennium to be brought about for the chosen race or class by the elect who holds this key; it must identify a host of ogres and demons to be overcome before this happy state is brought about; it must enlist the dynamic of hatred, envy and fear (whether of class or race) and justify these low passions by the loftiness of its aims; every means and every crime is laudable in overcoming the adversary, and the virtues of the enemy can be turned into vices by attaching some simple label, such as 'bourgeois', to them; in particular, truth is what is to the advantage of the chosen class or race, falsehood what is contrary to that interest; since this truth is scientifically demonstrable and since no two people are likely to agree about it, there must be a single interpreter, whose will is law, if the ideology is to be fully effective; as the bearer of all truth, the leader is entitled to expect from his followers religious devotion and every sacrifice and every crime that will promote his interest.

The requirements for the operation of a fully developed ideological system are complex. There should be in the first place a higher academic intelligentsia deeply imbued in the basic philosophy, whether it be Hegelian nationalism or Marxism-Leninism, which will promote the climate of opinion to gain acceptance in a wider circle of the practical consequences of these philosophies. Beyond this there must be a higher bureaucracy which need not be intimately acquainted with the basic philosophy, but which must be thoroughly well versed in its practical application in such documents as Hitler's *Mein Kampf* and his speeches, and Stalin's *Foundations of Lenin-*

ism and *Short History of the CPSU* (*Bolsheviks*). Such documents are the touchstones of the cohesive orthodoxy of the ruling class, enabling them to take routine decisions, while at the same time remaining alert for any basic change of line decreed by the leader. Below this there must be a widespread apparatus of minor bureaucrats, police and propagandists which needs only a sufficient acquaintance with the current application of the ideology to be able to evoke, by agitation or the necessary degree of terror, enthusiasm – or the appearance of it – or at least acquiescence, among the mass of the people. For the masses the ideology and its current application must be rendered down to a few basic slogans with topical variations which are dinned into them from earliest childhood.

Little has been said of the truth or falsehood of these ideologies, partly because they themselves interpret truth in terms of power and success, and partly because they have proclaimed so many different and contradictory truths at different times and places that they refute themselves. The nationalist ideologies make no claim to universality; therefore mutual contradiction is no evidence against them; the only principle they recognize is *Vae victis*. Communist ideology does, however, claim universality. Therefore when there are several different centres of Communist power each interpreting the doctrine differently, it is a real problem, a problem which was masked for many years by Stalin's domination of the Communist movement. He could after all excommunicate anyone who disagreed with him; and in any case the argument that every good Communist must put first the survival and interests of the Soviet Union had considerable force when the fatherland of the revolution was the only home of Communism. Thus Soviet nationalism could masquerade as proletarian internationalism. The masquerade could continue as long as all other Communist régimes were imposed by the Soviet Union and dependent on it for their survival. But when in 1948 Marshal Tito asserted his independence, the truth was out and it has been confirmed by nearly every development in the communist movement for the past twenty years.

Communists became nationalists and nationalists became communists. Gheorghiu-Dej, the Romanian leader who had seemed the most loyal, because the most dependent, of Moscow's supporters suddenly emerged as a nationalist leader in defiance of Khrushchev. Fidel Castro, who had fought his way to power as the leader of a nationalist movement, suddenly declared himself a communist. Whether he had been one in the past, whether in any strictly meaningful sense he ever became one, is not the vital question. He symbolized in his person the marriage of communism and nationalism, of the ideologies of Marx and Hegel.

It is in China that this union of the Marxist and Hegelian ideologies has achieved its consummation in the Great Cultural Revolution, although both Marx and Hegel must be turning in their graves at such an outcome. One can speak in this case of the *reductio ad absurdum* of ideology in a very strict sense. The Great Cultural Revolution claims to base itself on the Marxist laws for the development of society, determinist laws within limits; yet it has ended up in pure voluntarism. Lenin and Stalin having imposed a Marxist revolution on a society at a totally different stage of development from that postulated by Marx, tried to force the hand of history by driving Russian society towards that stage of development. This was voluntarism of a sort, in the sense that a revolution was launched by the will of a small conspiratorial group in conditions which varied widely from Marx's scientific predictions; further, in a second revolution, conditions – that is to say the means of production – were changed in such a way as to justify the previous revolution, again by the will of a small group of leaders. Mao Tse-tung carried this voluntarism a stage further by proclaiming that the will of the masses can overcome every obstacle and can carry on permanent revolution regardless of the stage of technical development. 'The people, and the people alone, are the motive force in the making of world history', says Mao's little red book. 'The masses are the real heroes.... The masses have boundless creative power.' Such rhetoric is part of the commonplace of Marxist-Leninist agitation; the novel feature in China is the attempt to put it into practice, by replacing the disciplined party organization by mass fervour. The shouting, chanting, young Red Guards waving their little red books resembled less the well-drilled, earnest Komsomols of the Soviet Union than the Hitler *Jugend*, both in their genuine enthusiasm and idealism and their dangerous mass hysteria.

The contents of the little red book itself bear little relation to the Great Cultural Revolution of which it is the gospel. Mingling the maxims of Confucius and Samuel Smiles with Marxism told to the children, it recommends self-help, persistence, industry and patient study of problems and facts rather than doctrinaire slogan-mongering, modesty rather than arrogance, peaceful persuasion rather than violent pressure. Yet, waving their little red books, millions of students and school children left their desks and their studies and their problems, bullied their teachers into inane repetitions of Chairman Mao's thoughts, shouted and wrote up slogans against the current 'devils and ogres' in the Maoist demonology, frog-marched foreign diplomats through the streets for refusing to kow-tow to Mao's portrait and mocked and manhandled dunces who were deemed to have strayed from the course of the infallible helmsman.

It is impossible to say whether this cult is promoted by the Chairman himself. On the face of it, the precepts of the little red book, the warnings against conceit, arrogance and the assumption of infallibility, the demands for modesty and self-criticism would seem to be against it. But we know that Stalin repeatedly issued similar warnings and, indeed, even (according to Khrushchev) made references to his own exemplary modesty in the *Short History of the CPSU (Bolsheviks)*. Yet in his latter days from his seventieth birthday on he was the object of a cult almost as extravagant as that of Mao. In fact when the leader lays down laws and rules for the whole of mankind except himself he is well on the way to becoming a god.

To judge from analogy, the aging Mao would seem to have

succumbed to the megalomania and paranoia, the desire to perpetuate and repeat the revolutionary mood and achievements of his prime in a new generation, which sometimes afflicts elderly dictators. Whether Mao himself was the moving force behind the Great Cultural Revolution, or whether an aspiring successor, such as Lin Piao, exploited his age, debility and vast reputation to dispose of possible rivals, does not affect the relationship between the leader and the ideology.

The dynamic meaning of the ideology derives not from its content, which bears little relation to the actions based on it, but from the personality of the leader. The doctrine of the little red book differs little from the rival work of Liu Shao Chi, 'How to be a good Communist', which is condemned as heretical, rather on account of personal rivalry between the two leaders than because of any fundamental divergence in their interpretations of Marxism-Leninism. Indeed the first edition of the little red book quotes with approval the leader who was later to be condemned as China's Khrushchev. Such differences as there are lie in the charismatic and religious character of Mao's utterances. While Mao was quite capable of writing the faceless dogmatic prose of communist bureaucracy, particularly when arguing with the Russians, the romantic revolutionary, guerrilla leader and poet kept breaking through.

The actions of the Red Guards correspond rather to these personal traits of Mao than to anything that could properly be called Marxist-Leninist doctrine. Mao sees Communists somewhat in the light of the seed that will fertilize the soil – the soil being the masses and in particular the young. The quasi-religious movement he has launched among them is reminiscent most of the Children's Crusade or of the young fanatics of Savanarola's Florence, who went around confiscating the ladies' trinkets and wrecking their hair styles, except that it is more highly organized, recalling, in this, the artificial fervour of the Hitler *Jugend*. Such a movement would not be possible unless its architect had control (although it was clearly not unchallenged control) of the state and party apparatus and the security police, whose role has been less studied in China than in any other dictatorship.

In one respect the Great Cultural Revolution diverges from the personality of its author, namely in its attitude to culture. Chairman Mao is, in his origins, a fairly typical sample of the revolutionary intelligentsia – peasant's son, school teacher, autodidact, poet and revolutionary agitator. But either he himself, or those who have been manipulating him have turned against his own class. In this he follows the dictatorial pattern of modern times. Lenin, Stalin and Hitler have all been more or less antagonistic to the intelligentsia who as a revolutionary class had helped to prepare the way for them. Chairman Mao found that they failed in his great test of them, in the campaign of 1957 to 'let a hundred flowers bloom', to let a hundred schools of thought contend. The thoughts that blossomed were often not those of Mao. In consequence the intellectuals have been under heavy pressure ever since. Teachers, professors, writers are sent out to work in the fields and factories and have now become the butts of the Philistine young, whose conduct recalls above all the burning of the books in Nazi Germany.

The grounds for this campaign are as obscure as most developments in Maoist China. The chronology was as follows: in 1956 Khrushchev made his denunciation of Stalin, divorcing the leader from the ideology, the earthly god from the secular religion. The effect of this disillusioning of the true believers, particularly the young, was shattering. Mao became conscious of this ferment among the young intelligentsia of Communist Europe which culminated in the overthrow of the Stalinist leadership in the 'Polish October' and in the Hungarian rising of 1956. The Chinese leader therefore determined either to demonstrate that there was no such weakness among the Chinese intelligentsia or, if there were such heretical thoughts, to uproot them. 'Correct ideas', he said, 'if pampered in hot-houses, without exposure to the elements or immunization against disease, will not win out against wrong ones.' The result was the campaign to 'let a hundred flowers bloom' which revealed a great many un-Maoist and un-Marxist weeds. There followed therefore the familiar process of lopping off the tallest blossoms, which in the peculiarly Chinese type of despotism takes the form of 'thought reform' or a so-called 'rectification campaign'. Intellectuals and bureaucrats were bullied and cajoled into confessing their errors and sent off to expiate them in farm and factory, to learn from the masses and to participate in the 'Great Leap Forward' which was to demonstrate that by Mao's thought and the will of the people China could leap straight towards communism, avoiding the deviations and heresies of Khrushchev's Europe.

The Great Leap Forward was the last word in revolutionary romanticism. Mao said of China's 600 million people: 'They are first of all, poor, and secondly blank. That seems like a bad thing, but it is really a good thing. Poor people want change, want to do things, want revolution. A clean sheet of paper has no blotches, and so the newest and most beautiful words can be written on it, and newest and most beautiful pictures painted on it.' With this philosophy Mao tried to make the Great Leap towards communism, by founding the People's Communes throughout China in which the efforts of the masses were to replace technical expertise. Predictably the experiment ended in chaos and famine. At the end of 1958, Chairman Mao resigned from the post of Head of State and, from later developments, it would appear that he was forced out by the party bureaucracy led by Liu Shao Chi. But he still remained the Chinese leader, devoting now his main attention to foreign affairs and above all to relations with the Soviet Union. The next two years saw the beginnings of the Sino-Soviet dispute. The differences were not fundamentally ideological. In 1960 the two great Parties were able to agree on a joint declaration in Moscow and, although it was possible to detect in this declaration the Chinese and the Russian hands, these differences in doctrine were by no means sufficient to account for the bitterness of the conflict that was to follow. These were explicable above all in terms of national antagonisms between two ancient civilizations aggravated by personal conflict between two proud and autocratic rulers.

An optimist might describe these years between 1956 and 1960 as the beginning of the end of the age of ideology. The nationalist ideologies of Fascism and Nazism had been shattered in war. The internationalist ideology of Communism was split between two great Parties struggling for power and a number of minor parties taking the opportunity to strike out on their own national courses. Finally, the intelligentsia, the natural carrier of ideology, had turned against it.

In Russia (where the term intelligentsia originated) this class had always played a specially important role. Russian writers were expected to give prophetic moral leadership; and although under Tsarist rule most of the leading ones were not themselves Marxists, many of them had sympathy with the ideology. In particular many of the young people, the students despairing of the idealistic Populism of the late nineteenth century, turned to a philosophy which offered an apparently simple and scientific account of society, and a decisive guide to action – the direct antithesis, in fact, of the ineffectual futility of Russian middle-class life so brilliantly depicted by Chekhov. In his latter years Marx found some of his most intelligent and active disciples among Russians and even began to learn Russian, in order to study their situation. Of course, the fashionable Marxism of the universities did not make all its devotees into revolutionary conspirators; but it certainly combined with the mystical apocalyptic expectations of such poets as Blok to contribute to the revolutionary atmosphere. And, although most writers and intellectuals were repelled by the excesses of the Revolution, some, such as Blok himself and Mayakovsky, were inspired by it; and for a brief time after the Civil War, under the lively cultural leadership of Lunacharsky, it seemed that the Soviet Union was going to combine with political revolution all that was most progressive and revolutionary in the arts. Maxim Gorki, the doyen of Russian writers and the friend of Lenin and Stalin, was won back. The period of the New Economic Policy – the middle twenties – was by far the most brilliant in Soviet literature. But the honeymoon did not last long; some 600 writers finished up in Stalin's prison camps, some of the most brilliant such as Babel and Pilnyak simply disappearing without trace, others committing suicide.

Thus by the whip – and by the carrot, since the rewards for conformist writers and artists were great – Stalin sought to produce a new Soviet intelligentsia, immune to 'bourgeois liberalism, objectivity and cosmopolitanism', a priesthood of the ideology. He failed; and a quarter of a century after the great flowering of Soviet literature in the middle twenties there arose a new generation of writers, not yet as brilliant as their predecessors who had been nurtured in the comparatively free and cosmopolitan air of the pre-revolutionary world, but of great courage in its search for artistic truth, integrity and free-dom. Boris Pasternak, who had, as by a miracle, survived from the earlier age was the prophet of this new generation, and his *Dr Zhivago*, circulating secretly in typescript from hand to hand, its prophetic book. That rich and many-sided work, may be interpreted as, in some measure, the *Pilgrim's Progress* of the Russian intelligentsia, symbolized by Dr Zhivago, poet and doctor, and by his love affair with Lara, the figure, as it were, of Mother Russia. The hero and his love survive the upheavals and hardships and brutalities of the revolution, the civil war, clinging tenaciously, as Pasternak did, to their native soil. In the Stalinist years Zhivago dies and Lara meets her end in some concentration camp in the north. But in the Epilogue after the Second World War there is the hint of resurrection: 'Although the enlightenment and liberation which had been expected to come out of the war had not come with victory, a presage of freedom was in the air throughout these post-war years, and it was their only historical meaning.'

This was true and prophetic, although it may seem a strange thing to say of the latter years of Stalin, when Zhdanov's rigid cultural repression, combined with Stalin's anti-Semitic cam-paign against cosmopolitanism, drove many of the most talented writers to silence. Even after Stalin's death, with the thaw that accompanied Khrushchev's de-Stalinization cam-paign, the limits of this loosening up were indicated by Paster-nak's own destiny. He supposed, during the thaw, that *Dr*

Zhivago might be published in the Soviet Union. When disappointed in this, he had the novel published abroad. Awarded the Nobel prize for literature, he was ostracized, expelled from the Writers' Union, subjected to all kinds of pressure and had to renounce the prize, as the price for continuing to live in the Soviet Union. The prime example of the Soviet method of handling cultural affairs at this time (1958) came from the leader of the Komsomol, the Party youth organization, Semichastny – who was later to become the security police chief – who said: 'If we compare Pasternak to a pig, then we must say that a pig will never do what he has done [Applause]. For Pasternak, this man who considers himself among the best representatives of society, has fouled the spot where he ate and cast filth on those by whose labour he lives and breathes. . . . Let him become a real emigrant and go to his capitalist paradise.' However – and this marks the contrast with Stalin's time – Pasternak survived to die a natural death in the writers' village of Peredelkino; and although his friend Olga Ivinskaya, who is said to have been the model for the heroine of *Dr Zhivago*, was, like Lara, sent off to a labour camp, unlike Lara, she survived.

The question arises why the authorities so feared the implications of *Dr Zhivago*, as to suppress it in the Soviet Union and to react so violently against it. It is not, essentially, a political novel, nor an attack on the Revolution and the Soviet system; more damaging indictments of aspects of the system have been published in the U.S.S.R., notably Solzhenytsin's remarkable picture of life in a labour camp, *One Day in the Life of Ivan Denisovich*. The essence of Pasternak's work is that it expresses an attitude to life that is entirely at variance with the official ideology, regarded as a secular religion, and an attitude which has a strong appeal to the younger generation of intellectuals who have been brought up entirely under the Soviet system. Generally speaking, they do not reject the system, but they do reject its deification. The students of Moscow university, the younger intelligentsia, turned out in thousands to attend Pasternak's funeral in Peredelkino, about which they had

heard from foreign broadcasts; and for many of the younger
writers Pastenak's independence of mind, wide-ranging
sympathy and courage is a model. Zhivago was both a poet
and a doctor; and it is the alliance between the rising technical
intelligentsia, on which Soviet society depends, and the writers
and artists, which gives the latter a power base for their struggle
against the authorities. This struggle has continued with varying degrees of intensity throughout the 1960s. Khrushchev
tried to restrain the independence of the intellectuals through
his ideological boss Ilychev. Khrushchev's successors (in 1966)
imprisoned the writers Sinyavsky and Daniel, the men who
had carried Pasternak's coffin at Peredelkino, for publishing
abroad works said to be slanderous of the Soviet people. But
this called forth a courageous protest from writers and from
the universities, as well as outspoken criticism from Communist intellectuals abroad. And when the Writers' Union met
for its Congress at the fiftieth anniversary of the revolution, a
scathing denunciation by Solzhenytsin of the 'Glavlit' system
of censorship, which is still more exacting than the Tsarist
censorship, and of police methods in persecuting writers, received the support of no less than eight signatories. Eventually
even the historians, always the most patient hacks of ideology,
showed signs of wanting to write the truth. The struggle con-
tinues. The intelligentsia are the only section of the population
who have the first of freedoms – the freedom to say that they
are not free – and are therefore able to play the same kind of
role of moral opposition as the intelligentsia under the Tsarist
autocracy.

Ideology, then, while still retaining vital force in such
countries as Mao's China and Castro's Cuba, where it represents the will of a leader, has become a bureaucratic necessity
in the Soviet Union and some of the other countries of Eastern
Europe. It supplies the element of cohesion for the ruling class
and party apparatus and the element of legitimacy in the succession. At the same time, the ideology acts as a brake on
necessary innovations in both domestic and foreign policy. The
reforms necessary to bring more flexibility and incentive to

enterprise into industry and the distributive trades, the changes vitally needed in the collective agricultural system, are hampered by doctrinaire considerations which provide an excuse for bureaucratic inertia. At the same time the relaxation of international tension which, by lightening the burden of armaments, could offer a way out of this economic impasse is blocked by the doctrinaire assumption of a necessary antagonism between the 'Socialist' and 'Imperialist' powers. Ideology, then, while a useful and often dangerously dynamic instrument in the hands of a single leader, promotes a perilous immobilism when a collective leadership takes over.

If, then, man were a rational animal and given to learning from experience, the optimist might be right in assuming that the age of ideology, and the clash of secular religions, might give way to more settled and reasonable ways, just as Europe's exhaustion by the wars of religion in the seventeenth century prepared the way for the Augustan calm and scepticism of the eighteenth century. But in the old-established ideological states there is, as we have seen, a powerful vested interest in maintaining the closed system of ideas. Further there are always new dictators in search of an ideology. Nkrumah had his Consciencism, which in his later publications developed into a hotch-potch of Leninist, Maoist and Pan-African ideas; Sukarno had his Nasakom, a combination of Nationalism, Islam and Communism. Both these ideologies have faded away with their authors; not surprisingly, since they were the projections of their personal ambitions. We live in fact in the age of the instant ideology; the deep philosophical roots of Marxism-Leninism or even of National Socialism are not deemed necessary, since it has been found that the desired result – a cohesive leadership capable of arousing organized mass enthusiasm – can be secured by far simpler methods. Gamal Abdel Nasser's sketch for an ideology, *The Philosophy of the Revolution*, contains most of the necessary ingredients. There is the self-pity and sense of grievance; of the first Palestine war he writes: 'We were cheated into a war unprepared and our destinies have been the plaything of passion, plots and greed. Here we lie under fire unarmed.' There is the paranoid sense of being the victims of a conspiracy; 'all our [Arab] nations seem, beyond our rear lines, the victims of a tightly-woven conspiracy which deliberately concealed from their eyes the facts of events and misguided them beyond recognition'. There is the encircling enemy: 'Imperialism is the great force that throws around the whole region a fatal siege', and there is the special devil, Israel, the agent of the forces of evil. There is the background of historic wrong: 'The Crusaders were the start of the Dark Ages in our country.' And, finally, there is the sense of destiny in the three great circles in search of a leading actor – the Arab world, Islam, and the African continent. Although *The Philosophy of the Revolution* has none of the turgid force of *Mein Kampf* – indeed, it has the charm of sincerity and self-doubt – it appeals to essentially the same emotions as Hitler's stab-in-the-back legend and world-wide conspiracy picture; and, every time he faced failure, President Nasser was able to turn defeat into personal triumph by appealing to these emotions of national self-pity.

Finally, although one might suppose that the disasters of the age of ideology had sufficiently discredited it among the intelligentsia of the more highly developed countries, the craving for such secular religions persists amazingly. J.-P. Sartre's strange flirtation with Communism illustrates the point: 'To keep hope alive one must [he says], in spite of all mistakes, horrors and crimes, recognize the obvious superiority of the socialist camp.' This is the *reductio ad absurdum* of the anti-bourgeois religion of the French revolutionary intelligentsia, a totally irrational act of faith in a political system. If a Christian declares: 'In spite of the crimes of the Crusades and the Inquisition, I still believe that Christianity is the hope of the world,' there is no logical contradiction involved, since secular crimes and mistakes cannot prove the falsity of supernatural beliefs. On the other hand a political or economic system can only be judged by whether it commits or avoids mistakes, horrors and crimes, and if it commits them, to go on recognizing 'the obvious superiority of the socialist camp', in order to keep hope alive, is to fall into contradiction and to make the wish the father of the thought.

However, the desire for certainty, for an all-embracing vision and system of rules is naturally strong in a sceptical, fragmented and highly specialized society and nowhere stronger than among the most alienated and frustrated section of the society, the intelligentsia. Thus ideological thinking, the search for a secular panacea for social evils, persists in the most unexpected quarters, and could easily reassert itself at times of stress and crisis. As 'an attempt to have in one way what can only be had in another', it tends towards tyranny. The time will doubtless come when men will recognize the idolatry of an '-ism', or a social system as being as absurd as our forefathers' worship of beasts and stocks and stones. That time is not yet. But it is certainly significant that the intelligentsia, the class which launched the great ideologies upon the world and was designated as their high priesthood, have been the first heretics and the most natural victims of these secular religions.

9. The Tyrant and Religion

'Puto ego Deus fio', jested the Emperor Vespasian on his deathbed. Unfortunately some tyrants tend to become convinced of their divinity earlier in their career, and in earnest.

The early Greek tyrants had little to worry about in this matter of religion. The ruler who gained control of the city would also master and, if he was prudent, enrich the state cult and secure the support of the oracles. In was part of his process of legitimation. The ruins of the treasury of the Cypselids, the wealthy sixth-century tyrants of Corinth, still stand at Delphi, and their offerings to the oracle were among the most splendid. Polycrates of Samos built the greatest temple of Greece. Pisistratus of Athens dedicated temples to Zeus and Athene Parthenos, instituted the Panathenaic Festival and made the Festival of Dionysus the nursery of Greek Drama, besides winning great credit by cleansing the island of Delos, sacred to Apollo. When he rode into Athens in a chariot with a majestic young lady dressed as Athene, he was presumably making an appeal to the religious emotions of the people and their awe of the miraculous. The early tyrants, then, kept on the right side of the gods. Sophocles' Antigone – braving the wrath of King Cleon in order to give due burial to her brother – indicates the kind of trouble men might incur by not doing so. Aristotle indeed regards it as the greatest subtlety of the tyrant to give such an appearance of piety that they will not dare to conspire against him, imagining that one who appears so reverently to serve the gods has their special favour.

Against the ancient tyrants then the general imputation was less one of formal impiety than of *hubris* – what we should perhaps call megalomania – the overweening pride which leads to 'nemesis', the vengeance of the gods. However, by the beginning of the fourth century, we find Dionysius of Syracuse stripping the statue of Zeus of its golden robe, on the ground that it was 'too cold in winter and too hot in summer' and selling the robe of Hera to the Carthaginians. The ruler who felt himself subject to no law divine or human first emerged at this time, under the influence of the sceptical and inconoclastic thinking of the Sophists. The godless ruler prepared the way for the God-King.

When Alexander the Great, at the age of twenty-three, visited the Temple of Zeus Ammon in Libya, and, being greeted by the priest as the son of Zeus, accepted the title, he started a new era in the relations of rulers and gods. It may have been a deliberate act of policy, the conqueror of Egypt and the East assuming the divinity which his subjects would expect of him. On the other hand classical antiquity drew no very sharp distinction between the divine and the human. Many great families claimed to be descended from demigods, the results of the intercourse of gods and mortals; and Alexander, seeing himself as the new Achilles and performing labours exceeding those of Hercules, could naturally assume the mantle of divinity. To many of his Greek subjects the assumption must have seemed the supreme example of *hubris*, the breach of the rule of moderation which they so much admired and so little achieved; and both Greeks and Macedonians resented the obeisances due to a divine King. However Alexander's achievements seemed to justify his claims; and his Oriental subjects could easily see in him a more divine figure than their own Pharaoh or Xerxes or Nebuchadnezzar. As the Greeks and Oriental 'barbarians' got more and more mixed up together, the citizens of the Middle East from Greece to India became inured to ascribing divine attributes to their rulers. Indeed, many of the names which the early Christians attributed to Christ are inherited from the Hellenistic successor Empires of Alexander; Pankrator (almighty), Autokrator (Dominus or Lord), Soter (saviour), Poimena Laon (the good shepherd), all were titles of Hellenistic kings.

The next great transformation in the relationship between religion and secular rule came with the advent of the Roman Empire. Julius Caesar had ample opportunity of studying the last example of Hellenistic divine monarchy with Cleopatra in Egypt. How far he practised what he had learnt before his death is hard to determine and his intentions remain a mystery. There may have been a cult of Jupiter Julius and certainly he was accustomed to associate himself with his divine ancestry. After his death his godhead was decreed by the Senate and people, and Octavian was accustomed to refer to himself as Divi Filius. But during the struggle for power with Mark Antony, he avoided any cult of himself, since he depended on Italian feeling for his support, and there was at this time a much more definite line between the divine and the human in Italy than there was in the East. Antony's position was different. While Cleopatra was identified with Isis, she also promoted a cult of Antony as Dionysus; and temples and statues were dedicated to them in this capacity in Athens and Ephesus.

After Actium, we may guess that Augustus could have achieved deification without offence to Italian opinion, such were the grateful expectations aroused by the new golden age of peace. But he proceeded cautiously. The title Augustus meant something more than human, but less than divine. At first there were shrines to his household gods and to his genius, but not to the Emperor himself. He refused to be one of the gods to whom his lieutenant Agrippa dedicated the Pantheon in Rome. In the east there were no such inhibitions and both provinces and cities raised shrines to Augustus. In the latter half of his reign an increasing number of temples were dedicated, to him and even to other members of the imperial family. In Europe however, death was the climax of Augustus' divine career, when a symbolic eagle was released at his funeral and the Senate decreed his apotheosis, a temple and a priesthood.

His successor, Tiberius, refused divine honours during his lifetime and indeed most of the Emperors were reluctant or posthumous deities, except for the insane Caligula, who insisted on his godhead and outraged the Jews by threatening to instal his image in the temple at Jerusalem, and the timid Domitian who atoned for his vices by reconstructing the shrine of the Delphic oracle and attributed to himself the title of 'Lord God'. Nor is the reluctance of the more reasonable Emperors for deification surprising; for as Gibbon puts it: 'We should disgrace the virtues of the Antonines by comparing them with the vices of Hercules or Jupiter. Even the characters of Caesar or Augustus were far superior to those of the popular deities. ... As soon as their divinity was established by law, it sank into oblivion, without contributing either to their own fame, or to the dignity of succeeding princes.' There was indeed little in the classic picture of the gods to tempt an educated Roman to become one, and still less in their behaviour to restrain him from any excess. The dignity was thrust upon the Emperors less by their own megalomania, which sometimes found other forms of expression, than by the adulation of their subjects and the need for a ritual symbol of the magnificence and cohesion of an Empire of so many races and cults. This ceremonial worship did not meet men's private religious needs, which were satisfied rather by the various mystery religions such as the cults of Isis and Mithras and later by Christianity. The Caesar cult with its priesthoods in each city served the purpose of an honours list and an incentive to civic effort. It was offensive only to the monotheistic Jews and Christians, who suffered persecution for resisting it, and also to those who, long after the collapse of the Republic, hankered after the ancient Republican virtues and the religion of their fathers.

Indeed the main restraint on the early Emperors was this *pietas*, the family religion of ancestors and household gods. Over a century after the foundation of the Empire, the work of the historian Tacitus is saturated with this respect for ancestral virtues and indignation at the Empire's decline from them. Augustus tried without much success to revive the traditional religion and virtue, and his respect for its deeply entrenched force determined the caution of his innovations and the care he took to conceal them in ancient forms. The conspiracies against his more tyrannical and dissolute successors, in so far as they did not stem from personal resentment and ambition, were inspired by this respect for Republican virtues, as personified in Marcus Brutus the tyrannicide and Cato the Censor.

This *pietas* or quasi-religious respect for the ancient ways of the forefathers is a bulwark against tyranny wherever it occurs. It was particularly strong in China, where Chairman Mao turned loose his young Red Guards on the streets partly in order to eradicate it; and one may guess that the resistance they have met among workers and peasants is due less to any ideological difference or lack of respect for Chairman Mao than to the sense of outrage that the young should so far forget the respect due to their elders.

In Rome the respect for Republican virtue was often strengthened by the Stoic philosophy, which, if it did not inspire any effective resistance to the tyranny, at least helped its victims, such as Nero's tutor the tragedian Seneca, to make a good end. It also inspired and restrained Antoninus Pius and Marcus Aurelius in their wise and beneficent rule.

In general, however, the Roman Emperors, although they took the office of Supreme Pontiff themselves, were subject to no religious restraint either from without or within. Religion was replaced by superstition. From the time of Tiberius to the dictators of the modern age astrology has always had an attraction for tyrants. If one is to seek a psychological explanation for their leaning towards this kind of superstition, it is perhaps to be found in a pathological extension of egotism which leads the ruler to suppose that every sign or unusual event has some reference to himself.

A new epoch in the relationship of God and ruler opened with the conversion of Constantine to Christianity. It might have been supposed that this would re-introduce some internal or external restraint on the conduct of the monarch. However this was not, at first, the case. As Gibbon observes:

The sublime theory of the Gospel had made a much fainter impression on the heart than on the understanding of Constantine himself. He pursued the great object of his ambition through the dark and bloody paths of war and policy; and, after the victory, he abandoned himself, without moderation, to the abuse of his fortune. ... As he gradually advanced in the knowledge of truth, he proportionately declined in the practice of virtue; and the same year of his reign in which he convened the council of Nice was polluted by the execution, or rather murder, of his elder son.

And since Constantine delayed his baptism until point of death, Gibbon remarks: 'Future tyrants were encouraged to believe that the innocent blood which they might shed in a long reign would instantly be washed away in the waters of regeneration.' The successors of Constantine were certainly not more notable for Christian virtues than their rival Julian the Apostate who attempted to restore paganism.

With the conversion of Constantine, the original sin of power entered into the Christian religion, and the Churches have ever since been subject to the third temptation in the wilderness, in which Satan took Christ up 'to an exceeding high mountain and shewed him all the kingdoms of the world and glory thereof' and said: 'All these will I give thee, if thou wilt fall down and worship me.' Up to the reign of Constantine Christians had, under threat of persecution, to resist the temptation to render unto Caesar the things that are God's, a problem which was no longer so simple when Caesar himself became the vice-gerent of God. Constantine was eulogized in terms which made him almost a member of the Trinity, and he was regarded as responsible for the 'peace of God' just as the pagan emperors had been responsible for the *pax deorum*. The novelty of this situation was that the Emperors were required to decide theological questions, to call the great councils of the Church, to make the final judgements at them, and to hear appeals of the Bishops against them. The proceedings of the Emperors during the Arian controversy may have been incompetent, but they can hardly be termed tyrannical, since they were only performing the function expected of them by the standards of the time.

This relationship between Church and State became traditional in the Eastern Empire, and provides the background for the attitude of the Orthodox Church to the autocrat, particularly in Russia. After the collapse of the Byzantine Empire, Ivan the Great at the end of the fifteenth century styled himself, 'the tsar autocrat chosen by God', and in the mid-sixteenth century Ivan the Terrible was crowned in the Byzantine style. The doctrine prevailed that the autocrat was responsible only to God and was entitled to absolute obedience. 'All Christian Tsardoms', it was said, 'have come to an end and have been gathered together into one Tsardom of our sovereign, according to the book of the prophets, that is the say, the Russian Tsardom; for two Romes have fallen, but the third stands, and a fourth there will not be.' The collapse of the Byzantine Empire, attributed to the weakness of the autocrat, was used as a salutary warning and an argument for terror. The Church asserted some independence and even predominance over weak Tsars during the seventeenth century, but Peter the Great brought it under the control of a department of state, a position of dependence from which it never escaped.

Moscow's inheritance of the Byzantine tradition in its widest form has largely determined the Russian political consciousness up to our time. It is not only that the church did not and could not restrain the excesses of the Czars. It did not generally feel any obligation to do so. Thus there never arose the notion that the political conscience of the citizen should, under law, put a limit on that of the autocrat. Those who for conscientious reasons objected to either Church or State government had no separate organization from which to promote reform. They were compelled to retreat into sectarianism – a sort of internal emigration, involving the rejection of all established authority rather than any attempt to reform it. The foundations from which Western political theory and practice have developed, the twin notions of a *Civitas Dei* to which the earthly city should – as far as possible – be made to conform, or a natural law to which both the monarch and the people are subject, were lacking in Russia.

This could have happened in Western Europe too. It is easy to imagine, for example, that the Emperor Frederick II Hohenstaufen might have become a more cultured Ivan the Terrible and the founder of an autocracy in thirteenth-century Western Europe, had it not been for his lifelong struggle with the Popes. Pope Gregory IX was often in the wrong in the implacable war which he waged against the Emperor. The papal propaganda against him was sometimes a good deal more monstrous than his own against the Popes. This propaganda may account for some of the blasphemous opinions attributed to him – as that 'the world had been deceived by three deceivers, Jesus Christ, Moses and Mohammed, of whom two died in honour, but Christ upon the cross', and 'All be fools who claim that God could be born of a Virgin.' But some of his ideas about his own divine nature certainly went well beyond the standards of his time. On the other hand some notions which seem repugnant to later generations were the orthodoxies of his time; when he declared, for example, on the setting up of the state of Prussia under the Order of Teutonic Knights: 'God ... hath chosen the Roman Empire for the preaching of his gospel; let us therefore bend our minds to the conquest, no less than the conversion of heathen peoples' he was only expressing the ideology of the Crusades. When he crowned himself in the church of the Holy Sepulchre in Jerusalem and issued a manifesto attributing all his success to God and to himself as God's agent, Frederick was speaking the proper language of his age.

However, when he referred to his birthplace, Iesi, as Bethlehem and his mother, Constance, as being the equal of the Virgin Mary, he carried his self-exaltation to the point of blasphemy. Perhaps, as we have seen, he saw himself as destined to fulfil, as the ruler who united East and West, the prophecies of the millennium that were widely believed at the beginning of the thirteenth century. Some of the language in which his courtiers addressed him would support this. 'Our forefathers', declared one of his governors, 'looked no more eagerly for the coming of Christ than we do for thine.' Again, 'Thy power, O Caesar, hath no bounds; it excelleth the power of man like unto a god.' His chronicler writes: 'This Emperor, the true ruler of the world, whose fame extends through the whole circuit of the earth was convinced that he could approximate his own nature to the heavenly nature, perhaps by his experience of mathematics.'

This elevated view of himself was carried through in Frederick's administration. It was regarded as sacrilege to discuss the Emperor's judgements or decrees, or the worthiness of his officers. Frederick, like other rulers who have put themselves above all laws, human and divine, yet had superstitions of his own, believing in astrology which would disclose to him 'the iron necessity of things'. He rejected all the conventional restraints of the religion and morality of his time, keeping his wives and mistresses in a harem, imprisoning and driving to suicide his elder son and his chief adviser, and roasting his enemies in molten lead.

Finally, this infidel monarch, in so many ways in advance of his times, was the father of the Inquisition. His officers first carried out on a large scale the trials of alleged heretics who were accused of unorthodoxy in those beliefs which the Emperor privately scorned. Thus he sought to make religion an instrument of his secular rule, with the aim of a complete tyranny over the minds of men. His opponent Pope Gregory IX, friend and patron of St Francis, was not slow to follow this example by introducing the Papal tribunals of the Inquisition.

Dante puts Frederick among the arch-heretics in Hell. Yet, writing fifty years after his death, Dante supports the Emperor's cause against that of the Popes, whom he blames, because of their usurpation of secular power, for the sad state of Italy torn by strife between the Guelphs and Ghibellines, the papal and imperial parties. Some of the arguments in the poet's treatise on Monarchy are those which Frederick used in his debate with the Pope. And the language in which Dante greeted the Emperor Henry VII as the ruler of the world is almost as Messianic as the blasphemous eulogies which Frederick encouraged.

Dante held that the Emperor's authority derived directly from God and not from the Pope as the Vicar of Christ. He saw in the Empire the fulfilment of God's purpose 'If [he wrote] the Roman Empire was not founded upon right, then Christ by his birth assented to an injustice'; and again, 'There is no doubt that victory among those contending for world-empire must have been in accordance with God's judgement.' One may perhaps see Dante here as anticipating Hegel's deification of the state and justifying the principle that might is right. But this would be to take him out of his historical context. He believed in a Natural Law and justice, which represented the will of God; he held that only one authority could be responsible for the peace of God and that this must be the Emperor and not the Pope. In view of the position and conduct of the Popes of his time, this was hardly a surprising conclusion.

Dante's doctrine is, perhaps, a logical extension of St Paul's teaching, in the Epistle to the Romans: 'There is no power but of God; the powers that be are ordained of God. Therefore he that resisteth the power, withstandeth the ordinance of God; and they that withstand shall receive to themselves judgement.' It was a very ancient doctrine which is to be found in the Old Testament; thus Daniel describes Nebuchadnezzar as 'King of Kings unto whom the God of Heaven hath given the kingdom, the power and the strength and the glory'. And Christ himself, in St John's gospel, told Pilate: 'Thou wouldest have no power against me except it were given thee from above.'

This tradition of obedience to the powers that be, even when they do evil is, therefore, very deeply ingrained in Christianity. But Christ's injunction to 'render unto Caesar the things that are Caesar's and unto God the things that are God's' has proved more influential in western Christendom. The struggle to establish the correct demarcation and interaction of the two kingdoms has largely determined the judgement of the western world as to what is or is not tyrannical behaviour. The saints and martyrs of the early Church struggled against what they regarded as the encroachment of Caesar on the things that were God's. They had their precedents not only in the New Testament, but also in the relations of the prophets to the kings in the Old Testament. For St Augustine the pagan state, because it did not render unto God the things that are God's, was no more than a great robbery. Unless the state promoted the faith and the glory of God, it was necessarily evil; only if kings and princes and their subjects all observed the precepts of the Christian religion could the republic secure felicity in the present life and ascend aloft to reign in bliss through life eternal.

St Augustine, then, believed in the primacy of the church, in the sense that unless the state followed Christian aims and promoted the Christian faith it could not be a just state, justice being taken to mean rendering their due to God and man. However he did not, for that reason, believe in a theocracy or a hierocracy or the supremacy of the Church over affairs of state. Indeed he drew a clear distinction between the spiritual and temporal spheres. But it was a distinction that broke down, as it was so often to do in later ages, on the question of the means by which the state should promote the faith. St Augustine approved of the suppression by the state of pagan rites, though not, at first, of forced conversions. In his arguments with the Manichaeans he relied on persuasion; and he sought, at first, to deal with his principal opponents the Donatists in the same way; but later and perhaps reluctantly he argued that the Church was justified in demanding that the state should take action to suppress heresy.

Thus the origins of the Inquisition go very far back in Christian teaching even if the institution itself was introduced some eight centuries after St Augustine. While to later generations the whole procedure appears outrageous and tyrannical, by the standards of the time it was not so. The Church, the highest moral authority, operated it. The soul of the heretic would be damned eternally; it was therefore better that his body should burn, as a means perhaps of saving other souls from temptation; and the scriptural authority of some of the more terrible of the parables could be quoted. Its purposes were, therefore, the most exalted. Not for the first or last time exalted purposes were held to justify means that would be regarded as illegitimate in any other cause – a presumption of guilt, an increased use of torture, and a one-sided treatment of evidence exceeding the abuses of contemporary lay tribunals. Finally, the penalty of death by fire was so cruel that the Inquisitors when handing the victim over to the secular officials would urge them to avoid 'all bloodshed and all danger of death', in order formally and hypocritically to clear the Church of responsibility for the atrocious end – a formula which showed the uneasiness of the Papacy and clergy at exceeding the scope of their spiritual authority.

Since the saving of souls by orthodox belief, the extinction of heresy was, for that age, an end so lofty as to justify any means whatever, the Inquisition became an example of the tyranny into which authorities fall when they claim a monopoly of such aims and identify themselves totally with them. It was an instrument as lethal in the hands of the saint as of the sinner – indeed more so since against the sinner's corrupt motives of avarice and lust for power there might be some redress; against the saint there could be none. Gregory IX, who introduced the Papal Inquisition, was not one of the evil, or weak, or corrupt Popes; as the friend of St Francis of Assisi, he was aware of the abuses of the Church and of the positive means of remedying them; but he was a frightened man. He had reason to fear Frederick's threat of secular tyranny over the Church; but he feared, too, the criticism of the Church which had become prevalent after a century of relatively settled conditions had brought increased prosperity, of which the Church was one of the chief beneficiaries. The spread of education, promoted by the Church, yet gave many the means of questioning its authority. As a consequence, the weapon designed for the protection of divine truth was abused as the instrument of preserving the privileges of an all-too-human institution.

In so far as the design was to promote Papal supremacy it

failed. The struggle for Papal control of the temporal power reached its zenith after the great Roman Jubilee of 1300, when Boniface VIII proclaimed, in the Bull *Unam Sanctam* (1302), that 'all human creatures are subject to the Roman Pontiff'. Within a couple of years of this proud claim to supremacy over all kings of the earth, Pope Boniface – who in the words of Gibbon 'entered like a fox, reigned like a lion, and died like a dog' – was hounded to death by his secular adversary Philip the Fair of France and the Papacy became for a time the pawn of the French monarch. In 1350 the poet Petrarch reported in grief from Rome: 'The houses fall down, the walls collapse, temples are overthrown, shrines wrecked, the laws trodden underfoot. The Lateran palace is rased to the ground and its basilica, mother of all churches, stands roofless, open to the wind and rain.' The sequel was the Great Schism which was to bring the Papacy to its lowest ebb in its long history.

Such was the Nemesis which attended the attempt of the spiritual power to avail itself of the secular sword. The secular power was now able to abuse the Inquisition for its own purposes. The Crusade against the Albigensian heretics served to extend the power of the King of France. The Inquisition served the King of Spain in dealing with his minority problems of Jews and Moriscos, and later with his disaffected subjects in the Low Countries. The Emperor Charles V established the Inquisition in the Netherlands; and King Philip II of Spain when he succeeded wrote in 1545: 'As to the Inquisition, my will is that it be enforced by the Inquisitors as of old, and as is required by all law, human and divine. This lies very near my heart and I require you to carry out my orders. Let all prisoners be put to death, and suffer them no longer to escape through the neglect, weakness and bad faith of judges.' Lord Acton comments that by this scheme of violence Philip II turned the Reformation into revolution. Meanwhile in Rome itself temporal power had been on the brink of usurping the spiritual authority. Perhaps only the accident – or providence – of sickness and death prevented the realization of Nietzsche's atrocious ideal of Cesare Borgia as Pope.

The nemesis of power did not cease its action there. The savage temper of the Inquisition passed its infection to its opponents, and absolved the temporal power of traditional restraints. Once the Popes had descended into the political arena, the spiritual authority could restrain neither the abuses of the clergy nor the excesses of monarchs. The Catholic Church having by its abuses – and its failure to correct them – provoked the Reformation, became dependent on absolute monarchs to maintain its power and to launch its counter-attack against the reformers. The Counter-Reformation might re-establish some of the spiritual authority of Rome, but this authority was inextricably entangled with the temporal power of the absolute monarchs (as was that of the Lutheran churches). So that, when the revolution against absolutism came, it was a revolt also against the Church.

It is against this background that we must judge the greatest of the English home-grown tyrants, Henry VIII. He demonstrated many of the classic features of tyranny, above all the progressive corruption of power, aggravated by disease, which converted the brilliant and popular monarch of his younger days into the bloated, morose and suspicious despot executing his advisers (including Sir Thomas More, the best and wisest) and potential rivals (not to mention his queens), burning for heresy and religious treason those, whether Catholic or Protestant, who disputed 'Henry, being next under God, the only supreme head of this Catholic Church of England.' But in making this claim he was doing no more than asserting in principle what the other monarchs of Christendom were acting out in practice. From his observation of the behaviour of the monarchs of that revolutionary age Machiavelli concludes: 'A prince, especially a new one, cannot observe all those things for which men are esteemed, being often forced in order to maintain the state, to act contrary to fidelity, friendship, humanity and religion.' Of religious devotion, he concludes: 'There is nothing more necessary to appear to have than this last quality, in as much as men judge generally more by the eye than the hand.' But he is equally convinced that to have religious scruples and always to observe them is injurious. Machiavelli had in mind his great models the Borgias, Pope Alexander VI, 'who never did what he said', and his son Cesare, 'who never said what he did'. But in the long run these were tyrants who failed. The more successful despots, such as Ivan the Terrible, have often had genuine religious belief and a sense of their divine mission, which puts them above all laws – a rather more effective weapon of tyranny than the cool hypocrisy recommended by the wily Florentine.

King Henry VIII, in fact, had according to the curious manner of his time a genuine and learned religious belief, which helped him to carry out an ecclesiastical revolution without giving too deep offence to too many of his subjects. A tyrant in the strict sense, no doubt he was, but one with a saving moderation and instinctive understanding of his people which enabled him to carry great and important bodies of opinion with him, to maintain contact with them through Parliament and to save them from the horrors of religious war which were shortly to rage across the Channel and also from the fanatical extremes of the reform movement.

It is against the background of the wars of religion that we must judge what is seen by some as an example of theocratic tyranny, by others as a model of Christian republican virtue, namely Calvin's Geneva. When we consider the holocausts of Calvin's supporters across the border in France who perished at the stake or by the sword – as for example the massacre of 3000 Waldensian heretics and the destruction of their villages in Provence – the reformer's rule in Geneva must be regarded as comparatively humane. It is true that Calvin played a culpable part in denouncing the Spanish heretic Servetus to the Inquisition and in finally bringing him to the stake in Geneva. But, by the standards of the age, there was nothing outrageous in this. It was indeed a gruesome way of 'living up to the Joneses'; for one of the deciding factors was to prove that Geneva, so often accused of being a nest of heretics, was not less orthodox than her opponents in punishing them. The numerous burnings of witches, sorcerers and alleged spreaders of plague were also in no way peculiar to Geneva. Where Calvin went beyond the standards of his time was in the detailed religious control over moral and political life. The consistory, the spiritual authority, made up of pastors and lay elders, supervised every detail of moral and religious conduct and even speech. It saw to it that the magistrates should, in the words of the Anglican prayer-book 'truly and indifferently administer justice, to the punishment of wickedness and vice and to the maintenance of true religion and virtue'. This had been the principle of both Catholics and Protestants, but it was left to Calvin to practise it in its full rigour.

Calvin himself was very conscious of what his Ordinances describe as 'the distinction shown to us in Holy Scriptures between the sword and authority of the Magistrate and the superintendence that the Church should exercise, to bring all Christians to the obedience and true service of God and to prevent and correct scandals'.

The results were certainly irksome. Every ecclesiastical offence, absence from church, blasphemy, singing profane songs, defamation of Calvin, praise of the Pope, possessing unsuitable books, dancing, wearing the wrong kind of clothes or wrong length of hair, might involve examination by the consistory and punishment by the magistrates. Inns and theatres were banned. Informers were active; anyone was liable to be examined on his religious knowledge, his attitude to the pastors, his church attendance, his superstitions and his family affairs. The pastors and the elders had their self-criticism sessions and this practice spread to the civil governing body, the Small Council. 'With love and charity each and every one was censured, from the highest to the lowest, revealing every man's imperfections and vices. May the Lord give us all the power to profit by it!'

Calvin, in fact, was engaged in creating a 'new man' and he used totalitarian methods to do it. He was conscious of doing the will of God in this great task. Both convictions are very conducive to tyranny, and there were moments when he seemed in danger of going over the edge, as when one of the magistrates was made to do public penance for an attack on Calvin, which was treated as an insult to the honour of Christ and when a pastor was unfrocked for criticizing this procedure. Again, when two of his opponents attacked his doctrine of Predestination, not only were they exiled, but also it was ruled that 'no one now or in the future may dare to speak against the said book [Calvin's *Institutes*] nor against the said doctrine [Predestination]'. Calvin's Geneva, in fact, represents one of the most successful systems of thought-control the world has ever seen. At the same time it was perhaps the only genuine 'totalitarian democracy'. Within certain limits, it was more genuinely democratic than subsequent examples of that species, and certainly, in its detailed control of every aspect of life, totalitarian. Must we for that reason classify Calvin's régime as a tyranny? In the circumstances of the time and place, probably not.

Even before Calvin took over, Geneva had been under ecclesiastical rule, and the Prince-Bishop could, and did, enact the kind of moral and sumptuary laws which seem to a later age an unjustified interference in the private affairs of the citizen. Such laws were not uncommon at the time. The difference was that under Calvin they were thoroughly and efficiently enforced. This could not have happened without the consent of a great number of the inhabitants or, alternatively, more force than was ever used. The consent (and indeed enthusiasm) was there. When Calvin came to Geneva, there were some 10,000 inhabitants; during the next two decades there were at least 5,000, probably more than 7,000, immigrants. Most of them enthusiastically embraced Calvinism. Although only a minority became citizens, they were able to control the consistory or religious authority, and supply the majority of the pastors. They provided, too, most of the missionaries or agents whom Calvin sent abroad in their hundreds to convert Christendom to the true faith, which he considered at least as important as his work in Geneva. They regarded Geneva as the Holy City. As one of the most notable of them, John Knox, said: 'In other places I confess Christ to be truly preached, but manners and religion so sincerely reformed I have not yet seen in any other place.' This sense of being the elect of God spread among the citizens of Geneva, although some of them found restrictions intolerable and were driven into exile. The fact that it was, for a generation, a beleaguered city, threatened and attacked by hostile neighbours, but sustained by the support, both material and spiritual, of an expanding world-wide movement helped to rally spontaneous support for the Calvinists. Finally there was the personality of Calvin himself. Although he had started his career with a commentary on Seneca's *De Clementia* and a letter of intercession to the King of France for toleration of the reformers, tolerance was not among his virtues. He regarded himself as expressing the will of God and was certain that he was right, with the true believer's confidence that his beliefs would prevail by moral rather than physical force. But his rigidity of mind and hasty temper were accompanied by a saving humility, so that he could say on his death-bed, 'but still I say that all I have done is worth nothing and that I am a miserable creature'.

Thus, while most of the circumstances of tyranny were present in Calvin's Geneva, and while many of his followers elsewhere were to act tyrannically so that men would say, 'new presbyter is but old priest writ large', Calvin's career yet indicates the kind of way in which religion can act as a restraint on tyranny. Self-discipline and firm principle saved Calvin both from the corrupting influence of power and its arbitrary use. The consensus between the religious and civil authorities and people, hostile pressure from outside, and the exhilarating sense of being the centre of an expanding missionary movement, enabled the Genevans to succeed, for a limited time in a tiny community, in the aim (which has been a fruitful source of tyrannies in subsequent larger totalitarian societies) of making men virtuous and creating 'a new man' by decree.

Calvin laid down that 'magistrates are ordained of God and must be obeyed even if wicked; but if they command what God has forbidden we must fear God and disobey the King'. Tyranny at this time had above all a religious connotation and resistance to it was justified on grounds of religion. Calvin's argument that since the powers that be are ordained of God, they must do the will of God and where they transgress it they may be resisted, is elaborated with great power by the late sixteenth-century author of *Vindiciae contra Tyrannos*, Junius Brutus, who was probably Duplessis-Mornay, a young Huguenot adviser to Henry IV of France. He carried the argument further: 'We have showed that it is God that does appoint kings, who chooses them, who gives kingdom to them; now we say that the people establish kings, puts the sceptre into their hands, and who with their suffrage, approves the election. God would have it done in this manner, to the end that kings should acknowledge that after God they hold their power and sovereignty from the people.' The people here was not the mass of private citizens, but magistrates, estates and parliaments. The author was aware of the dangers of the growth of absolute monarchy, based on the doctrine of the divine rights of kings and he warned: 'Let us therefore reject these detestable, faithless and impious vanities of the court marmosites which make kings gods and receive their sayings as oracles; and, which is worse, are so shameless as to persuade kings that nothing is just or equitable of itself, but takes its true form of justice or injustice according as it pleases the King to ordain; as if he were some god, which could never err nor sin at all.'

The author of *Vindiciae contra Tyrannos* did not anticipate Locke in demanding freedom of conscience, but he argued most cogently that 'Of the two things if the one must needs be done, it were much better to forsake the King, than God'.

This traditional Christian belief was practised on both sides, by Protestants and Catholics alike, but a long time passed before the various sects were to admit each others' right to freedom of conscience. The recognition of this in practice was the great contribution of Oliver Cromwell to the development of the Church-state relationship: 'I beseech you, in the bowels of Christ', he wrote to the General Assembly of the Church of Scotland, 'think it possible that you may be mistaken'; and it was the fact that despite his very deep, even fanatical, religious convictions, he was able to consider this possibility in his own case, and to respect the different beliefs of others that generally held Oliver back from the brink of tyranny. A combination of deeply held religious beliefs with toleration of the beliefs of others is indeed the greatest restraint on arbitrary rule and the soil from which modern political liberties have grown.

The work of John Locke, the philosopher of England's Glorious Revolution and the inspirer of the United States Declaration of Independence, arose from this struggle for religious toleration. Indeed he himself drew up a Constitution for Carolina guaranteeing religious toleration, which, however, was not put into practice. It was still possible in Locke's time for people who could not accept the social compact in their native land to go and set up a republic, as he put it, in *vacuis locis*. Indeed this was what the Quaker, William Penn, did at the time when Locke was writing his *Treatise on Civil Government*. The last religious body to take this course and to set up the latest of the 'theocratic' states were the Mormons, who made their great trek to Utah under the leadership of Brigham Young to seek refuge from the hostility excited by the curious Mormon doctrines and practices. The early history of Utah is a remarkable example of what can be done by a body of likeminded men under a common religious impulse and under pressure of persecution. It also illustrated in the later days of its polygamous patriarch, Brigham Young, the dangers of tyranny in such a 'theocratic' system, and also the bitter feuds that may arise in it.

In general, the countries in which religious toleration was established at the end of the seventeenth century have so far escaped any home-grown tyranny. Those in which a single church, whether Catholic or Lutheran, prevailed and made common cause with absolute monarchy have sooner or later succumbed. In the period of comparative tranquillity which followed the decline of the fanatical passions of the religious wars, the ideas of the Enlightenment affected most nations more or less. But in the countries of absolute monarchy where the court and the church shared the privileges and blocked the roads to reform and advancement, the intelligentsia of the Enlightenment was driven into anti-clerical if not anti-religious courses.

This was particularly the case in France where the Church was completely identified with the *ancien régime*, and with many of its abuses. The revolutionary leaders were, therefore, more or less anti-clerical, whatever their attitude to religion – not least the apostate bishop Talleyrand and the seminarist Fouché, the 'butcher of Lyons' and the future chief of police. Robespierre and Saint-Just who attacked the clergy and the atheist Hébert, impartially, were the first (though not the last) revolutionary dictators to attempt to replace the old church with their own national church. They were also not the last to fail in the attempt.

Robespierre himself not only believed in a Supreme Being, but also thought that such a belief was necessary to maintain national morality. Among the dogmas which he thought necessary to his national religion were the existence of a powerful and benevolent divinity, of a future life in which the good are rewarded and the bad punished; and the sanctity of the social contract and the laws. It was a religion with its own ritual and sacraments such as federative oaths at the altar of the country, dancing and singing round the tree of liberty, processions, banners, hymns and sermons, incense-burning before the altar of the law. There were confessionals and purges in the clubs. In June 1794 the Cult of the Supreme Being was launched with personal homage to the High Priest of Jacobinism and pageantry arranged by the artist David. Robespierre declared: 'To me God is he who created all men for equality and happiness, he who protects the oppressed and exterminates tyrants.' However he had to act tyrannically to establish his 'constitutional' 'national' church, and in the long run his attempt did not prove any more successful than subsequent attempts, for example in Nazi Germany and in Gomulka's Poland. The most savage civil war which the revolutionaries had to fight was against the Chouans of Britanny who were inspired by their priests.

The revolutionary religious settlement was a failure and it was left to Napoleon to draw the necessary consequences. Most of the people whom he intended to use for his purposes were Catholics. He had no strong religious views himself, wavering between materialism and a general belief in a deity in the style of Rousseau. But religion was a necessity for social order. 'My policy,' he told his Conseil d'État, 'is to govern men as the great majority wish to be governed.... It was as a Catholic that I won the war in the Vendée, as a Moslem that I established myself in Egypt and as an Ultramontane that I won the confidence of the Italians. If I were governing the Jews, I should rebuild the Temple of Solomon' – which was what another tyrant, Herod the Great, had done before him. It was in this spirit that he entered on his negotiations for a Concordat with Pope Pius VII, which he was later to describe as the most difficult enterprise of his career.

His aim was to reunite the country by ending the schism between the revolutionary constitutional church and the Catholic church, while at the same time bringing the church under his control. Formally, at any rate, he succeeded. The Church's endowments, confiscated in the Revolution, were not restored. The clergy received their stipends from the state. Under the Organic Articles of Administration the clergy were subject to police regulation and their training required state approval. But the Mass could again be celebrated openly throughout France, the hierarchy was restored, and the church could operate without persecution. In 1804, the Pope gave Napoleon the legitimation he required by anointing him as Emperor, while he asserted imperial supremacy by crowning himself. The only price he had to pay was a religious marriage ceremony with Josephine. Two years later the Church had, with the approval of the Papal legate in Paris (though not of the Pope), to accept a catechism which described the Emperor as 'the agent of God and his image on earth' and which declared those who failed in their duty towards him as 'worthy of eternal damnation'.

It looked as though Napoleon was winning all along the line. He had the temporal power and he had only to push forward step by step to control the spiritual power too. The Pope's temporal state lay within his grasp. 'For the Pope's purpose,' he declared, 'I am Charlemagne. . . . If he behaves well, I shall make no outward changes; if not, I shall reduce him to the status of Bishop of Rome.' Behaving well would mean joining the continental Confederation against England. Pius refused. 'We are the Vicar of a God of peace,' he declared, 'which means peace towards all, without distinction between Catholics and heretics, or between those living near at hand and those living far away, or between those from whom we expect benefits and those from whom we expect evil . . .'

In 1809 Napoleon declared the annexation of the Papal states. Conscious of his strength and having, as he believed, done more for the Catholic Church than any other man, he was outraged when Pius replied with a Bull of Excommunication. Although the Emporer later denied that had ordered the arrest of the Pope he certainly wrote to Murat that Pius was a dangerous madman and should be shut up. He was taken at his word.

There followed the long imprisonment and isolation at Savona, as the Emperor sought to reduce Pius to the status of a puppet Pope. Napoleon failed to get what he wanted, and in 1812 he annulled the Concordat.

It was a bad moment for the break. The Emperor was just about to advance on Moscow through Catholic Poland, raising a Polish army *en route*, and Catholic Spain was in revolt in his rear. Before he departed, he commanded that the Pope should be brought from Savona, from which the English might take him off by ship, to Fontainebleau, where the Emperor might hope to compel him to accept a settlement. Pius nearly died on the journey. Then the Emperor returned defeated. There followed one of the most dramatic confrontations in history of which, alas, no details are preserved to us. There were various reports of physical violence by Napoleon, which, however, Pope Pius denied. But we know from other occasions how the great man could alternate charm and bullying; and we can imagine the pressures he brought to bear on the aged, enfeebled and isolated Pontiff. For six days the unequal battle continued and then the Pope signed the heads of a new Concordat, only to retract it later.

However, the end was now near. The Pope's return to prison in Savona became a triumphal progress. The Emperor's banishment to Elba was a furtive flight in fear of the anger of his own people. Napoleon had, to all appearances, won every round of the contest; but in the end it was the monkish, retiring Pope who gave members of Bonaparte's family refuge in Rome and interceded with the British on behalf of the prisoner of St Helena. Napoleon had understood the importance of spiritual power, but never its nature. Mohammedanism, he maintained at St Helena, was more simple and superior to Christianity, in that it conquered half the world in ten years, while Christianity took 600 years to establish itself. His greatest hero was Alexander the Great; he admired him for going to the temple of Zeus Ammon, where he was proclaimed a god. If he had stayed in Egypt, he declared, he would have become Emperor of the East and made a pilgrimage to Mecca. In Egypt he had studied the Koran and had professed hostility to the Pope and Catholic Christianity, and if such a line had helped him to extend his conquests he would, no doubt, have put it into practice; he even discussed the possibility of converting his army to Islam. To him the Pope was merely a means to an end. As he himself put it: 'After all, I only care for people who are useful to me and as long as they are useful.' And again: 'I am not a man like other men; the laws of morality and decorum could not be intended to apply to me.'

The internal defence against *hubris* or megalomania which is provided by religion was, in fact, largely, though not entirely, lacking in Napoleon; but the Pope and the church provided a formidable external restraint. In the case of more modern dictators the internal defence has often been entirely lacking and the external restraint has been much weakened. Recent confrontations between dictators and religion have been enacted at an altogether lower level of civilization than the clash between the adventurer of genius and the monk; the struggle has for that reason been all the more savage.

Not so in Italy, however; there Mussolini reached a concordat with the Vatican which was a great deal more favourable to the Church than Napoleon's. The *Duce* was one of those revolutionaries who became strongly anti-clerical, following a religious upbringing. At the age of nine, unable to control the violent boy, his atheist father and devout mother sent him to school with Salesian Fathers in Faenza. They tried, without success, to preach and beat some discipline into him. At the end of a year masters and pupil parted with mutual relief, and enduring resentment on his part. As a young socialist journalist he thundered against the Church, 'that great corpse', against the Vatican, 'den of intolerance and robbers', against Christianity, 'humanity's immoral stigma', against 'a vindictive, cruel and tyrannical God', who does not exist. When he came to power he launched the blackshirts against the Catholic organizations and then, in order to appease the Vatican, ordered the prefects to apologize to the Bishops. Before long his public image was that of the practising Catholic, the champion of Christendom against atheist Bolshevism. It was in this guise that in 1929 he signed the Lateran Treaty recognizing 'the Catholic, Apostolic and Roman Religion as the sole religion of the State', 'the sovereign independence of the Holy See in the international field' and in the Vatican state. The attached Concordat also authorized Church religious teaching in schools and social (though not political) work by Catholic Action. Mussolini may have regretted the agreement when Pope Pius XI spoke against extreme nationalism and racial ideology, and when his successor advocated Italian neutrality in the war and sent messages of sympathy to the Catholic monarchs driven out by Hitler in 1940. But he had to accept this limitation on his power, which was one of the reasons why he was never able to become a totalitarian dictator in the full sense. In religion, as in most other matters, his approach was impulsive and opportunistic; and although in his final days of despair and defeat he philosophized a good deal about God, he never gave evidence of any firm belief. In the tradition of other great despots of the past he was a believer in magic charms, fortune telling, interpretation of dreams. Indeed, when he described the Italian people as superstitious rather than religious, he was projecting his own image upon them. In the last despondent days he had even lost faith in his own destiny.

This never happened to Hitler. His one supernatural belief was in his own destiny (*Schicksal*) or Providence (*Vorsehung*); 'I go the way Providence dictates with the certainty of a sleep walker,' he said just after he had brought off the re-militarization of the Rhineland. Each new success, each act of folly or weakness by his opponents – whether German or foreign – added to his conviction that the force of omnipotent Providence had streamed down upon him, that his greatness and that of the German *Volk*, with which he identified himself, was a world-historical mission and that anyone who frustrated his mission was an enemy of the *Volk*. These supernatural concepts, *Volk* and *Vorsehung* were abstractions without content. Hitler's *Volk* was not the actual people. It meant – if it had any precise meaning – those racially pure persons who gave the Fuehrer fanatical support. Hitler's Providence was not God, who – whether one believes in him or not – acquires a certain concrete and objective character from the qualities, laws and powers which men down the ages have attributed to him. 'Providence' is a windy abstraction into which the believer can blow what content he likes – in the case of Hitler his own insatiate will to power. It enabled him to identify his own destructive impulses with the 'creative force' of history.

Hitler had no more precise supernatural beliefs than this. He was not the dupe of the efforts of earnest ideologues to revive pagan rites and the worship of Nordic gods. He had, in fact, not much interest in religion, apart from an old-fashioned rationalist belief that the progress of science would prove the absurdity of Christian doctrine and finish off the Churches. In the style of Nietzsche, he despised Christianity as a religion for slaves and failures. This was only in private; in public he was prepared to stand up as the champion of Christian civilization against godless Bolshevism. He left anti-Christian statements to such subordinates as Bormann who declared: 'National Socialism and Christianity are irreconcilable.' And he showed little interest in Rosenberg's plan for a 'national Reich Church' with *Mein Kampf* replacing the Bible, the sword instead of the Cross on the altar, and National Reich orators instead of pastor and priests. Hitler certainly had every intention of settling with the priests and the pastors, but that could wait till after victory.

He had an admiration for the Catholic Church as an institution, its survival value, its genius for propaganda, and its grip on men's hearts and minds. One of his first actions was to sign a Concordat with Cardinal Pacelli, later to become Pope Pius XII. It helped Hitler towards the respectability which he needed to prove the constitutionality of his rule and to bring the army under his sway. He did not, however keep the Concordat any more than any other agreement. Before long the leader of Catholic Action had been murdered, in the Night of the Long Knives, and hundreds of priests were in concentration camps. In 1937 the old Pope Pius XI found it necessary to issue his Encyclical, *Mit Brennender Sorge*, in which he accused the Nazi movement of violating the Concordat and sowing hatred against Christ and his Church and warned of the danger of new religious wars of extermination. This did not prevent the Austrian Cardinal Innitzer, a year later, from urging Austrians to vote 'yes' in the plebiscite on the *Anschluss* with Germany. When a few months later he preached a critical sermon, the Nazis repaid him for his pains by sacking his cathedral.

During the war individual Catholic leaders, such as the Bishop of Muenster, Graf Galen, spoke out bravely against various Nazi measures. Individual Catholics played a noble part and gave their lives in the resistance to Hitler, including the brother and sister Scholl of Munich who in 1943 led the first student demonstration against the régime, and Count Stauffenberg the leader of the 1944 bomb plot. However, Pope Pius XII has been criticized for not speaking out unequivocally against Nazi crimes and in particular the *Endlösung*, the mass extermination of Jews.

The question for the Curia and the Catholic Church was an agonizing one. An outside authority can scarcely condemn the faithful of a country to martyrdom against their will. If the Pope had spoken out boldly, the hierarchy and clergy of Germany would have had to follow and the laity too would have been committed. It is arguable that in the midst of a war, when national unity and army discipline were vital, such an intervention of the spiritual power could have been made both effectively and with impunity, and that, if the spiritual power was not deployed against such monstrous crimes as this, it would never be worth using at all. It is also possible that, with the madness of war aggravating that of the dictator and with the powers of the Gestapo being what they were, intervention would have provoked yet another massacre, as well as infringing the neutrality to which the Vatican state owed its survival and any good it might do in the world. The decision which was actually taken – to do whatever good could be done by stealth – was perhaps the logical outcome of the position of the Church and the Curia over the centuries. One should not, of course, expect the Curia – as a political authority – to show any more courage or sagacity than the other governments who allowed themselves to be repeatedly bamboozled or terrorized by Hitler over the years, but one could expect it, as a spiritual authority, to show a greater sensitivity to the moral enormity of what was being done. The Church authorities were partially blinded to this by the menace of Communist atheism which Hitler skilfully exploited; they were therefore slow to realize that it was much more dangerous to have Hitler for a friend than Stalin for an enemy. In this they shared the blindness of most of the German ruling class; and part of the reason for this was that, through the centuries of the age of absolutism the Church, whether Catholic or Protestant, had got very much mixed up with the powers that be. Often great prelates had been the agents of monarchs in power politics, witness the machinations of Cardinal Richelieu and Père Joseph; there was a tradition of Machiavellianism in the Church's operation in the temporal sphere, in which it had great interests to protect. This identification with established authority also determined the role of the Church in the Spanish civil war. That the existence of a supra-national spiritual authority can be a great strength to Catholics in resisting tyranny has been proved again recently in Poland where the Church has been the chief limiting factor on Communist totalitarian power. But in dealing with Nazi tyranny this spiritual power was never employed to the full, which has been one of the factors in reducing the Church's influence in the post-war world.

The German Protestants had no such outside support. Hitler despised them for their subservience and was confident that he could bring them under control. Martin Luther himself had been a virulent anti-Semite and had founded a church with a tradition of conformity to the State authority. However the process of *Gleichschaltung* did not prove as simple as Hitler had expected. When he came to power it was estimated that some 3,000 of Germany's 17,000 pastors supported the Deutsche Christen, who championed Nazi racialism and the *Fuehrer-prinzip*. After the seizure of power the numbers increased rapidly. Hitler had reason to suppose that, with a judicious mixture of terror and patriotic appeal, he would have no difficulty in making the fanatical army chaplain, Pastor Mueller, bishop over a Reich church. He did get him elected with the aid of Gestapo and S.A. terror. But the famous ex-U-boat commander, Pastor Niemöller – at that time a nationalist from whom the Nazis might have expected support – formed the Confessional Church with a considerable minority of the Pastors. Hitler's answer was the Gestapo. In 1935 some 700 pastors were sent to concentration camps. Mueller had evidently failed in his task of proving that National Socialism was Positive Christianity. The subsequent efforts of the Nazi Minister of Church Affairs also proved unsuccessful; and in 1937 another 800 pastors and Church leaders were arrested, including their leader Pastor Niemöller himself. There was individual resistance after that and both Protestants and Catholics played a great part in the anti-Hitler conspiracy of 1944, providing with their deaths some of the great martyrs of the twentieth century, such as Pastor Bonhoeffer, and in their letters from prison some of its most moving and relevant documents of devotion. The fact remains that if the majority or even a large minority of professing Christians had lived up to their principles the worst crimes of National Socialism would not have been possible in Germany. But, then, perhaps the same could be said of most of the great catastrophes of Christendom. The church organizations did not provide a sufficient framework of moral resistance to keep the tyranny within limits, although the existence of the churches and the sense that they were not alone no doubt helped to give courage to the martyrs.

This question of keeping the church in being and what price should be paid to keep it in being arises just as acutely in Soviet Russia. The Concordat which Stalin reached with the Russian Orthodox Church in 1943 was, at any rate symbolically, an event of greater importance that that of Napoleon or Mussolini or Hitler. For he alone of these dictators was openly and avowedly a militant atheist, dedicated to the destruction of religion in his country. His training in an Orthodox seminary in Tiflis had made him, like so many other seminarists from the French Revolution onwards, a fanatical enemy of the Church. His accession to the supreme power in 1928 heralded an intensification of the Communist anti-religious drive which coincided with the great collectivization, religion being seen as the ideological superstructure of the peasantry. Religious persecution reached new heights at this time, and the anti-religious organization, the League of the Militant Godless, attained its peak membership of over five million. But when the census of 1937 was taken it was reliably reported that some 50 million people registered themselves as believers. As a result the census figures were not published; the census officials were arrested; both the Church and the League of the Militant God-less suffered mass arrests and deportations during the great purges. Anti-religious propaganda was again intensified, particularly in the newly occupied territories from the Baltic to the Black Sea, right up to the time of the German invasion.

Then when it became necessary to mobilize all patriotic forces for the Great Fatherland War, the League of the Militant Godless was disbanded, its journal was suppressed, and the support of the Orthodox Church with its mass following and great national tradition was enlisted for the war effort. The Concordat of 1943 was the reward for the Church's patriotic efforts. The Church was recognized as the principal religious body of the U.S.S.R. and allowed to elect its own Patriarch, to have its own ecclesiastical government, the Holy Synod, to publish its own journal, to have a legal right to its own property, and to take over the schismatic church hitherto favoured by the Communists.

Needless to say, this did not represent a change of heart on Stalin's part, nor even an intention to fulfil the rather limited guarantees of religious freedom in the Stalin Constitution. The motto was not so much, 'If you can't beat them, join them', as, 'If you can't beat them, use them'. Stalin set up a special ministry to make use of the Orthodox Church (headed by a former secret police official who had previously been engaged in spying on the hierarchy) and he found that even after the war there was much usefulness to be got out of them. This was particularly so in the foreign sphere. The Patriarch as the Head of the most numerous Orthodox Church – indeed the second most numerous Church in the world – had great prestige with other Orthodox Churches, particularly in the Middle East which the Soviet Government has been trying to penetrate ever since the war. Furthermore, the toleration of the Church gave the Soviet Government an unprecedented respectability with the Western Churches. Finally, since every Christian is in favour of peace and against sin, the heirarchy could be relied on to support the World Peace Council – one of the main instruments of Soviet propaganda and foreign policy – and to denounce the sins of the imperialists (such as alleged American germ warfare in Korea) without too nice an inquiry as to whether these sins had actually been committed. The hierarchy, in any case, had no means of ascertaining the truth in such matters and the Orthodox tradition of nationalism and submission to the powers that be would naturally incline the bishops to the régime's point of view. Anyway, the Communists had ample means of penetrating the Church at every level, so that it served to keep the fervour of the faithful in safe channels.

Stalin and his successors have, therefore, been able to gain certain advantages from their limited toleration of the Church; but, by any standards, the faithful have got the better of the bargain. For the existence of some form of organized religion has been one of the main obstacles to that complete tyranny over the minds of men which Stalin sought by every means to establish. Their freedom may seem small enough by the standards of the non-communist world. They can celebrate their liturgy; that is all. The missionary, teaching and social activities which are the normal rights of religious bodies elsewhere are forbidden. Under Khrushchev, who seems to have had strong personal feelings on the subject, hundreds of churches were closed down; monks, pilgrims and church congregations were subjected to arbitrary police interference and hooliganism. Under Khrushchev's successors there was less arbitrary persecution, but the regulations against any religious activity apart from the church services were tightened up. There are, however, limits to government pressure. Already in 1966 two priests wrote to both Church and government authorities, complaining of the subservience of the hierarchy to atheist pressure and their betrayal of the faith. It is a feeling that is fairly widespread among believers; and if, as a result of persecution, it were to grow, there would probably be a schism and a formidable increase in underground religious opposition. Already the Baptists have split into official and unofficial bodies, the latter accusing the former of selling out to the

Communist authorities. Hundreds of the schismatic Baptists have been arrested. The régime has reason to fear a growth of such activity since Russia is traditionally the land of fanatical sects; and even totalitarian police measures have not been able to suppress them. The area on the Ukrainian-Moldavian border, for example, has ever since the war been particularly fruitful of millennial sects which regard Communism as anti-Christ. Recently, according to the local press, one of these sectaries issued a warning that the end of the world was at hand and that only those who retired with him into the caves would be saved. No less than 5,000 people followed him and stayed in the caves for some weeks until removed by the police. A régime which cannot prevent such an extraordinary demonstration as that cannot afford to drive more reasonable believers into a mood of desperate defiance. The protest of the two priests was a warning of just such a mood. The controversy was similar to that between the followers of the African Bishop Donatus and St Augustine after Diocletian's persecution; the Donatists argued that the '*traditores*' – those who had handed over the holy things to the pagan authorities – were not worthy to administer the sacraments. Similarly some of the Soviet believers must feel that clergy and prelates who have been intimidated or bribed by the K.G.B. or are actually in a few cases K.G.B. agents or who live in rich plenty on the generous offerings of the congregations are not worthy to handle the holy things. However anyone who has experienced the fervour of the congregations of one of the packed churches of the Soviet Union is liable to put aside such doubts; for these are the exploited and downtrodden standing at the gates of heaven. The contrast between the worn hard-bitten faces, the drab shabby clothes of the congregation and the ancient, glorious liturgy of the Orthodox Church recalls the words of St Paul on the primitive church: 'How that not many wise men after the flesh, not many mighty, not many noble are called. But God hath chosen the foolish things of the world to confound the wise; and God hath chosen the weak things of the world to confound things which are mighty' (1 Cor. 1.23).

For the Communists, religion remains officially a capitalist survival; and it is true that the majority of the people who pack the fairly small number of churches that are still open are elderly, with a large proportion of old women. But the same observation has been made for nearly half-a-century, which means that each new generation of the elderly provides a new generation of churchgoers; those whom one sees in Church now are those who have experienced in their prime the horrors of collectivization, the mass purges, and the war; one sees their sufferings etched on their faces; but one sees, too, an inner faith which has helped them to live through the greatest experiment in 'social engineering' the world has ever experienced, Stalin's attempt to create the New Soviet man. In externals Stalin became as near omnipotent over the people under his rule as any ruler in modern times ever has been. He could to a large extent make people act as if they were new men. But the survival of the Church is the outward and visible sign that a great multitude of his people, whatever their apparent conformity, retained an inner integrity, which the will of the tyrant could not break.

The state of the Church in Russia, battered and corrupted, persecuted and infiltrated, recalls the line of Boris Pasternak in *Dr Zhivago*: 'I am conquered by them all; that is my only victory.' It is a victory which Pasternak himself has helped to pass on to a new generation. The leading spirits of this new generation are not for the most part, in any strict sense, believers, but many of them are God-seekers, looking far beyond the official code of historical materialism, which has failed to supply any adequate basis for men's moral and spiritual existence. In that sense, the baptism of Stalin's daughter, Svetlana, although by no means an orthodox believer, into the Church of her forefathers, is, if not representative, at least symbolic. A new generation is seeking an aim in life; some feel the need of a religious basis for living; and after the struggles of two generations seekers and believers are united in what Walter

Kolarz in his fine book on *Religion in the Soviet Union* called the 'oecumenism of suffering'.

No communist Constantine is yet on the horizon; indeed it is conceivable that such a figure could be the greatest danger to the Christian Church. But now the wheel, that took a great turn with the conversion of Constantine, has come full circle again. The Churches have to operate, for the most part, in states that are thoroughly secularized under governments that are either neutral or sometimes hostile towards religious belief. The churches no longer strive to:

> prove their religion orthodox
> By apostolic blows and knocks.

The freedom and tolerance which were hammered out in the terrible fires of religious struggle now have a mainly secular basis. Men are never likely to agree about how far religious belief has restrained and how far it has enhanced the tyranny of rulers. However, on the face of it, the old distinction between the things that are Caesar's and the things that are God's presents a greater problem to men who no longer believe in God. The private conscience often no longer has the support of an organized body of belief in resisting the temporal authority. The ruler often no longer has the inner restraint of such beliefs to limit his exercise of power; and since modern technology has put in his hands quasi-divine powers of creation and destruction, the ruler who believes in no transcendental God is under special temptation to cast himself in that role. 'Nothing', writes St Augustine, 'renders men so anti-social in the perversity of their lives as the imitation of Gods.' Clearly he had in mind the pagan gods of Rome, but they have their modern equivalents. The temptations to the arrogance of power, that *hubris* which to the Greeks was supreme quality of the tyrant, are greater than ever before; and for the same reason – man's enormously increased control over his environment – the common man's sense of being subject to supernatural powers, and with it the restraining influence of religion, is reduced.

It used to be the boast, as Lord Acton observed, 'that religion was the mother of freedom, that freedom was the lawful offspring of religion'. Even in lands where this boast once held good, the maternity is now little recognized. The political offspring has come of age and stands on his own feet. He has travelled far and has sought with varying fortunes to establish himself far from the motherland. There the motto may be 'Seek ye first the political kingdom', and the temporal ruler may claim back the title of 'Redeemer'; Chairman Mao's little red book may play the role of bible and prayer-book. Where God is no more feared, other men and other powers are the chief limit and restraint on tyranny. Therefore it is logical now to turn to the tyrant and foreign policy and war.

10. The Tyrant and his Fellows

'L'enfer, c'est les autres'; to no one is Sartre's famous phrase more apt than to the tyrant. In the most extreme stages of his development, everyone who is not just an extension of his own ego, a mere means to his ends, is hell to him. Anyone who checks the extension of his power must, if possible, be crushed. His relationship with the outside world is one of power; his vital question, that posed by Lenin: 'Who–whom?' Therefore the natural relationship between tyrants, although there are important exceptions, is that of master to puppet.

The two most famous puppet tyrants in history are Herod the Great and Quisling – the one distinguished by the divine coincidence of the birth of Christ, the other by the temporal accident of being the first of many satellites in the modern age. But the breed was born very early in history, on the coast of Asia Minor, where the Persian conquerors installed dependent rulers in the Greek cities in the sixth century B.C. The relationship is well illustrated in the story told by Herodotus about Histiaeus the tyrant of the greatest of the Ionian cities, Miletus.

In 513 B.C. King Darius launched an expedition against the Scythians. He built a bridge of boats across the Danube and left the Ionians behind to guard it. When Darius retreated, the Scythians reached the bridge first and urged the Ionians to destroy it, thus recovering their freedom. But Histiaeus dissuaded his fellow rulers, pointing out that they all owed their positions to Darius and, if he were to fall, they would fall with him. His ten fellow tyrants were convinced. Thus they observed 'rule one' of the puppet-ruler. Histiaeus was rewarded for his services by being awarded a colony which he proceeded to fortify. Thus he observed 'rule two' of the puppet-ruler – that he increases his power when he can. This caused Darius' advisers to distrust him, with the result that the King sent for Histiaeus to join him in the capital of Susa, flattering him that he would be the King's closest friend and adviser. This is 'rule three' for the satellite – that the stronger he grows, the less his master will trust him. Histiaeus, desiring to escape from his gilded cage, sent a message (tattooed on the head of a slave) urging his deputy at Miletus to raise Ionia against the Persians. This he did, by handing over the government to the people and stirring up the people of the other Ionian cities against their tyrants. This is 'rule four' for the puppet-ruler – that he must win popular support before he can assert his independence. Finally, Aristagoras went first to Sparta, where he failed, and then to Athens, where he succeeded in gaining outside help for the Ionian revolt, which is 'rule five' for the puppet when he wants to cease being one. When Histiaeus returned to Miletus, the people having tasted freedom refused to have him back. The revolt failed, costing both Histiaeus and Aristagoras their lives, thus demonstrating that the path of the puppet to independence is both tortuous and dangerous, calling for cunning as well as courage.

Another problem of the puppet-ruler is to choose the right master. It was in this that Herod the Great showed supreme skill. His power like that of his father depended on Rome; but to choose the right Roman in the era of civil war was a difficult task, but rewarding, since the struggle of the dynasts gave the client king a reasonable freedom of action. Herod resisted the temptation of playing one against another, which can prove either profitable or fatal. He served Mark Antony loyally until the end, and then, after Actium promptly switched his allegiance and loyalty to Octavian, who at once recognized his usefulness. Herod's troubles came not from his masters but from his subjects and family. Although a believing Jew, he was a foreigner, a Nabatean, and not all his services to his people, such as magnificently rebuilding the Temple of Solomon and securing a measure of peace in troubled times, could counteract the hatred of the Jews for a foreign ruler imposed by Gentiles; particularly one whose dissolute way of life flouted the canons of their Law. His own family plotted against him, and although Augustus supported him against the claims of his sons, the corruption of power and hardening arteries combined to reduce him to paranoiac suspicion and fits of insane rage during which he killed his favourite wife, most of the high priestly family to which she belonged and, later, her two sons. His fear of his subjects and the impression of the Messianic prophecies of the time on the tyrant's insanely jealous mind gives colour to the gospel story of the massacre of the innocents, perhaps in 4 B.C., the last year of Herod's life and a probable date for the birth of Christ.

Herod had survived one master and died at the age of seventy under another. It is a more general fate of client kings to fall with their masters. None of the Kings created by Napoleon kept their thrones after Waterloo, except for Bernadotte who had prudently changed sides three years earlier; and he alone legitimized himself among the people he ruled. The rest, mostly Napoleon's brothers and brothers-in-law, had to withdraw, as the Emperor's military power collapsed.

The family bond between Napoleon and most of his client kings was conducive to loyalty, rather than efficiency. It cannot be said that the more modern ideological bond produces either. The names of the rather numerous puppets who appeared in Hitler's Europe – Doriot, Déat, Degrelle, Antonescu, Pavelic, Hlinka, etc. – are scarcely remembered today. Vidkun Quisling alone retains an unenviable notoriety as the first of the breed. He started his career by working with Nansen's relief mission in the Soviet famine of the 1920s; impressed by what he saw, he tried to join the Norwegian Labour Party, at that time affiliated to the Comintern. Disillusioned with the Left, he turned right and in the early 1930s formed his own Nasjonal Sammling in imitation of Hitler's Nazi Party, and became befuddled with Rosenberg's Nordic racial doctrines. These doctrines gained trifling support from the most Nordic of peoples, although the aged writer Knut Hansen developed a senile passion for Hitler. Quisling seems first to have volunteered treachery to Rosenberg very early in the war. The ideologue's memoranda on the subject seem to have been ignored by the military; but Hitler saw the potentiality of this fifth column, however tiny, and exploited it. Quisling received little reward for his betrayal; when he became puppet Prime Minister he was unable – with all the trappings of power – to secure any substantial support from his people. He was, therefore, of little use to the Germans who chose to rule through their own tough *Gauleiter*. Both Quisling and the *Gauleiter* paid with their lives when their master fell.

Quisling was for Hitler a lucky accident, which he exploited with typical opportunism. Stalin, on the other hand, systematically developed a school for Quislings, in the Comintern, and the most successful of the Communist puppet-rulers is a graduate of that school, namely the East German dictator, Ulbricht. Having survived, as a Comintern official, both Stalin's and Hitler's purging of the leadership of the Communist party in the 1930s he was well qualified to take the position of supreme trust in Stalin's post-war European empire – a trust which he had fully justified. For, in survival value alone, he had out-Heroded Herod, having made himself indispensable to three successive Soviet leaderships – Stalin's, Khrushchev's and Brezhnev's. The task of ruling a rump Germany, overshadowed by the free Germany of the Federal Republic, rendered him dependent on Soviet support for his survival, and has denied him that measure of nationalist appeal which has enabled most of his fellow rulers in Eastern Europe to exert some measure of independence. The same circumstance long rendered Ulbricht indispensable to his masters; for, while they might have preferred a German leader who could rally at least some popular support as a magnetic attraction to the West Germans, they were compelled to recognize that any change from their point of view would inevitably be a change for the worse. It would involve the risk of an explosion which would remove the cork from the East European bottle.

At the opposite extreme in the East European spectrum we

must place Gheorghiu-Dej of Romania. From 1945 to 1960,
for most of his reign in fact, any objective observer would have
placed him among the most abject of the East European
satellites. Certainly he owed his position entirely to the Soviet
invasion of his country. At the time when the Red Army was
sweeping down on Romania in 1944, the Communist Party there
numbered perhaps a thousand and most of its leaders were in
gaol in Romania or in exile in the Soviet Union. In the *coup
d'état*, which King Michael led to overthrow Marshal Antonescu's dictatorship, the Communists played a minor, if effective,
part which is now naturally represented as the leading role. By
the end of 1945 the Communist Party membership had grown
to half-a-million. It was the governing Party of the state with
Gheorghiu-Dej as its titular leader. This government had been
imposed by direct Soviet threats to the King, reinforced by the
presence of the Red Army. Every aspect of Romanian life was
under Soviet control. This was particularly true of the economy, which was milked dry first by heavy reparation payments,
secondly by the Sovrom joint companies which under Soviet
management exploited the most valuable Romanian economic
assets including the vital oilwells and finally by paying specially low prices for Romanian trade. Soviet advisers ran everything, including the Secret Police who were among the most
brutal in Eastern Europe. When President Tito broke with the
Cominform in 1948 and trials of allegedly 'nationalist' communists were held in other Communist countries, the
Romanian leaders did their duty by purging one of their
number, Patrascanu, who was later to be executed in 1954.
Two years later, when the Hungarians rose in revolt, in
Romania nobody stirred except to take sterner disciplinary
measures against the Hungarian minority in Transylvania. It
was in Romania that the dissident Hungarian Premier Nagy
was held before his trial and execution.

For the first fifteen years of Communist rule, therefore,
Romania appeared as the most faithful of satellites and
Gheorghiu-Dej as the most subservient of puppets. However,
even there, appearances may have been deceptive. Gheorghiu-

Dej was not a Muscovite Comintern product but a home-grown Communist, a leader of the railwaymen who had spent most of the period of Iron Guard and military dictatorship in prison. He was later to argue that, although from 1944 he was the official leader of the party, it was Anna Pauker the Moscow-trained Foreign Minister who both controlled party recruitment – largely from the Iron Guard – and kept the rest of the Politbureau under surveillance and sometimes humiliating control. Be that as it may, the Romanian leader took advantage of Stalin's anti-Semitic mania in his last year, 1952, to get rid of Anna Pauker. The Russians had consolidated Communist Party control over Romania; now Gheorghiu-Dej was able to consolidate his control over the Party. When in 1954 Stalin's successors found it no longer possible to continue the full exploitation of his East European empire, they dissolved the joint Sovrom companies. Gheorghiu-Dej now consolidated his hold on the Romanian economy which was to be the basis of his bid for independence. After 1956, Khrushchev strove to put Soviet relations with Eastern Europe on a new footing; he was also engaged in the last stages of his struggle with his rivals at home, which strengthened the satellite rulers' bargaining position.

The events of 1956 had indicated to Gheorghiu-Dej just how far he could go. In Hungary the rising had threatened to overthrow Communist rule altogether, which was not what the Romanian leader wanted anyway, and to take Hungary out of the Warsaw Pact; therefore it had been crushed by Soviet tanks. In Poland the national Communist leader had been able to take over and break the Soviet grip on Polish domestic policy without any military intervention. When in July 1958 the Red Army withdrew from Romania, the scene was set. Already Gheorghiu-Dej had chosen the battlefield and was preparing his reserves. He knew from Hungary's experience that he could expect no support from the West in the event of military action and that, in any case, the Russian bear could crush him in a few hours. But he put out feelers for economic support. In 1959 Romania placed orders for 100 million dollars' worth of goods in the West and began to re-orientate her trade which up to then had been exclusively with the Soviet bloc.

At this very time, Khrushchev having renounced direct control over the Soviet East European empire, was seeking some form of cohesion by converting the Comecon, which had been set up as a Communist response to the western Organization of European Economic Co-operation, into an effective instrument of joint planning and co-ordination. For the Romanians, who were just beginning to feel their economic strength, this might have meant relegation to the 'colonial' position of a supplier of raw materials to the more developed Communist countries. They would have none of this. The Comecon, therefore, was the chosen battlefield.

The Romanian leaders had two advantages. However unpopular Communist rule might be in many respects, in any struggle with the Russians the leadership can rely on overwhelming popular support. This was due not only to the plunder and humiliation which the Romanians had suffered at Soviet hands after the war and to the recent loss of territory which they regarded as Romanian, but also to ancient historical causes and traditions and to the picture they have of Romania as an island of Latin civilization in a Slav sea. Secondly, the struggle developed just when the Soviet Union had become involved in a far more serious conflict – with China. The Romanian leaders have exploited the Sino-Soviet split with great skill to secure a greater area of manoeuvre for themselves. When in 1960 the Sino-Soviet argument broke out in Moscow the cracks were papered over with a declaration which asserted the principle of national sovereignty, independence and full recognition of rights. This was just what Romania wanted; the Russians needed Romanian support in their argument and were willing to pay for it with an advantageous trade agreement. When finally in 1962 Khrushchev put his plan for economic co-ordination to the Comecon the Romanians rejected it and despite a visit by Khrushchev himself they went on doing so.

The chief Romanian fear was Soviet economic pressure. What if the Russians were to withdraw their resources and experts from the great Galati steel combine, the greatest project in Romanian economic development? The Romanians, therefore, went ahead with seeking support from elsewhere, Austrian, British, French and German investment. They joined with the Yugoslavs in a great hydro-electric project at the Iron Gates. Then at the height of the Sino-Soviet dispute in 1963 they doubled their trade with China and increased it with Albania at a time when all the other Comecon countries were cutting down. At the same time they condemned the polemics between China and the Soviet Union and maintained resolutely friendly relations with Peking. Not that they had much in common with Chairman Mao; indeed nothing could be more alien to the regimented order of Romania than the excesses of the Red Guards. But in practice Chinese support might be useful in case of Soviet pressure, and in principle every Communist government should be able to act as it pleased.

This was the principle which the Romanian Communist Party asserted uncompromisingly and skilfully in its declaration of independence of April 1964. From that time the process of eradicating Soviet influence in culture and in politics has proceeded steadily under both Gheorghiu-Dej and his successor Ceausescu.

This story of a captive chrysalis turning into a free-flying butterfly illustrates the main difficulty in relations between totalitarian states, namely that friendship and hostility between them tends to be total. A critical article in the press, or even a few rude remarks in private become a political offence justifying economic sanctions and even ideological excommunication. One may say that the underground struggle between Bucharest and Moscow represents in this respect a highly encouraging advance in civilization compared with the Tito–Stalin conflict.

Yugoslavia was never a satellite state in the same way as other East European countries. In so far as Tito's rise to power was attributable to foreign aid it was due to that of Britain which in the crucial guerrilla struggle of 1943–4 far exceeded that of the Soviet Union. Stalin later argued that, had not the Red Army come to Yugoslavia, the Communist Party would no more have been able to achieve power there than in France or Italy. There is a partial truth in the argument, which is completely true of all the other East European countries. But, owing to the Partisan struggle, Tito had around him a solid nucleus of loyal supporters; neither the party nor the secret police were infiltrated by Soviet agents to the same extent as in other East European countries. When the break came only two high Party members were imprisoned for betraying Yugoslav secrets to the U.S.S.R. Stalin, in fact, grossly overestimated his power when he boasted that he need only lift his little finger for Tito to fall. There is no need to go into the charges which formed the excuse for the Cominform break with Yugoslavia. Criticisms of Red Army behaviour, failures in collectivization, fractionalism and deviation, all these were mere pretexts. The key to Stalin's motives is to be found in the conversation in Moscow early in 1948 – vividly described by Djilas who was one of the leaders of the Yugoslav delegation – in which the Soviet leader rudely attacked the Bulgarian leader Dimitrov, most famous of Comintern figures, for proposing, without consulting Moscow, a Bulgarian–Romanian federation. Dimitrov had to admit he had been in error. But, said Stalin: 'Your trouble is not errors, but that you are taking a line different from ours.' It was not that Stalin objected to federations – he was indeed urging a Bulgarian–Yugoslav–Albanian federation in order to control Tito through Dimitrov – but that he objected to federations which he had not promoted. He was capable of telling the Yugoslavs to swallow up Albania, then reproaching them for planning to send troops in, because Moscow had not been consulted. 'You don't consult at all,' complained Stalin. 'That is not your mistake but your policy – yes, your policy.'

When the break came into the open in June 1948, Stalin attempted to crush Tito by every means short of war – above all economic pressure and propaganda. The propaganda, while ostensibly appealing to the masses, was only designed to convince Communist bureaucrats. The kind of charges which Stalin launched were likely to make Tito more popular with his people. Both the propaganda and the economic pressure were aimed at making the charges of heresy and deviationism come true and in this they were largely successful. First Tito had to take measures – such as de-collectivization of the farms – which would both reduce popular resentment and add to economic efficiency; secondly he had to seek aid from outside and this involved getting mixed up with Western nations to an extent which had never before happened to a Communist country. These two factors led to the profound transformation of Yugoslav society which is still in progress. The transformation was speeded by the contrast with what was happening in the other East European countries, where the purge trials of Stalin's prime were being repeated against so-called nationalists and followers of the so-called 'Tito–Rankovic Fascist clique' such as the Hungarian communist leader, Rajk, and the equally eminent Bulgarian Kostov, and where collectivization of the farms on the Soviet model was rushed through regardless of economic sense. No reconciliation was possible in the tyrant's lifetime and, when he died, the Yugoslav leaders having tasted independence and friendly relations with the Western powers – whom, however, they never ceased to abuse – were in no mood to return to the old dependence on the Soviet Union. Khrushchev's attempt to patch up the quarrel was the first step in establishing a new relationship between the Soviet Union and the East European Communist régimes, a more complex relationship between societies which are gradually becoming less totalitarian and monolithic – a process which suffered a tragic, but not irreversible, setback with the Soviet invasion of Czechoslovakia.

Tito, therefore, may in part have owed his position to Stalin, but as soon as he could he asserted his independence. The same was true of General Franco *vis-à-vis* Hitler and Mussolini. While his rising was not inspired by them, without their

support it could well have failed. Most of his arms and
supplies came from his fellow dictators. It was the first example of what was later to become a well-known dictatorial
gambit (or at least a threat) – the use of so-called 'volunteers'
on a major scale. The Italian divisions, which were by no
means volunteers, performed miserably, at which Franco himself was reported to be as pleased as most other Spaniards. The
Condor Legion was used to 'blood' German airmen in war. It
is now pretty well established that the annihilation-bombing of
Guernica was carried out as an experiment on purely German
initiative, to the fury of Franco.

From the first, then, it was a question of who should use
whom. The Germans and Italians in return for their support
tried to force trade concessions and valuable raw materials out
of Spain. Franco slowly and grudgingly conceded. He also
joined the anti-Comintern Pact and entered into treaties of
friendship with the dictators. Hitler wanted Spain as a friendly
or dependent power in order to outflank France. Mussolini
wanted the same in order to control the Western end of the
Mediterranean, Mare Nostrum. But when the moment came
for Hitler to collect on his IOU, Franco politely, even ful-
somely, declined.

In October 1940, just after Hitler, now the conqueror of
Western Europe, had abandoned any early invasion of Britain,
the two dictators met on the Spanish frontier at Hendaye. In
order to set the scene the Generalissimo kept him waiting for
an hour. Hitler on this occasion was the suitor. He wanted to
enlist Franco's support for Plan Felix which would involve
seizing the straits of Gibraltar and North Africa, in order to
secure Axis control of the Mediterranean. 10 January 1941
was the appointed date. The Caudillo did not refuse but he
made conditions. Spain must have food; modern equipment,
too, since it could only be Spanish troops who would storm
Gibraltar and would hold the coastline against British naval
raids. With clear, yet hostile, eye, Franco perceived that the
British would never give in, either on the sea or in Africa.
Hitler was offering him spoils in Africa which were not his to

give and refusing to offer the French territories which Franco coveted. Hitler, by now at the height of his power and accustomed to get his way in everything, became more and more nervous and restless as the steady stream of objections flowed quietly on. The two dictators reached no conclusion and left their foreign ministers Suñer and Ribbentrop to reach an agreement which indeed committed Franco to enter the war, but did not say when. Ribbentrop went off cursing the 'Jesuit' Suñer and the ungrateful and cowardly Franco, while Hitler later told Mussolini: 'Rather than go through that again, I would prefer to have three or four teeth pulled out.' Mussolini when he met Franco in February 1941 had no better luck. Franco went on sending Hitler effusive messages and conducted negotiations through Suñer, his brother-in-law, who genuinely believed in the ideology of the Falange and the aims of the Axis. It is probable that Franco really did desire an Axis victory and sent the Spanish Blue Division of some 20,000 men to fight in Russia out of genuine conviction. But when it became clear that they were not going to win, he very quickly trimmed his sails to the western wind, getting rid of his Axis-orientated Foreign Minister, Serrano Suñer, and replacing him with a less doctrinaire minister. He himself never took ideology very seriously, treating the Falange as merely one of the pillars in his power structure. It has been one of the fallacies of the left to classify him with Hitler and Mussolini as a Fascist. Whereas they were radical dictators, he is a profoundly conservative one, which combined with a shrewd sense of self-preservation has made him the most long-lived of modern tyrants, with the exception of Dr Salazar of Portugal.

Where, then, tyrants start dependent, they will not long remain so without constraint. Where tyrants start equal, they will not long remain so without hostility. The record of the relationship between Hitler and Mussolini in the ten years between their first and last meetings is a cautionary tale in the corrupting influence of power. Mussolini came to their first meeting with a contempt for the Fuehrer. He regarded him as an upstart, his racial theory as nonsense, the Germans as barbarians. Hitler on the other hand deeply admired the *Duce*, acknowledged himself his disciple. He was always to show him as much affection and loyalty as was in his nature. Their first encounter in June 1934 confirmed Mussolini's impression; the Italian splendid in his uniform and boots and spurs regarded the insignificant figure in the yellow raincoat as 'a silly little clown', an impression which the Fuehrer's pretentious and gradiloquent monologues did nothing to remove. A month after their meeting, the disciple showed his mettle by causing the assassination of the Austrian dictator, Dolfüss, at a time when Frau Dolfüss was Mussolini's guest. Such brutal episodes are not uncommon in the dictatorial jungle. But they do not long affect the relations between dictators, since it is the behaviour they expect of one another. Mussolini, helped by the weakness of British diplomacy, by Hitler's moral support in his Ethiopian adventure and by their combined intervention in the Spanish Civil War, soon recovered from the resentment and fear caused by Germany's designs on Austria. In September 1937 he visited Germany and the theatrical display of highly organized power and disciplined mass enthusiasm wove a spell on him from which he was never to be free. He returned home to introduce the *Passo Romano*, a more dignified term for the German *passo d'oco*, and racial laws which though they were never rigidly enforced, signified the *Duce*'s submission to Nazi doctrines which he had previously despised. There followed the Anti-Comintern Pact and Mussolini's connivance, contrary to all earlier pledges, at the Anschluss with Austria. Thus he brought the power which fatally hypnotized him right to the borders of Italy.

It was a curious and one-sided alliance. According to 'the pact of steel' there should have been prior consultation on any action which might involve armed conflict. But Hitler seized Czechoslovakia without warning to Mussolini, who then invaded Albania equally without consultation. Hitler's partner in the anti-Comintern pact was taken by surprise by the Nazi–Soviet treaty. The invasion of Poland was contrary to the wishes of Mussolini who held that Italy would not be ready for war until 1943–4. When Italy entered the war it was not due to any requirement on Germany's part, but to the desire to secure the spoils of victory before the fighting ceased; and, in fact, the two allies fought separate and parallel wars, except when the Germans had to intervene to get the *Duce*'s forces out of trouble. Although Italy had a special interest in the Balkans, Hitler occupied Romania without any advance notice. 'Hitler always presents me with a *fait accompli*', complained Mussolini. 'This time I will pay him in his own coin. He will find out from the papers that I have occupied Greece. In this way the equilibrium will be re-established.' It was not; for within a few weeks Hitler had to mount an expedition to get the Italians out of trouble in Greece. German influence was firmly established in Italy's Balkan sphere of influence.

When Hitler invaded the Soviet Union, Mussolini was dragged from his bed by a telephone call an hour and a half after the event. He had not approved of the Nazi-Soviet pact; now he did not approve of its reversal. But still he was so much impressed by this grandiose display of power, that he insisted on Italian participation in it. An Italian army corps was sent rather against the wishes of the Germans. When the front broke after Stalingrad, the Germans blamed the Italians and left them in the lurch, seizing most of the transport, just as Rommel's Afrika Corps had done after Alamein. Italian military advice was to withdraw the shattered divisions; they were by now badly needed in Italy; the Germans wanted to get rid of them and refused to equip them; but Mussolini, out of hurt pride, obstinately insisted that they should stay. Yet he was by then beginning to argue, under the pressure of defeat in North Africa, that the only salvation was a separate peace with Stalin. In the face of Hitler's fanatical rejection, he did not press the matter. Indeed the balance of power had now shifted so far, and repeated Ialian defeats had so humiliated the *Duce*, that he was reduced to the position of a puppet.

It was the failure in his own theatre of war, Mare Nostrum, and in North Africa which had broken Mussolini's spirit. The 'pact of steel' had never brought any of that close co-operation, joint commands and co-ordination of planning which characterized the Anglo-American alliance. Even when Mussolini's advice was good, as when he pressed for the seizure of Malta to secure lines of communication to North Africa, it was ignored. After defeat, the Germans refused to re-equip Italian divisions and insisted on sending their own formations. When the Axis had completed the retreat to Tunisia, Mussolini as was his right relieved Field-Marshal Rommel of his command, only for Hitler to restore him at once as Commander of the Army Group Africa.

The only real contact was at the summit. The meetings became more and more one-sided. Hitler would launch into one of his rambling, pretentious monologues (on one occasion he spoke for two and a half hours). Mussolini would play the unaccustomed and repugnant role of listener. It may be doubted whether the Fuehrer ever realized how much his friend resented the relationship.

When in July 1943, after the invasion of Sicily, the two dictators met at Feltre near Venice, there was but one way of saving Italy from all the horrors of invasion – to sue for a separate peace and neutralization – and only one man who might have some chance of persuading the Fuehrer to accept such a course. Some of Mussolini's advisers hoped he might attempt it; but in vain. The *Duce* was in his own way an Italian patriot; but he was above all a power-worshipper; Hitler had the power, and beneath all his bluff and braggadocio Mussolini was realist enough to recognize it. So his last words at Feltre were: 'Ours is a common cause, Fuehrer.' He had, in effect, consented to become the figurehead of a German-controlled Italy. When the conspirators removed the figurehead Hitler was determined to put him back again. 'I cannot and will not fail Italy's greatest son in his hour of need,' he told Skorzeny, who was designated to rescue the *Duce* from his imprisonment. Mussolini, now worn out and drained of will-power, did not want to be rescued; but he allowed Hitler to talk him into resuming the leadership. 'I have come for my instructions', he said bitterly. He succumbed, partly because he hoped to save his country from the worst consequences of German occupation, but partly because he had no more will of his own. Right up to the end, Hitler was able to animate his puppet, to galvanize the corpse.

What did Hitler get out of this strange relationship? The man who can live alone is either a god or a beast; and it would be insulting to either species to describe Hitler as one of them. Mussolini was a friend who was officially his equal. The Fuehrer could demonstrate his loyalty to him; he could patronize the man he had previously hero-worshipped; and he could not allow another dictator who proposed the same principles as himself to fall, could not even admit the possibility. So, his 'friend and ally' became a projection of Hitler's own ego, a vehicle for his daemonic will.

This survey of the relations between tyrants would not be complete without a reference to Hitler and Stalin. They eyed each other warily but respectfully from afar. If ever two men should have understood each other, these should have. But it is doubtful whether Stalin ever fully understood Hitler. The Fuehrer's intentions towards the U.S.S.R. were clearly set out in *Mein Kampf*, but Stalin, who had so skilfully juggled with Marxist-Leninist ideology for his own purposes, was unlikely to take anything another dictator had written at its face value. The joint attack of Communists and Nazis on the Weimar Republic helped Hitler to power; and it was not until after the Reichstag Fire Trial that Stalin seems to have realized the kind of menace that confronted him. The Comintern then switched its main attack from the Social Democrats, and adopted the tactics of a United Front against the Nazis, while Litvinov developed his collective security policy under the slogan, 'Peace is indivisible'.

However, Stalin shared with Hitler a contempt for the Western democracies, which up to 1940 proved all too justified. It is certain that he did not put all his eggs in the 'collective security' basket. The view that he was all the time planning a deal with Hitler, and that the great purges were carried out partly to remove those in the Party and Army who would

oppose such a deal, is attractive from the psychological point
of view. It would illustrate that characteristic dictatorial
phenomenon of 'projection' by which the dictator accuses
others of his own guilty designs. Did Stalin accuse his victims
of plotting with the Nazis because he intended to do so himself? There is some evidence that he did try to maintain a
tenuous personal connection in Berlin; and it is reasonable to
suppose that the cautious Stalin wanted to keep his options
open. But there is not enough evidence to support the view
that Stalin was planning his pact with Hitler from the start. It
was not until his total disillusion with the Western allies after
the surrender of Czechoslovakia that he began openly, if
cautiously, to signal his invitation of a reversal of alliances to
Hitler. Even then, if the Western Powers had been willing and
able to meet his defence needs and imperialist claims in
Eastern Europe, there is no certainty that he would have
chosen Hitler, although, in general, a dictator is more to be
trusted in doing deals at the expense of other nations than any
democratic government.

Whatever the motives for the pact, Stalin's behaviour towards Hitler thereafter was ambiguous. He told Churchill that
he knew that the Nazis would eventually attack the Soviet
Union, but that he hoped to expand the period of preparation
for defence by a year or so. If this was all he wanted, he certainly played his part with gusto. Indeed, it is hard to interpret
the strange negotiations which Molotov conducted in Berlin in
the autumn of 1940 except on the assumption that he thought
some longer-term arrangement with Hitler would be possible
after the destruction of the British Empire. It is true that
Molotov hinted that they were dividing the lion's skin while
the lion was not yet dead, and R.A.F. bombers over Berlin
reinforced the point. It is true, too, that every time Hitler or
Ribbentrop tried to divert his eyes to the alluring prospects of
India and Iran, Molotov would pin them down to some more
immediate issue such as the German troops in Finland or the
Soviet interest in Bulgaria or the Straits. But the Soviet
government seems to have regarded such settlements in the

frontier areas as the condition for a wider agreement, of which they later sent a draft to Berlin.

Molotov did not realize that he had talked away his chance of peace; Stalin still less. There is nothing more curious than the series of gestures towards Germany which Stalin made as the war clouds gathered. He publicly embraced the German Ambassador, exclaiming: 'We must remain friends and you must now do everything to that end'; he rejected and ignored the British and American warnings of the forthcoming invasion, as well as that of his own espionage service; making himself premier six weeks before the invasion, he expelled the envoys of the exiled Belgian, Norwegian and Yugoslav governments, with the last of which he had a few months before concluded a treaty of friendship; he fulfilled the Soviet commitments under the trade pact with Germany more zealously than ever before; finally, a week before the invasion he publicly and indignantly denied rumours, said to have been circulated by the British Ambassador, of a forthcoming German invasion and described them as provocative; similarly frontier units had orders not to shoot back in shooting incidents for fear of provocation, and when the attack actually came some of them could not get orders to resist. Stalin in fact had moved strong forces to the frontier and then allowed them to be taken by surprise.

How was it, then, that the least trusting of men had somehow persuaded himself to trust the least trustworthy? His first calculation was presumably that either Britain and France would fail in their commitments towards Poland and try to turn Hitler eastwards, in which case the Nazi–Soviet pact would frustrate them; or there would be a prolonged and exhausting struggle between Germany and the Western Powers, in which case the Nazi–Soviet pact would give him a breathing-space to build up Soviet strength either to intervene at the most advantageous time or to dictate the peace terms. When Hitler scored his rapid victory in the West, the situation needed re-assessing. Stalin attempted to secure a permanent frontier between the Soviet and German Empires by seizing the Baltic

States on the north flank and the Bessarabian province of Romania in the south. With a secure front from the Baltic to the Black Sea and even the Straits, he could quite easily agree with Hitler and Japan on partitioning the remains of the British Empire. The arrangement would be as permanent as any agreement between Communist and capitalist states could be. Stalin had in any case found Hitler much easier to deal with than the British and French governments, which had refused to give him *carte blanche* in Eastern Europe. Hitler had everything to gain by such an arrangement, at any rate until he could dispose of Britain. Therefore the pathologically cautious Soviet dictator, judging his German colleague by himself, came to the conclusion that Hitler would not make an attack when he could secure most of what he needed without one. The German preparations and troop movements seemed to Stalin, therefore, to be merely the means of establishing a strong bargaining position; and his final acts of appeasement before the invasion were clear signals that he was ready to bargain.

He failed, in fact, to reckon with the gambler and fanatic in Hitler's nature, since these characteristics were alien to him. He trusted his fellow tyrant, in the sense that he assumed that he would act rationally in his own interests; and when Molotov asked the German Ambassador as the German troops swept across the frontier: 'Do you think we have deserved this?', he was probably reflecting the true disillusionment and bitterness of his master who had done all in his power to make it worth Hitler's while to keep the peace. Stalin continued to be fascinated by his great adversary – to such an extent that he at first refused, contrary to all the evidence, to believe in Hitler's death, and thereafter took on some of his characteristics in the increasingly pathological anti-Semitism of his old age.

Relations between tyrants, then, are normally only amiable when remote; closer relations tend to lead to mutual exploitation or conflict. Yet dictators do not learn from this bitter experience. It has now become the settled policy of the Soviet leadership to attempt to capture nationalist dictators for Communism. The policy was launched under Stalin, when in the early 1950s the Communists tried to appropriate the left-wing Guatemalan military dictator, Colonel Arbenz, only to be defeated by a U.S.-supported military *coup*. The model is now Fidel Castro who seized power in Cuba at the head of a nationalist movement and subsequently declared that he was a Marxist-Leninist. This declaration had several advantages; for Communist institutions and the nationalization of all the means of production guarantee the dictator a totalitarian power which he could secure in no other way; further, membership of an international revolutionary movement enables the dictator to intervene in the affairs of other countries far more than would be possible for the simple leader of a small power; finally, declaring himself a Communist guarantees the dictator Soviet support against the U.S.A. or any other so-called 'imperialist power', as well as economic aid. It is rather more dubious whether the Soviet government gets value for its very considerable expenditure. For Castro has rarely followed the Soviet line, and has denounced the Soviet policy of dealing with Latin-American governments, against whom he seeks to stir up guerrilla revolts.

However, the Soviet leaders seem to regard the policy of seeking revolution from above as worthwhile, since they have sought to follow it elsewhere – so far without notable success. To judge from his writings and utterances shortly before his fall, the Ghanaian dictator Kwame Nkrumah was close to accepting a Communist role at that time, indeed, his book on neo-colonialism might almost have been written in Moscow. In Algeria Ben Bella was moving increasingly into the Soviet sphere when he fell; and his successor Colonel Boumédienne has moved rapidly in the same direction since the Middle East war of 1967, although, from the Moscow point of view, he displays an alarming affinity with Peking.

In fact the two great Communist centres compete with each other in supporting and seeking to capture for their purposes nationalist socialist dictators. Peking seemed to be on the verge of success in Indonesia when the Communists attempted their *coup d'état* against the army, only to be crushed in their turn by the army *coup* which toppled Sukarno. Such dictatorial states, provided that they are anti-Western, above all anti-American or, in Soviet language, anti-imperialist, are now styled 'independent states of national democracy' and it is Soviet policy to support them, even when they ban the Communist party.

Thus, while the relationship between tyrants has commonly been brutal and unsatisfactory, there is a natural affinity between them – almost, one might say, a dictators' international. Ever since King Darius sought, in the Marathon campaign, to restore the ex-tyrant Hippias to Athens, despots have from time to time sought to overthrow democracies and constitutional governments in order to impose their fellows upon them. Between tyrants there is a natural state of distrust and rivalry. Between tyrants and free men there is a natural hostility, which often finds expression in subversion, cold war or war.

11. The Tyrant, the Army and War

'A prince', writes Machiavelli, 'ought to have no other aim or thought, nor select anything for his study, than war and its rules and discipline.' An equally important principle, and one nearly as widely practised, is that, if you are preparing war, you should talk peace. These two principles sum up the approach of most tyrants to democracies and constitutional governments.

Here a word must be said about one of the commonest forms of government at the present time – the military dictatorship. It is almost by definition tyrannical; for when the military usurps the civil power it is acting beyond its scope. In extreme emergency the politicians are sometimes glad to let this happen; but even war is normally regarded as too serious a matter to be left to the generals. However, even if by nature tyrannical, military despotism is not generally the most tyrannical form of government, nor the most warlike.

The last point is illustrated by the history of Latin America. This sub-continent has experienced during the past 150 years more military dictatorships than any other corresponding area, but less international wars. This happy immunity is partly due to geography. Isolation has enabled the Latin-American countries to keep out of the two Great Wars of this century – at any rate until it was too late to take any active part in them. The vast areas of mountain, swamp and jungle make it difficult for the various nations to get at each other and reduced the scale of such hostilities as the Chaco War between Bolivia and Paraguay. However, men in their more bellicose moods have not normally been deterred by geographical obstacles. And there does seem to be something paradoxically peaceful in the nature of military dictatorship.

The exception seems to prove the rule, since the most terrible war in Latin-American history, that waged by Paraguay aainst Argentina a century ago, was launched not by a General or Colonel who had seized power by *coup d'état*, but by Francisco Solano López, who had inherited absolute power from his father, and with it Napoleonic ambitions and very strong armed forces. By methods which look forward to modern totalitarian dictatorships he completely isolated and controlled his people and drove them to fight fanatically for four years, until nearly all the men had perished and only about a quarter of the population survived. Between this war and World War I the unhappy country experienced no less than fourteen civil wars. Paraguay however was the exception in Latin-America. In general, although military dictators may often admire the great conquerors of the past, it has been mostly the civilian tyrants who in our time have sought to emulate them. Thus we have seen how General Franco, who spent many of his younger years fighting in North Africa and then came to power in a very bloody civil war, yet played Penelope to his German and Italian suitors when they sought to involve him in the world war. Similarly, although Kemal Atatürk was a soldier, came to power in war and maintained strong armed forces, Turkey, under him and his successors, has enjoyed nearly a half-century of peace; his military successor General Inönü has been the chief restraining influence, whereas his civilian successors have had greater difficulty in restraining the military from going to war over Cyprus than any military dictator would have done. In the 1967 crisis the Greek military junta, just because it was a military dictatorship, was able to withdraw General Grivas and the Greek troops from Cyprus, a concession which would certainly have brought rioting crowds on to the streets under a democratic régime and would probably have brought down the government. To take another modern instance, it was Sukarno, the civilian dictator, who, egged on by the Communists and in the erroneous supposition that he could thus keep the armed forces under control, launched the warlike confrontation with

Malaysia; it was the military dictatorship of General Suharto which took over from him and promptly ended the confrontation. On this showing, the Generals and Colonels might almost riposte to Lloyd George: 'Peace is too serious a matter to be left to the politicians.'

The reasons for this apparent paradox are not far to seek. The soldier does not need to follow the maxim of Machiavelli because he is assumed to have done so from his youth up. He does not need to pursue military glory, because he is already the representative of the army which is the repository of the nation's military glory. He does not have to struggle for the support of the armed forces, and to seek it through military adventure, because he assumes, often mistakenly, that he already has it. Finally, the armed forces are the instrument of his power; he wants to keep them in being and not to squander them in a war which may well bring glory to other officers and raise up rivals to himself.

It is not, therefore, surprising that Latin-America under a series of military dictators has been among the most internationally peaceful areas of the world. It is more difficult to explain why military dictatorships should have become endemic there. But perhaps we should first tackle the question why they are not endemic everywhere. After all the majority of states in the world today have experienced military rule and most of them, since they are fairly recent formations, within the last two generations. The armed forces are, in physical terms, normally the strongest body in the state; they are also the most highly organized and usually show an *esprit de corps*, a hierarchical respect and obedience to their leader which makes them a natural and effective instrument of rule. Why then since military dictatorship is the rule of the strongest, and may at any given time prevail in the majority of countries, do we regard it in most circumstances as abnormal, as an abuse of power, in fact as a form of tyranny? The answer is historical, moral and practical. Historically, a professional standing army, the armed forces as a separate entity in society, emerge only at a fairly late state of development. By then certain legal or moral sanctions for government have normally become established, be it the traditional prerogatives of a ruler or ruling-class, the divine right of kings, a constitution, or the will of the people, or some classes of them, expressed in elections. With this degree of complexity, civilian government will have acquired certain skills, which the military with their own progressively more specialized craft will not possess. The military when seizing power will frequently pay lip-service to the primacy of the civilian power, by promising elections or a constitution within a given time, a promise which should generally be treated with scepticism.

However, these conditions for constitutional government had not emerged at the time of the liberation of Latin-America. There was an alien authority based on the right of conquest and maintained by a fairly rigid military caste system. The authority was overthrown in a long war of liberation. A military caste, with a tradition of strong-man rule – or 'Caudillismo' – overthrown by military means at a time when Bonapartism supplied the revolutionary model – all this is a constellation favourable to the birth of a long series of military dictatorships. The Liberator himself was aware of the danger. 'We were left in a sort of infancy', wrote Bolivar, 'a permanent minority in all public affairs. If we had been allowed to control our internal affairs, to administer the country, we should have had experience of the course of public affairs and their machinery and we should enjoy at least a personal consideration, a certain automatic respect on the part of the people, sentiments very necessary in the case of revolution.' Bolivar, deprived of these advantages became reluctantly the first of the great 'charismatic' liberation leaders, as they are now called. Only absolute necessity and the imperative will of the people, he said, 'constrained him to accept the terrible and perilous charge of supreme dictator of the Republic'. He was aware too of the perils of the liberation struggle: 'Struggling after an impossible liberty, you will only find yourself thrust back into an extreme tyranny.'

The prophecy was fulfilled. The process was started by the

Liberator's own lieutenants and successors. It has been calculated that between the liberation and the First World War
there were 115 successful military *coups* in Spanish America.
Since World War II Latin-America has suffered on average
about three military *coups* a year – nearly half the world total.
Where military despotisms are so common, it is dangerous to
generalize about them, and certainly the old-fashioned picture
of the military dictatorship as a right-wing régime upholding a
reactionary ruling-class is misleading. The nature of the dictatorship varies with the time and place. During the 1930s,
when the big landowners and wealthy capitalists felt themselves threatened by revolutionary agitation and the rise of
labour movements, they often had recourse to military *coups*
out of fear. But the period around World War II was one of
very rapid economic growth in many Latin-American countries and in the decade 1943–53 more or less left-wing movements seized power through military *coups*. During this period
social reforms of one sort or another were carried out in
countries comprising three-quarters of the population of the
area. Military dictators may be generals who identify the glory
of the nation with the established ruling-class and its shame
with corrupt and inefficient politicians, or they may be colonels
or majors who regard the backwardness of their people as an
affront to themselves and the national dignity. However they do
have certain techniques and tendencies in common.

The Spanish language has contributed a whole range of
terms for the technique of seizing power. Professor Finer in
his comprehensive study of military dictatorships *The Man on
Horseback* describes the *Cuartelazo* or barracks rising in which
officers combine, having as they hope (by *trabajos* and *com-
promisos*), negotiated among themselves a common programme and a superiority of forces which will compel the
government to give in, raise a garrison or barracks in revolt,
issue a *pronunciamiento* and seize the centres of communication or march on the capital. Sometimes this involves fighting
but sometimes the Head of State can be removed by a bloodless
golpe. In countries where military *coups* are endemic they are

not normally very bloody. The Praetorian Guard may surrender after a token resistance and some random shooting; a few generals or politicians may go into exile in a neighbouring country to plot their return at some suitable opportunity.

Sometimes as in the case of Fidel Castro in Cuba the *pronunciamiento* will lead to a long civil war and a good deal of killing – Castro shot some 500 army officers in his first six months of power – and finally a social revolution. But, in general, 'Latin-American Revolutions' are not revolutions at all. *Plus ça change, plus c'est la même chose.* The military conspirators may blackmail the existing government, replace it by another civilian government or take over the rule themselves. But the result generally tends to be a certain immobilism accompanied by inflation of the military budget. Indeed in Mexico for the first quarter century after the liberation the military budget exceeded the civilian in most years and in Mexico City there was one officer to every two private soldiers. This was an extreme example of a general tendency of military rule, and if any socially reforming colonel or general tries to change it, he will be overthrown by other members of the armed forces jealous of their privileges. The military ruler has the advantage of having a ready-made machine; he has the disadvantage, unless he is a great leader or conqueror, that this machine is not his own creation or his own instrument, and can as well be used by another against himself.

To escape from this military squirrel cage, unless as in Chile or Costa Rica there is a tradition of constitutional government to return to, is exceedingly difficult. There are three possible escape routes: personal tyranny, radical dictatorship and genuine revolution leading to constitutional government.

The first is the commonest. As a counterweight to the armed forces which brought him to power, the ruler tries to arm a workers' militia and to set up a secret police – apart from the military police and intelligence – or a personal terrorist force like the hoodlums of the *tonton macoute*, the kind of *oprichnina* which asserted the personal power of the Haitian tyrant Duvalier. Military rule, in itself, being dependent on order and discipline, and very often coming to power in protest against the corruption and self-interest of politicians, may at first lack this personal and arbitrary character; but it very soon becomes corrupt in this way; the tyrant will enrich himself, his family and a whole group of hangers-on; such an incubus on the state may prove very difficult to get rid of – witness the long rule of the Trujillos in the Dominican Republic and of Batista in Cuba.

The second way out of military rule is through some kind of radical dictatorship. This is what Colonel Perón attempted in Argentina. He came to power at the head of a military junta pledged to build up the military machine and to assert Argentine leadership of Latin-America. But he very soon attempted to widen the basis of his rule by calling in organized labour. In the first few years of his dictatorship the strength of the labour unions rose from 300,000 to 800,000; he made them the basis of a workers' militia under the control of the Peronista party. At the same time he corrupted the army officers with high pay, tried to play off the armed forces against each other and to bring them under control of the Peronista party. However in his appeal to the poor, the *descamisados*, under the influence of his remarkable wife, Evita Perón, he alienated the more conservative elements of the armed forces and of the Church. This for any Spanish-style Caudillo is a most perilous position; and after suppressing a military *coup* in 1951, Perón succumbed in 1955 to an armed revolt backed by the upper and middle classes. He lasted longer than other radical dictators. In Guatemala, Colonel Arbenz tried to diversify his support by arming a workers' militia with arms from Poland and by turning to the Communists. Having thus alienated the army he could not resist the exiles who returned with the help of the United States. A dictator who relies on mixed support does well to stay to the right of centre like General Franco.

The third, and most difficult, form of escape from military rule is towards constitutional government, and a radical change in the social structure. This has been achieved in Mexico, but only by the efforts of four Generals from Obregón in 1920 to Cardenas in 1940, who worked for twenty years to bring the armed forces under control and to give the social revolution in their country a solid constitutional basis.

The question now is whether other Latin-American countries will embark on this long hard road or whether they will follow the path pursued by Fidel Castro and the late Ché Guevara, of social revolution imposed by the bayonets of a guerrilla uprising. The Cuban model at first had a certain attraction. It offered independence of the great northern neighbour and liberation from the corrupting influence of United States capital. It combined a real change in the structure of society, such as no military *coup* can ever achieve, with the kind of personal rule which is acceptable and familiar in Latin-America. In a continent where most of the conditions for revolution prevail in many countries – extremes of wealth and poverty, vast estates and landless peasants, rapid urbanizaton and growth of population and a weak middle class, a humiliating semi-colonial dependence on American capital – Castro's attempt to spread his revolution was bound to raise an echo. But the echo has become feebler rather than stronger. For despite his noisy affirmations of independence, Castro has become very visibly dependent on Soviet aid; and East European experts and technicians are no more popular than American capitalists. The economy of a relatively small island, supporting the largest armed forces in Latin-America, has not made that rapid progress which is supposed to be one of the main benefits of Communism. Further, Castro's perpetual meddling in the affairs of other countries, his acceptance of Soviet rockets has threatened the international tranquillity which has for so long been the one great asset of South America. The prospect of a dozen Vietnams on the continent may excite romantic revolutionaries like Ché Guevara or Régis Debray, but it can have little appeal to the damned of the earth, the downtrodden peasants and proletarians, whose cause they affect to champion.

Latin-America is not the only home of military despotisms; indeed they proliferate at an alarming rate elsewhere. After the

First World War from the Baltic to the Balkans the newly liberated territories of eastern Europe very soon fell under one form or another of military rule, until most of them were forced out of this particular frying-pan into the fire of totalitarian communism; and right up to the present day, as the recent experience of Greece shows, even the most sophisticated societies can relapse into this primitive form of rule. Nor, since President de Gaulle was brought to power in response to the threat of a military *coup* and civil war, can even the most advanced societies of the Western world be regarded as immune to this disease. It is not therefore surprising that nearly all the Arab states 'liberated' since World War II and a very large proportion of the African and Asian states have succumbed to military dictatorship.

It would be comforting to believe that this is just a phase through which every society has to pass as it grows to maturity. However, in the light of 150 years of Latin-American history, no such facile assumption is possible. When we see that most promising creation of British imperial rule, the great state of Nigeria, involved in civil war between two military dictatorships, the maces and the wigs, the speaker's handbook, so proudly handed over to many a parliamentary assembly, begin to look forlorn and even ridiculous. Indeed, to hand over one of the most sophisticated systems of government, evolved in a thousand years of stormy history, to peoples who have perhaps enjoyed no more than a generation of modern government, may well seem the triumph of hope over experience. However, it is a source of hope, albeit a slender one. As we have seen, one of the reasons why the Latin-American states find it so difficult to escape the treadmill of military tyranny is that they have no tradition of constitutional government on which they can fall back. It is not surprising that African states barely emerged from tribalism should, under stress, succumb to dictatorship. But if there is a short period of constitutional government to act as a model, if there are a few civilian politicians and experienced administrators, freedom is more likely to be established by the return to such customs and traditions than by any appeal to abstract human rights. Congo can have little prospect of emerging from military rule; Nigeria should have a more hopeful future. And where there has been a longer period of constitutional government and civilian administration, as in India, some form of democracy can, as we have seen in the past twenty years, survive in the most adverse conditions; but as the experience of Pakistan demonstrates, there can be no guarantee of such a constitutional outcome.

To sum up, then, military dictatorship is the most common form of modern tyranny; and one could argue, on a purely statistical basis, that it rather than Communism or any other 'ism' is the wave of the future. However this would be to treat as a unity very many widely different developments; the military dictator may as we have seen be radical or conservative, arbitrary or conventional, a representative of the old military caste or of the new nationalist intelligentsia. He is likely to emerge in the first place in a country of relatively low political culture and this will normally go with a fairly primitive stage of economic development. This limits the amount of damage he can do. He is only likely to become a menace to peace when he has the dynamic of revolutionary nationalism on his side, when this spreads across frontiers, and when he is supported or exploited by some great power. President Nasser had acquired these characteristics and they enabled him to survive a series of disasters which would have brought down any purely military despot. However, by himself he remained, like most other military dictators, a comparatively minor predator in the international jungle. We must now turn back to *tyrannosaurus rex*.

The great tyrant will always be a good deal more than a military dictator, but whether he comes to power by military or constitutional means he will follow Machiavelli's maxim by making war his study, whether 'shooting' war, civil war, or class war, or cold war. But he will, if he is wise, relate his study to its purpose; when he fails to do this, when war becomes an end in itself, *un beau métier*, the writing is on the wall for the tyrant.

Yet it is of the essence of the tyrannical character that he should come to this; for whatever his professed – or even genuine – aims his pursuit is power and war is the supreme exercise of power. In so far as he restrains himself from this he falls short of complete tyranny. This is the great distinction between Cromwell and Napoleon; both were great soldiers; both had fashioned the finest instruments of power of their time, but whereas Napoleon used his to destroy in a perpetual restless desire for power after power, Cromwell did not follow the poet's advice, 'Like a Caesar he to Gaul, to Italy a Hannibal.'

'War alone,' said Mussolini, 'carries to its highest tension all human energy and sets the seal of nobility on the people who have the courage to face it.' Such sentiments might in the nineteenth century relieve the tedium of the professor's study or compensate for the frustrations of academic life. In our time they have served the indefinite inflation of the dictator's ego and the projection of his unbounded egotism on whole peoples. Mussolini failed in the first essential, that of creating or securing the instrument of power. Indeed he had not the raw materials. Napoleon and Hitler had.

The French revolutionary armies had astounded Europe by their successes even before Napoleon came on the scene. To a great military tradition they had added the revolutionary mystique and *élan*, and the enthusiasm that comes when a career is opened to new talent, when a new class of young men marches out, each with a field-marshal's baton in his knapsack. It was Napoleon's greatness to be able to use this instrument for his own purposes. His military genius was the basis, but he exploited it with an equal political genius.

The first necessity was to gain all the credit for victories and disclaim responsibility for defeats. Though generous in rewards, he was grudging in praise of his subordinates and prodigal in blame if anything went wrong. He blamed Admiral Brueys for the defeat by Nelson at Aboukir Bay, Villeneuve for the failure of his invasion projects against England and Ney or Grouchy or anyone but himself for Waterloo. In 1800

he vaunted his own victory at Marengo and played down
Moreau's battle at Hohenlinden which finally brought Austria
to her knees. Marengo indeed was a decisive event in his
career; and he treated it as such, three times in the next five
years rewriting the story of the battle to his own greater credit.
In fact, it had been one of his most fortunate victories owing
more to chance, to the dilatoriness of the enemy and to the
brilliance of his subordinates than to his own skilful planning,
since he appears to have misjudged the intentions of the
Austrian commander. Napoleon's myth-making reshaped
Marengo as the model for future great battles at Friedland,
Austerlitz and Wagram. It was necessary, too, that the credit
should go to him, since the victory enabled him not only to
force peace on the Austrians and to conclude the treaty of
Amiens with the English, but also to consolidate his position at
home, to disarm the opponents both of the right and the left,
to destroy humanely the one military conspiracy against him
and to crown himself Emperor amid practically universal
acclaim. It is rare that a ruler can present himself as both the
great war-leader and the great peace-maker at the same time.
After Marengo Napoleon could do so, fully justifying the
prophecy of Régnier, who described him at the time of the
coup of Brumaire as 'A hero, whom France holds dear not so
much for the number of victories as for the desire he has so
patently expressed to become the peacemaker of the world.'

Had the Emperor died in 1802 that verdict would have
stood. Even as it was, the English bore the formal responsibility for the breach of the Treaty of Amiens, although considering how Napoleon used the peace to extend his domination of
Europe, the breach was bound to come sooner or later. It was
indeed Napoleon who first in modern times eroded the sharp
distinction between war and peace, and from whom Clausewitz
learnt the maxim that war is the continuation of politics by
other means, the maxim which was later to be most fully put
into practice by Hitler.

The parallel emerges clearly in their relations with Russia.
Both Napoleon and Hitler sought the Russian alliance in order

to have a free hand in the West, and particularly in order to finish off Britain. Napoleon after Tilsit tried to divert the Emperor Alexander's attention from Finland and the Balkans towards India and Mesopotamia, just as Hitler unsuccessfully tried to divert Stalin during the Molotov visit to Berlin in 1940. Napoleon tried to convince Alexander as Ribbentrop later tried to convince Molotov that England was on the verge of collapse, both equally unsuccessfully. Napoleon perhaps had more excuse for his attack, since Alexander had failed in his agreement to assist him in his war with Austria and showed signs of turning towards England, whereas Stalin, as we have seen, kept his agreement meticulously. But basically their motives were the same – to round off their conquests, Napoleon by dictating peace in Moscow and Hitler by securing the Lebensraum in the East which had been his constant aim since he wrote *Mein Kampf*. For, both conquest and war had become a necessity. Both assumed that a quick campaign would settle everything; and when they failed, they refused to accept the reality of defeat. For Napoleon, Borodino, the Pyrrhic victory which sealed his fate, remained his best battle. From then on, although during 1813–14 there was no decline in his military skill, the Emperor refused to face his true position or to negotiate on realistic terms, pursuing always a military solution.

Such a flight from reality is the logical last stage of the tyrant. What is surprising is that both in the case of Napoleon and Hitler their armies – with the exceptions of some Marshals, Generals and often high officers – were ready to follow them to destruction. For Napoleon the task of securing the allegiance and devotion of the armies was easier, because they were in a very special sense his armies. He had grown up with the revolutionary army, had been identified with its glories and had risen to power by leading it to victory. He might ungenerously begrudge his high officers credit for any independent action which he did not regret; he might treat the rank and file with appalling callousness, riding comfortably by in his coach while they died in their thousands in the snowy wastes of the

Beresina and Pripet Marshes. But, right to the end, he could rely on the heroic devotion of his veterans and their children.

For Hitler it was more difficult. His relations with the armed forces were strictly on the 'who-whom' basis. The officer caste, once owing exclusive allegiance to the Kaiser, became with the Republic an independent and disastrous force in politics. Insisting on the armistice of 1918, and turning round to accuse the politicians of stabbing them in the back; advising that the Versailles treaty must be observed and denouncing the politicians as traitors for observing it, the military interventions in politics were – with the exception of the Machiavellian manoeuvres of General von Seeckt – as inept as they were ill-intentioned. Unwilling to take responsibility for the sad state of Germany themselves, the military leaders saw to it that no one else should be able to govern.

The notion of the military that they could use Hitler was natural enough. They had launched him on his career as a political propagandist; it was as 'an education officer' employed to restore the morale of the army that he had first made contact with the Deutsche Arbeiter Partei; army funds had helped to launch the party newspaper *Voelkischer Beobachter*; and the party in its early days at Munich was infiltrated by army officers. Moreover Hitler himself always showed the utmost deference to the army leaders and to aged Field-Marshals such as Hindenburg and Ludendorff. Even the wily Hans von Seeckt believed himself to have the same purposes as Hitler, however much he might deplore some of his methods.

Hitler, indeed, realized that, in order to achieve his purposes, he must come to power with the support of the Generals; but he had no intention of being used by them. On the contrary he saw the Wehrmacht as a magnificently tempered sword of power, if only he could lay his hands on it. His method in gaining control of the army was similar to that by which he overcame political opponents at home and abroad, by exploiting their weaknesses which he diagnosed with a keen and malevolent eye. The class interest of the Junkers, with which the Hindenburgs father and son were so much involved, the total lack of civic principle which was regarded as compatible with the strict officers' code of honour, the superstitious reverence for the paste-board figures who were held to embody this code, the personal weaknesses of such lamentable figures as Schleicher, Papen, the 'Gummi-Loewe' or india-rubber lion, Field-Marshal von Blomberg, all this was grist to Hitler's mill.

The decisive day was 30 June 1934. It was, as we have seen, a classic manoeuvre: with the support of the army to destroy the S.A. and thereby liquidate a potential rival centre of power; with the support of the destroyers of the army – the S.S. – to reduce it to dependence on himself. The army leaders connived at their own abdication; by the pact on the cruiser *Deutschland* they had pledged themselves to the Fuehrer on condition that he should liquidate the radical wing of the party. By their approval after the event, they mantled with their code of honour one of the most treacherous acts of political gangsterism in modern times, making themselves at least passive accomplices. Thus although the governments of the Weimar Republic could rely on little but disloyalty from the High Command Hitler, who least deserved it, could depend on ten years of grudging obedience from the collective military leadership, who might share the misgivings of the small dissident group led by Colonel-General Beck, but could never be brought to action.

Hitler never fully trusted the High Command. He wanted to make sure of them, to base his ascendancy not simply on an oath, but on proved successes and counter-balancing forces. Unlike Napoleon, his victories must be won not on the battlefield but in the council chamber. Hitler had not the experience of the generals in battle, but in psychological warfare he knew no master. He felt a boundless – and generally justified – contempt for the democratic politicians of the West. After each successful *coup*, the departure from the League of Nations, the proclamation of German rearmament, the remilitarization of the Rhineland, he sang his lullaby of peace and in each case the charm worked. The Generals, in the case of the Rhineland calculated that their French – and British – opponents would use their superior forces as the German High Command would have done. Then the three battalions Hitler had sent in would have to be smartly withdrawn; and that could well have been the end for the Fuehrer. The Generals' misgivings were contemptuously swept aside; France and Britain failed to react. Instead western leaders eagerly swallowed the bait of peaceful aspirations and sweet reasonableness salted with offers of non-aggression pacts which the Fuehrer held out to them.

Hitler's intuition had proved right, the Generals' science wrong. Their position was weakened for the next engagement. In this the code of honour of the officer caste was exploited to bring it under closer control by the Fuehrer. Since the army could not be expected to intervene in matters of domestic discipline in Germany, Himmler had been able to build up his own Praetorian Guard in the S.S. and was seeking with his chief assistant Heydrich, a disgraced naval officer with a personal grudge against the officer corps, an opportunity of bringing the Army under Party control; attempts at Nazi indoctrination of the rank and file, something equivalent to the Soviet political commissar system, had been successfully resisted. Now the Minister of War, Field-Marshal von Blomberg himself gave them their chance. Recently widowed, he re-married in the presence of Hitler and Goering. Then the Gestapo produced the evidence that the lady had a police record as a prostitute. Indignation among the generals; resignation of the Field-Marshal; but from Himmler's point of view nothing would be gained if the pliant Blomberg were to be succeeded by the more formidable army Commander-in-Chief, Colonel-General von Fritsch. So the Gestapo framed a grotesque homosexuality case against von Fritsch.

Hitler was probably not himself a party to these intrigues. He had no intention now, any more than in 1934, of handing over the control of the army to the Party, or to anyone else but himself. But here was an opportunity of reinforcing his own control. He had in November 1937 revealed his intention to extend Germany's Lebensraum in the first place by overrunning Austria and Czechoslovakia, later in 1943–5 by a military decision. The generals, and in particular von Fritsch, who still exaggerated the strength and resolution of Britain and France, were alarmed and had even dared to argue against the Fuehrer. So in these morality charges Hitler saw the opportunity for the complete *Gleichschaltung* of the High Command.

There was no serious resistance from the generals. For a time in January and February 1938 there seemed to be a threat of a military *coup*. Colonel-General Beck, the chief of staff, tried to rally his fellow Generals to resist the take-over – the first step in a long and courageous career of conspiracy. But von Fritsch resigned and was replaced by the wavering von Brauchitsch, with Hitler as supreme commander and defence minister for the whole Wehrmacht. The court of honour which cleared von Fritsch and showed up the filthy methods of the Gestapo might have been the occasion for a reassertion of the position of the High Command. But it was overshadowed by Hitler's bloodless victory in Austria. Again he had been proved right.

This, indeed, was the weakness of the generals' position. They had no grounds of principle on which to oppose Hitler's career of aggression, only grounds of expediency. And when his plans succeeded that ground was cut from under their feet. Few people are prepared to go to the stake on a question of tactics, and a 'limited liability' conspiracy is never likely to succeed. The more formidable conspiracy which arose during the Czechoslovak crisis seems to have been of this nature.

The most resolute of the conspirators, Colonel-General Beck, resigned as Chief of Staff; but although many of the generals including the army Commander-in-Chief Brauchitsch and the new Chief of Staff Halder shared his view that France and Britain would intervene and that this would mean ruin to Germany, and although for the last time some of them actually dared to argue with Hitler, not one of them took action. Even Beck's resignation could be concealed until after the crisis. Halder maintains that everything was prepared for a *putsch* before Hitler's D-Day for invading Czechoslovakia, 30

September, but that it was called off when Mr Chamberlain flew to Munich. Such a 'conditional' *putsch*, even if it ever reached the stage of preparedness which was claimed after the war, was never likely to succeed against a determined and ruthless adversary. There are many sound reasons for condemning the Munich surrender; but the expectation of a German generals' revolt is not one of them. At best the moral is that the front of totalitarian dictatorship is rarely so monolithic as it appears, and those who stand against it on grounds of principle may gain an unconvenanted advantage from its internal fissures.

The bloodless victory in Czechoslovakia increased the Fuehrer's prestige with the army. The resistance, it is true, continued, inspired by Beck, now in retirement, and by such unexpected figures as Canaris, head of the *Abwehr* or security service. Not surprisingly, since the dissidents had up to now been proved wrong and Hitler right, the generals at the top were little interested, wherever their private loyalties lay. What is more remarkable, they did not betray the conspirators. The army despite the surrender of its High Command remained a state within a state and therefore the only possible field for effective resistance to Hitler.

Up to the outbreak of war Hitler's successes were political, being based on a shrewder assessment of his enemies' weaknesses than that of the generals. But when he launched the war he at once began a similar ascendancy on the battlefield. The change of the command structure in 1938 gave him the machinery through the O.K.W. (*Ober kommando der Wehrmacht*) to by-pass the Army High Command. He took advantage of this to launch the invasion of Norway and Denmark which the Army staff regarded as a reckless, dangerous and fruitless campaign. The success consolidated his leadership. Still more did his invasion of Holland, Belgium and France in a Blitzkrieg which the army leadership had argued against. This long string of triumphs in the Council Chamber and in the field convinced the Fuehrer of his omnipotence and the army leaders of their impotence. Hitler's directives and commands ranged from the most general strategical principles to the most detailed tactical instructions. When he began to run into difficulties, when, for example, his offensive against Moscow was held in the winter of 1941, his prestige was such that he was able to blame the generals for a blunder which was due to his own contemptuous assessment of the Russian powers of resistance; even then his decision to hold the line before Moscow probably saved the underclad and underequipped German forces from an even worse disaster.

Hitler's contemptuous and insulting treatment of the generals grew worse as the war went on. He accused them of cowardice, insisted on seeing all their orders in advance, sometimes countermanded the orders and often dismissed the generals. Of seventeen Field-Marshals ten were dismissed, of thirty-six Colonel-Generals eighteen. He built up the rival force of the Waffen-S.S. to thirty-six divisions and gave them priority in armaments. He still had his flashes of inspiration as when contrary to the view of his military intelligence he forecast Normandy as the scene of the allied landing. But many of his decisions now seemed military idiocy to the generals; for their aim was to keep in being the army which they identified with Germany. Hitler identified himself with Germany and was aware that he would not survive defeat. Hence from Stalingrad on, the constant stream of orders to fight 'to the last bullet', orders which were not obeyed at Stalingrad nor, for the most part, elsewhere; but they prolonged the war and increased the slaughter. This clash of aims between Hitler and his generals culminated in the July 1944 plot, which will be dealt with later.

To what then must we ascribe the ascendancy of the Bohemian corporal over the proud German officer corps, an ascendancy which continued even beyond the point of defeat? First, as we have seen, to success; the ancients ascribe this characteristic largely to chance; for example, the great Pompey as long as he earned his nickname Felix, the lucky, was able to hold his own against Julius Caesar, but when his luck began to run out his legions began to run away, too. The great Augus-

tus, though no great soldier, made a point of claiming a
triumph for himself whenever one of his generals won a
notable victory. Napoleon as we have seen begrudged his
subordinates credit for their successes and monopolized the
glory himself; Hitler did likewise and success bred success.
Secondly Hitler owed his ascendancy over the army to the fact
that he knew what he wanted and the generals had no principle to set against his systematic pursuit of power. They had a
private code of honour and tradition which gave them cohesion and a sense of superiority, but no public morality. Their
aim was the expansion of German power and in particular the
power of the army. They had certain rigid, cautious and
conservative ideas about how this should be achieved. Hitler
had both a grand design and the will and the cunning to
achieve it. So when Hitler's methods, the methods of the gangster and the gambler, proved successful the generals could
have no objection in principle to them. From the invasion of
Poland onwards, many officers were disgusted by the revolting
atrocities of the S.S.; and when in Russia the army itself was
made the instrument of these mass crimes against humanity,
some generals complained in private and attempted to mitigate
the worst effects of the Fuehrer's barbaric orders; but none
dared protest to his face; none resigned. Those who stayed the
course, enduring their master's increasing arrogance and contempt, often reaped the fruits of their ambition in honours,
wealth and estates. Finally Hitler had Himmler and the S.S.,
his own Praetorian Guard and the secret police to keep any
dissident officer in line. The energetic and sometimes indiscreet
activities of the 1944 conspirators show that the Gestapo was
not as efficient as was generally assumed at the time; but it
certainly was a deterrent against independent thought and
action.

As far as foreign policy and war are concerned, Hitler stands
out as the complete tyrant. He had one constant theme – the
domination of Europe by the master race based on Lebensraum
in the East. On this theme he was prepared to play any number
of variations as opportunity offered. Where the weakness of

others permitted, he would get what he wanted by the threat of war, deploying just the force that was necessary. He reckoned that he had to achieve his aims by 1943–5 since by then his superiority in force would be at its peak. For this purpose he regarded war as inevitable, conceiving it, however, as a series of lightning blows. Not only was war a necessary means to his ends, but also he came increasingly to delight in the destructive use of power.

In the case of his great opponent, Stalin, the picture is less clear-cut. There is a certain ambiguity both about his relations with the armed forces and his aggressive aims. It was one of the first principles of the Bolsheviks that the army must be under party control, in order to avoid the danger of a Bonaparte destroying the Revolution. The system of political commissars had been developed before Stalin came to power for this purpose and his own role in the civil war was on the political side. He developed associations with various of the army leaders such as Voroshiloff and Budyenny, and antagonisms with others, such as Tukhachevsky; but he never gained that ascendancy over the Red Army which his rival Trotsky at one time had and failed to use.

Stalin tackled the problem with a characteristic ruthlessness. On 1 May 1937 Marshal Tukhachevsky, indisputably the U.S.S.R.'s greatest soldier, stood beside Stalin on the Lenin Mausoleum in the Red Square, as the military parade filed past. On 12 June his execution was announced together with that of a number of high officers. Blücher and Yegorov, two of the Marshals who had signed the death warrant, followed soon afterwards. It was the start of a purge in the army which may have involved some 20,000 officers. Was there a plot? The answer must be 'certainly not the conspiracy with the Nazis which was alleged'. If it had existed there must certainly be some evidence in the German archives and none has come to light. But there may have been a purely domestic conspiracy. By 1937 Stalin's purges had hit practically everyone who had achieved any independent distinction in the Soviet Union, anyone who was not wholly dependent on Stalin for his position. The turn of the army commanders was clearly coming and they may have decided to anticipate it by acting first. They may have; but there is no evidence that they did. Marshal Tukhachevsky, the popular leader of an officer corps alarmed by the purges and a peasant army disgruntled by the collectivization, was the man best placed to carry out a *putsch*; and that probably was enough for the tyrant's suspicious mind. In addition the Gestapo have subsequently claimed to have planted evidence of a plot. President Beneš of Czechoslovakia passed on information about it to Stalin. It is even suggested that the N.K.V.D. itself planted the information which was passed back by the Gestapo. If so did Stalin instigate the whole affair, or was he the dupe of his own paranoia and the secret police? We may never know the answer. The purge of the army coincided with an enormous build-up of the security forces, which commanded in the concentration camps the Soviet Union's greatest single labour force, and, after the Nazi-Soviet pact, followed the Red Army into the Baltic states and Poland to carry out mass deportations.

Stalin's very characteristic method of bringing the armed forces under control had disastrous consequences. Taken together with the poor showing of the Red Army in the 1939 winter war against Finland, it led both enemies and possible allies to underrate the fighting qualities of the Soviet forces thereby making an attack on the Soviet Union more likely. When the attack came, the officer corps proved inadequate to its task. Stalin put three of his old cronies in charge of the main fronts – Marshals Timoshenko, Voroshilov and Budyenny – of whose loyalty he was sure, but whose competence he very soon had reason to doubt.

The start of the war was indeed a disastrous beginning to his career as Generalissimo. Despite many warnings, as we have seen, he allowed his armies and, above all, his air force to be taken by surprise. One should perhaps attach little importance to the reports circulated under his successors that he was in a state of panic and prostration in the early weeks of the war. He, in fact, seems to have learnt very quickly. He replaced his incompetent commanders with young and vigorous ones like Marshal Zhukhov or Marshal Rokossovsky, who was among those brought from a concentration camp to serve in the hour of need. Nor need we take too seriously Khrushchev's jibes at his qualities as a supreme commander, that he directed operations on a globe and made disastrous interventions in operations against the advice of those at the front. Sometimes, no doubt, his interventions were disastrous. Anyone directing operations by telephone from the Kremlin would be bound to make mistakes. Stalin never went to the front and never sought to inspire the troops by his presence.

However, such visitors as Churchill, Beaverbrook and Harry Hopkins were impressed by his detailed grasp of operations and of supply problems on the Eastern front just as they were occasionally shocked by his ignorance of problems that lay beyond his immediate experience. He once suggested to Churchill that thirty British divisions should be transported to Russia, and he always showed a total incomprehension of the difficulties involved in setting up a second front across the sea. Perhaps the verdict of history – if ever history has enough reliable information to pass a verdict – will lie somewhere between the all-wise, imperturbable, supreme commander of the Stalin legend, and the incompetent and hysteric bungler of the Khrushchev version. Like Napoleon and Hitler, he claimed all the credit for victories. He did not trust his Marshals and took the earliest opportunity to sidetrack the most brilliant of them, Marshal Zhukhov. This unfortunate soldier was brought out of obscurity by Khrushchev to be Minister of Defence and to help in his struggle against his rivals, and then, when he had served his purpose, thrust into retirement again on a charge of Bonapartism; it seems he tried to cut back the influence of the Party in the army on grounds of military efficiency. Soldiers who serve dictators well can expect little thanks.

Stalin, then, distrusted his army; but he knew how to use it for political purposes. Lenin had said that the Revolution was not to be spread by bayonets, although when he got the chance of spreading it towards Germany by the invasion of Poland he could not resist it. Stalin never believed that it could be spread by any other means. As an aggressor he differed from Hitler in his caution. When checked in his attempt to take over Berlin, no consideration of face or prestige prevented him from pulling back. Similarly he was quite capable of encouraging the North Koreans to attack and leaving them in the lurch. More than any other tyrant he systematized the techniques of the Cold War – particularly the technique of the 'peace campaign' which he employed on an unprecedented scale.

The modern tyrant then differs from his predecessors in that he need not study war from his early days on the battlefield. He can become a great war leader by telephone and radio. But he can only do so if the instruments are to hand – the Wehrmacht or the Red Army for example. Such leaders as Mussolini and Nasser found no such instrument and were not able to create them. He must also have a grand design and utter ruthlessness in pursuing it and adapting his forces to it; he must understand the techniques of subversion and cold war and the weaknesses of his adversaries, and he must be skilled in talking peace while waging war. More ruthless than constitutional rulers in his use of his forces and more willing to risk lives, he will gain more brilliant victories often at greater expense and suffer more sensational defeats. And since he lives by the sword – sometimes a double-edged one – he will often die by the sword.

12. The Fall of Tyrants

Nothing more clearly illustrates the progress of tyranny than the difference between the ends of ancient and of modern tyrants. In Machiavelli's view conspiracies against princes arise chiefly from personal grievances; above all the prince should abstain from his subjects' women and their property – particularly the latter, since 'a man more quickly forgets the death of his father than the loss of his patrimony'. Nowadays, however, a dictator can take over all his subjects' property and be applauded for it, while there is no modern example of a tyrant being assassinated on account of a woman.

Machiavelli in his *Discourses* devotes a whole chapter to conspiracies, which underlines the personal character of tyranny up to his time, and of the means of ending it. Such plots, he argues, are best carried out by one man alone; then there is no one to tell. Next best, if confederates are required, is that it should be done quickly; then no one has time to tell. Conspiracies against group tyrannies are more or less bound to fail, since all the tyrants cannot be killed at once and those who survive will be warned and wreak a terrible vengeance. Finally, if the prince has the love of his subjects, the conspirators are liable to come to a bad end, as happened to the most famous tyrannicides of all, Brutus and his fellow conspirators.

The first tyrannicides, Harmodius and Aristogeiton, of Athens, well illustrate some of Machiavelli's points. They killed Hipparchus, on account of the dishonour of Harmodius' sister, but did not kill his brother Hippias; thus, according to Herodotus, they merely exasperated the remaining members of the clan, without in any way checking their despotism. Nevertheless, tyrannicide was so rare in the first wave of tyrants that they won immortal honour.

It was under the Roman Empire that tyranny became endemic and tyrannicide a fine art. The mad Caligula was the first victim, having – contrary to Machiavelli's maxim – insulted and threatened his servants without actually killing them. His assassin was an officer of the Praetorian Guard, those 'formidable servants', who in Gibbon's words 'are always necessary, but often fatal to the throne of despotism'. His successor Claudius was the first Emperor to pay for the loyalty of the Praetorian Guard with a generous donative, thus setting a precedent which became an obligation for every subsequent Emperor. He succumbed, apparently, to poison, to be succeeded by Nero who was the first to be overthrown by that other great scourge of the Emperors, a rising of the legions. He was too paralysed by fear to raise any resistance and his final panic-flight and suicide make a tyrant's cautionary tale.

It was, however, after the Antonine age towards the end of the second century A.D. that the Praetorians became virtually the sovereign body of the Empire. The Praetorian Prefect having learnt that Marcus Aurelius' degenerate son Commodus was planning to murder him anticipated his master and appointed as his successor the worthy Pertinax; but eighty-six days of virtuous rule were enough for the licentious Praetorians. They murdered Pertinax and put the Empire up to auction. Tyrannicide, which from the days of Plato to those of Cicero had been a matter for serious and principled philosophic discussion, had under the Empire become a lucrative, if hazardous, profession.

The despots of the Renaissance lived precariously and went in perpetual fear of assassination, against which they took the most elaborate precautions. Filippo Maria, the last of the Visconti (1412–47) devoted the main resources of the state of Milan to his own security; living isolated in the citadel, not setting foot in the city for many years, travelling in secluded convoys only to his country estates, closely vetting all his courtiers and servants and controlling all their contacts with the outside world, his security system was as rigorous as Stalin's. Like Stalin his seclusion did not prevent him from waging wars and conducting diplomacy. But his *condottieri* and his ambassadors and ministers were spied upon and had to operate in pairs in order that they might keep an eye on each other. Death must not be mentioned in the presence of the superstitious tyrant and any dying courtier must be transported away from the castle. Thus, as the author of *Vindiciae contra Tyrannos* puts it: 'In the midst of their greatest strength the tyrannizer of tyrants, fear, makes prize of their souls and there triumphs in their affliction.' Visconti was only delivered from this tyranny by death, which he met with courage and dignity.

The Italian despots had plenty to fear. Not only did their own excesses tempt revenge, and their own rapid rise excite ambition, but also tyrannicide was approved in principle and Brutus was admired as a model. Boccaccio wrote: 'Shall I call the tyrant king or prince, and obey him loyally as my lord? No, for he is the enemy of the Commonwealth. Against him I may use arms, conspiracies, spies, ambushes and fraud; to do so is a sacred and necessary work. There is no more acceptable sacrifice than the blood of a tyrant.' Many young aristocrats acted in this spirit of idealism as well as from ambition and personal resentment. Machiavelli does not approve of conspiracies; he quotes Tacitus as saying, 'the past should have our reverence; the present our obedience; we should wish for good princes, but put up with any'. But if a conspiracy is entered upon he advises using experts who will not lose their nerve. Presumably he means professional assassins, of whom in Italy there was no lack.

With the growth of the modern state tyrannicide became a much less personal matter and was justified, as we have seen, by the sixteenth-century author of *Vindiciae contra Tyrannos* on religious grounds, the tyrant being one who 'holding the earth not great enough for his ambition will climb and conquer heaven itself'. The author held that magistrates and properly appointed assemblies might, if no other course was open, take up arms and depose the tyrant; he went further and, arguing on the basis of the unity of the Church and Christendom, said that other princes had a duty, if asked, to go to the help of people rising against lawless and persecuting rulers in other lands.

It is said, probably wrongly, that *Vindiciae contra Tyrannos* was translated into English by one of the regicides of King Charles I. Certainly it inspired the author of one of the most brilliant pamphlets of the Commonwealth, 'Killing no Murder'. The author was probably the Leveller Sexby, who had attempted unsuccessfully to organize the assassination of Cromwell. He argued the right of private men to kill a tyrant 'over whom every man is naturally a judge and executioner and whom the laws of God, of nature and of nations expose, like beasts of prey, to be destroyed as they are met'. His attack on Cromwell is doubtless unfair, but it is perhaps the most brilliant characterization of a tyrant in the English language. He mentions but one excuse for not killing the Lord Protector and for praying for his long life 'for the same reason that the old woman of Syracuse prayed for the long life of Dionysius of Syracuse, lest the devil should come next'. Indeed, he says prophetically: 'A tyrant is a devil, that tears the body in exorcizing; and they are all of Caligula's temper that, if they could, they would have the whole frame of nature fall with them.'

In fact, subsequent history was to justify the author of the *Vindiciae* in his championship of revolt by some organized body rather than Sexby in his plea for individual assassination. The latter whether executed by anarchists or by representatives of the National Will movement in Tsarist Russia usually had disastrous results. Either the tyrant was succeeded by a worse devil or, if the attempt failed, himself became more oppressive out of fear. The highly organized modern tyranny does not lend itself to the very individual and personal kind of conspiracy recommended by Machiavelli although such methods may work better in the newly independent states. Indeed he himself points out the danger of leaving alive any kinsman or possible successor of the prince. But in a highly organized modern state there are bound to be a number of survivors who have a vested common interest with the assassinated tyrant and may hope to succeed him. The development of professional standing armies and police forces, above all secret police, is mainly responsible for this difference. It has had the effect that conspirators must be able to rely on some organized force in the nation; otherwise in the ensuing chaos the leaders of the police or the army will instal another tyranny.

In general, the great dictators of the modern world from Napoleon onwards have fallen only as a result of defeat in war. Against Napoleon despite intrigues by Fouché and Talleyrand there was no conspiracy. As long as his armies were victorious he was in no danger, although he had at the time reached a hazardous stage in the career of any dictator, when those who have risen to power with him have become either complacent or disgruntled, and the impetus which has carried him to the top is exhausted. Otherwise he might perhaps have continued the struggle; but his fear of the mob restrained him from calling for a *levée en masse*; and in any case, although the army remained loyal, it may be doubted whether the exhausted nation would have responded to such a call.

However great his flight from reality in the latter years, he took a realistic view of the source of his own power. 'I shall know how to die', he told Metternich in 1813, 'but never to yield an inch of territory. Your sovereigns, who were born on the throne, may get beaten twenty times and yet return to their capitals. I cannot. For I rose to power through the camp.' In fact, he did not die, although he later felt he ought to have done so at Borodino or Waterloo. In 1813, after his abdication and before his exile to Elba, he tried to poison himself, but afterwards was pleased that he had failed, since suicide would have gratified his ill-wishers and done no good to his well-wishers.

From then on, in defeat, he ran remarkably true to form and to the form of other dictators too. As he made his way south to Elba he showed a terror of the mob. Once there he ruled the tiny island as if it were an Empire. When he escaped he proclaimed to his troops: 'We have not been beaten, but betrayed.'

And this was the constant theme of his declining years. He would never admit that he could be beaten in battle. After Waterloo, he said, he should have had Fouché shot or hanged, should have shot Soult, and beheaded Lafayette and thirty or a hundred others. France had let him down. 'She has been violated; she is henceforth only a cowardly dishonoured country. She has only had her deserts, for instead of rallying to me she deserted me.' England too had let him down. He had devoted much study to his principal adversary, but, as Metternich said, he believed what he wanted to believe and his ideas were totally false. His attitude like Hitler's was ambivalent. He was infuriated by British press criticism, yet admiring. 'Had I an English Army I should have conquered the universe.' If he had been victorious, he declared : 'I should have entered London not as a conqueror but a liberator.' After defeat: 'Had I been allowed to go to London in 1815, I should have been carried in triumph.'

Yet, despite his monstrous egotism and vanity and perhaps because of his gross self-deception he was more successful than any other in that final objective of dictators, leaving behind him a time-bomb for posterity. The myth of himself as the champion of a Europe of nations as opposed to the Europe of dynasties, although it had little to do with the facts, was well calculated to appeal to the next generation of young liberals and romantic nationalists. This myth and the military glory, which left an enduring mark on the nation which he accused of betraying him, enabled his adventurer nephew to carry out his own Brumaire, and to become Napoleon III, tragedy repeating itself as farce after half a century.

Napoleon differed from later dictators and harked back to an earlier age in devoting real attention to the problem of succession, and attempting to found a dynasty, with as little immediate success as most tyrants. The man who thought he could arrange the succession was his police chief Fouché, in this showing nearly as much optimism as later secret police chiefs Himmler and Beria, who aspired personally to succeed their masters. In fact the police chief would probably have made a better job of it than the actual successors, who having learnt nothing and forgotten nothing, caused people, by contrast, to remember the Emperor's virtues and to forget his vices, thereby contributing to the undying Napoleonic legend.

The fall of Mussolini was also due largely to defeat in war, but there were other factors, too. The *Duce* had failed to follow the counsels of Machiavelli to a degree astonishing in one of his countrymen and disciples. He had not made war his study, but had merely talked about it, and been fascinated by its external trappings as an exercise of power; if he had studied it, he might have followed General Franco's example and kept his country out of a conflict for which its resources were plainly inadequate. He had, over the years, humiliated the King but had not isolated him or rendered him powerless, and had even trusted him to the end. By his constant 'changes of guard' he had indeed prevented anyone beside himself from becoming great, but he had left many half-great still retaining power and influence, yet disgruntled.

His failure to study war meant that, although he could, and frequently did, dismiss his generals he could never completely control them either in office or retirement, although he quite rightly distrusted them. He also allowed the King to act as an independent focus of loyalty, thereby depriving himself of the advantage of the oath of allegiance which Hitler enjoyed. His personal method of rule, balancing between powerful subordinates, had prevented him from forming a monolithic party which could control both army and nation. The Fascist militia was by no means the equivalent of Himmler's Waffen-S.S. as a counter-balancing force to the army.

In addition, the military defeats, the humiliating dependence on German forces for the conquest of Greece, the loss of the African Empire to a handful of British Empire troops, the defeat and annihilation of the Italian forces in North Africa, the successful Allied landing in Sicily shortly after the *Duce* had declared that no enemy would set foot on Italian soil, all these came at a very difficult time for the *Duce*. The dynamic of Fascism had run out; the young were not interested; their elders had bred a profound cynicism in the nation by their enjoyment of the corrupting fruits of power. The normal course of a dictator in such circumstances is to try to whip up public opinion against an external enemy. The entry into the war in 1940 might perhaps have achieved this result if it had led to the anticipated swift and relatively bloodless victories. But it produced the reverse effect. Consequently all the *Duce*'s sins of omission and commission began to build up against him.

In Turin and Milan the workers went on strike; the leading industrialist Count Cini, whom Mussolini had brought in to strengthen the government, had questioned the very basis of his policy and rule; the army Chief of Staff, General Ambrosio, had represented that Italy must make a separate peace; the pre-Fascist politicans were meeting at the house of former Prime Minister Bonomi; they were in touch with the Count and with the dismissed and disgruntled generals; the *gerarchi* of the Fascist party were divided, with Grandi, at one extreme, preparing for a negotiated neutrality and Farinacci, at the other, urging struggle by Germany's side to the end; the rot had even spread to the *Duce*'s own family, Count Ciano, his son-in-law, having been dismissed from the Foreign Ministry and sent as Ambassador to the Vatican, the ideal centre for intrigue. All the ingredients for a conspiracy were there, and Mussolini knew it. The normal tyrannical reaction is to assume that where there are the ingredients there is also the conspiracy and to act accordingly.

Mussolini did not do so. Why? The reasons are complex. Some of these advisers were pressing him to an action which he alone could accomplish, to get Hitler's consent to a separate peace. He revealed to his advisers during his final meeting with Hitler before his fall, at Feltre, that the problem had been in his mind for a long time. But it could mean 'to wipe out at one stroke a régime of 20 years ... to disappear from the world scene.... And what attitude will Hitler take? Perhaps you think he would give us liberty or action?' In fact Mussolini never dared to broach the matter with Hitler. But he could hardly regard as treason a course which he himself had been seriously contemplating, and which was certainly favoured by many who were not involved in any conspiracy. He might, however, have drawn the logical conclusion that when he rejected this course and became the main obstacle to a separate peace, a conspiracy to remove him was almost inevitable.

Why, then, did he not draw that conclusion? The answer is to be found in his own physical and psychological state at the time. In July 1942 the *Duce* had crossed to Africa in high hopes of leading the Axis march into Alexandria. He had returned disappointed and when the Axis forces were defeated at Alamein, the Germans leaving the Italians in the lurch and stealing their transport, his hopes of rapid and easy victory were smashed, particularly when the German Sixth Army collapsed at Stalingrad too. From October to December he suffered a physical collapse. He spent most of his time at his country estate suffering from stomach ulcers. The wild swings of mood from deep depression to irrational elation which now characterized him have been attributed by some to the syphilis he contracted when young. However that may be, the nine months from October 1942 to July 1943 were a period when blow after blow must have aggravated any psychosomatic complaint he was suffering from. If Napoleon's conduct at Waterloo can be in part be attributed to the state of his stomach ulcer, the same may be true of Mussolini's management of his final political crisis.

It is not quite true to say that Mussolini and Khrushchev were the only two modern dictators ever to be ousted by majority vote; for the *Duce* never accepted the Fascist Grand Council's nineteen to seven vote in favour of Grandi's motion to transfer the military command from himself to the King as final or binding. The Grand Council was a purely consultative body; and Mussolini when he went to see the King the next day, 25 July, seems to have had some political manoeuvre in mind to overcome what he regarded as just another political crisis, albeit a very serious one. For the King however the

Grand Council vote gave just the constitutional excuse he wanted to order the *coup d'état* that had long been planned.

It was a copy-book example of the *coup d'état*. General Ambrosio, the Chief of Staff, was the key figure; he brought the necessary troops to Rome, put them under reliable generals, ordered the Chief of Military Police to arrest Mussolini as he left the Palace, took control of the telephone exchanges and the radio so that the general secretary and the commander of the Fascist militia could take no action. The conspirators had only the Germans to fear and hoped that they would disarm them by declaring their determination to continue the war – a ruse that did not deceive Hitler and which later cost Italy dear.

The most puzzling question is why the *Duce* was not warned of a conspiracy so thoroughly prepared with so many people at least on the edge of it. True the recently deposed chief of police had been close to the plotters and the new one was neutral; but one cannot but feel that if he had really wanted to find out he could have. As it was, immediately after his arrest, he pledged his co-operation to Marshal Badoglio, the new head of state, and his continuing loyalty to the King; and he seems to have been content with the prospect of retiring to some St Helena and dictating his memoirs. He was sick and weary and approaching his sixtieth birthday. However, Hitler very promptly sent him as a birthday present the complete works of Neitzsche, and very soon made it clear that he was not to escape so easily the destiny of the Superman.

A year later, by a strange coincidence, the *Duce* – after his rescue by Hitler, the puppet dictator of a ramshackle republic – arrived at the Fuehrer's headquarters at Rastenburg just in time to congratulate Hitler on his escape from Stauffenberg's bomb. It is instructive to compare the plot that failed with the one that succeeded; for there is no reason to doubt that, but for the German intervention, the King and Badoglio could have controlled all Italy and taken it out of the war. The essential differences lies not in the courage and skill of the conspirators but in the régimes against which they operated, and these régimes were the projection of the personalities of their leaders. Hitler often congratulated himself that he had no king to deal with and was critical of the *Duce*'s attitude to the King; he never trusted the German royalists. His attitude to the German officer corps was one of great and growing distrust. The débâcle at Stalingrad when von Paulus, having been created a Field-Marshal on the assumption that he would fight to the last bullet, surrendered with 90,000 men raised his suspicions to pathological levels and the collapse in Tunis, again contrary to his orders to fight to the last bullet, confirmed him in these suspicions. After each defeat he dismissed or switched around his commanders, using every inducement of ambition to make them compete for his favours. He had, as we have seen, established his ascendancy over them in the years of victory and he maintained it by his detailed military control in the years of defeat. Mussolini had never exercised this detailed military control over his generals, and while he distrusted them – and the Gestapo reported their unreliability back to Germany – there was not much he could do about it. He had not built up the same countervailing force as Hitler had created in the Waffen S.S., nor were the series of rather unreliable officials who controlled the police in any way the equivalent of Himmler. The Gestapo had penetrated nearly every German institution, and had thrown nearly all figures capable of independent action into concentration camps or into exile. Consequently there were no Bonomis or Orlandos, eminent elder statesmen to give a political backing to the *coup*. Nor were the Nazi leaders in a position to play politics as the Fascist *gerarchi* with their own private and competing empires were. Mussolini trusted in his ability to outmanoeuvre these potentates at their political game. The Nazi leaders, Himmler and Goering, Bormann and Goebbels, had their private empires, but they were all dependent on Hitler, and only in the last days of collapse of the Reich did the first two try to play some independent role. Hitler in fact had created the substance of an absolutely arbitrary tyranny, Mussolini only the shadow.

In these circumstances, it is surprising that a conspiracy

could develop in Germany at all and still more surprising that the nucleus of it was able to survive for six years from 1938 to 1944. This is partly due to the fact that the *Abwehr*, the Army Counter Intelligence Agency, under its enigmatic chief Admiral Canaris remained beyond the grasp of the Gestapo until early in 1944, and gave some cover and freedom of action to some of the plotters. At the centre of the conspiracy throughout was Colonel-General Beck who resigned as Chief of Staff in 1938, a general who realized too late, but still a good many years before his fellow generals, where Hitler was leading Germany. He was joined by a devoted group; there were politicians such as the former mayor of Leipzig, Goerdeler, the social democrats Leber and Leuschner, released from concentration camp, and some retired diplomats and younger civil servants; there were Catholic and Protestant priests such as the indomitable Pastor Bonhoeffer, who believed that Hitler was anti-Christ and must be overthrown by force by the German people as an act of penitence, and on the fringe of the conspiracy the idealistic young men of the Kreisau circle around Helmut von Moltke who made plans for a better Germany, but would not use force to remove the tyrant. These supplied the political and moral background to the conspiracy, the deep Christian conviction that inspired it and also the foreign contacts which would have been of great importance if the *coup* had succeded. But success depended entirely on the military. During the first five years the manager who supplied the cover and communications for the conspiracy was General Oster of the *Abwehr*. When he was forced to retire by the Gestapo in 1943, the courageous, brilliant and energetic Count Claus von Stauffenberg took on the dangerous role. He and a number of other young officers with cool gallantry launched attempt after attempt on Hitler's life, but always luck or the increasingly stringent security precautions defeated them. But although, as the war went on, more and more generals realized that only by removing Hitler could Germany be saved from utter ruin, all those in key positions made excuses – such as the oath of allegiance – when any opportunity arose for action.

Colonel-General Halder, for four years Chief of the Army Staff, was associated with the conspiracy from an early date. He laid down three conditions for a successful *coup* – clear and resolute leadership, willingness of the masses to follow and the psychological moment. Until Hitler dismissed him in 1942 he was in a position to play the role of General Ambrosio, to give resolute leadership, but he never did. The only senior officers ready for action were retired by Hitler, notably Field-Marshal Erwin von Witzleben, scheduled to be commander-in-chief if the *coup* succeeded. All that the plotters could rely on was a precarious footing in the Home Army, whose commander the infamous Colonel-General Fromm betrayed them when he learned that Hitler had survived the bomb attack. When the attempt was actually made the Gestapo was closing in on the conspirators. It is therefore not surprising that in these adverse circumstances they botched the job, neglecting the most elementary precautions of a modern *coup* such as cutting communications with the Fuehrer's headquarters and failing to seize the radio and central telegraph exchange. If they had managed this much they might have induced the double-faced Field-Marshal von Kluge, commander of the Western army group, to march.

The sequel vividly illustrated the difference between Mussolini and Hitler. The *Duce* had shown little resentment at the conspirators who had overthrown him and had to be urged by the Germans to bring them to trial and execution. Hitler, on the other hand, at the macabre tea party after the attack at which Mussolini saw him for the last time, suddenly burst into a tirade of hatred and vengeance. He would destroy utterly those who had dared to raise their hands against the instrument of divine Providence; he would uproot them and their wives and families too. The German people had shown themselves unworthy of his greatness.

Such was Mussolini's last impression of his friend and master, and such was the maniacal character of Hitler's last year. His terrible threats of vengeance were fulfilled with tortures and barbarous hangings, which he caused to be filmed in order that he might gloat over the fate of his enemies and warn others. He suspected betrayal and conspiracy in all around him. Occasional moods of irrational optimism – as when President Roosevelt's death raised hopes of dividing the allies – alternated with outbreaks of savage and sanguinary rage. The mixture of megalomania, persecution mania, self-pity and flight from reality provide a classic picture of the tyrant in his last stage. In August 1944 he told his Gauleiters that: 'If the German people was to be conquered in the struggle then it had been too weak to face the test of history and was fit only for destruction.' Again, in his final interview with his Minister of Munitions, Speer, who alone in his entourage acted with sanity and tried to save what he could of Germany's resources, Hitler said: 'If the war is lost, the nation will also perish. This fate is inevitable. There is no need to consider the basis even of the most primitive existence any longer.'

Isolated in the Chancellery Bunker in Berlin with the Reich falling to pieces around him, a physical and mental wreck sustained by the drugs of a quack doctor, he was yet able to impose his will to destruction. This was due in part to his personal magnetism; although his whole personality showed the symptoms of premature senility, his eyes apparently could still exercise their baneful hypnotic influence. But above all he had drained every department of German public life of the ability and will to independent action. The revenge on the July conspirators which destroyed the last men capable of active resistance merely completed the process of *Gleichschaltung* which had started with the seizure of power. As early victories had increased the power of the dictator, they had accelerated this process of inanition until German science which might so easily have produced the first atomic weapons was reduced to the superstitious dabblings of the pedants of racialism, the astrologers, cranks and charlatans who duped the masters of Europe, and the process of total mobilization fell as far behind that of the democracies in efficiency as it exceeded them in brutality. Now no one dared gainsay Hitler when he ordered imaginary battalions into impossible attacks. When his illusory plans failed it could only be because he was betrayed. His courtiers fed his illusions. At his side there was Goebbels, his twisted mind revelling in the destruction and preparing the myth of a heroic end; and Bormann, feeding the Fuehrer's suspicions in order to poison his mind against his own rivals, the successor-designate Goering and Himmler. Goering, by now a degenerate voluptuary who had done more than any one man to ruin the Luftwaffe, was still able to grasp at power when Hitler declared that he would stay and die in Berlin; and, cut off in his Bunker, the Fuehrer was still able to have him arrested for his pains. When the news came through of Himmler's wildly unrealistic attempts at a separate peace with the West it was the final betrayal, a conspiracy which explained why all his plans for the relief of Berlin had failed. Hitler deprived Himmler of all offices (although the order never got through), shot his representative Fegelein who had tried to sneak away from the Bunker and prepared his testament, his suicide and his funeral pyre. His insane rancour outlasted the grave and determined his choice of Admiral Doenitz as successor, since the navy was the only body that had not betrayed him. 'Disloyalty and betrayal,' he complained in his last message, 'have undermined resistance throughout the war. It was thus not granted to me to lead the people to victory.'

Hitler's last days, the supreme object-lesson in the corruption of absolute power, illustrate also the tyrant's attempt to project his ego beyond the grave. In societies where the hereditary principle is accepted the solution of the problem should be simple, but the result is often corrosive of the life of the family and the court. For the heir apparent either is or, to the jealous tyrant, seems a menace. To give a few samples from many, Periander the seventh-century B.C. tyrant of Corinth killed his wife and quarrelled with his son; Alexander, as we have seen, was suspected of complicity with his mother in the murder of his father, Philip of Macedon; Augustus said of Herod the Great – in a rather crude Greek pun, that he would rather be his pig than his son and Herod by slaughtering his sons justified the jibe. Augustus himself, with his wife Livia – the first of

a long line of formidable imperial matrons – spent a great deal
of his later life searching the Julian and Claudian families for a
suitable heir and had to settle reluctantly for his stepson,
Livia's son, Tiberius. The outrages of that suspicious tyrant
were traceable in part to the stresses and strains of the problem
of succession to Augustus and the intrigues surrounding the
succession to himself.

Indeed his ambitious favourite Sejanus may serve as the
prototype of those police chiefs, such as Himmler and Beria,
who aspired to succeed their masters. Of comparatively
humble birth he became commander of the Praetorian Guard
and first established their camp at Rome. At the same time he
ingratiated himself with the populace by urging liberal and enlightened policies and wormed his way into the imperial
family by seducing the Emperor's daughter-in-law, Livilla.
Next he proceeded to eliminate the potential heirs to the throne,
Tiberius' son Drusus was poisoned, the Emperor's adopted
grandsons and their mother exiled and doomed to death.
Sejanus now sought Tiberius' permission to marry Livilla. But
he had overreached himself. As a low-born minister and favourite he was useful; as a member of the imperial family, a
dangerous rival. Although he had induced the Emperor to retire from Rome leaving him in control, Tiberius now struck.
Sejanus was executed; all his associates, including Livilla, and
his own children succumbed in the ensuing purge. The satirist
Juvenal later described the destruction of Sejanus' statue in a
passage which could well be applied to the fate of future
tyrants, Mussolini's body hanged upside down from a butcher's
hook in Milan, Stalin's statues dragged down all over Russia
and Eastern Europe in 1961, his body removed from the Lenin
Mausoleum, his name from Stalingrad, the Stalin Allee and all
the other places:

> Down go the Titles; and the Statue crown'd
> Is by base hands in the next river drowned
>
> .   .   .   .
>
> The smith prepares his hammers for the Stroke,
> While the lung's bellows hissing fire provoke;

Sejanus, almost first of Roman names,
The great Sejanus crackles in the flames;
Formed in the forge, the pliant Brass is laid
On Anvils; and of Head and Limbs are made
Pans, Cans and Pispots, a whole kitchen Trade.
Adorn your doors with Laurels; and a Bull
Milk white and large, lead to the Capitol;
Sejanus with a rope is dragged along,
The Sport and Laughter of the giddy throng!
Good Lord, they cry, what Ethiop lips he has,
How foul a snout, and what a hanging Face;
By Heaven, I never cou'd endure his sight;

   .   .   .   .

I fear the rage of our offended Prince
Who thinks the Senate slack in his Defence;
Come let us haste, our Loyal Zeal to show,
And spurn the wretched Corps of Caesar's Foe;
But let our Slaves be present there, lest they
Accuse their Masters, and for Gain betray.

(*Juvenal Satire X*, J. Dryden's translation)

With the fall of the tyrant, begins the re-writing of history. The process had started with Augustus who had rewritten his own history, but had taken a civilized view of the history of the past. It was now carried further by Sejanus himself; he inspired the prosecution of the historian Cremutius who had dared to praise the tyrannicides Brutus and Cassius. After a courageous defence which concluded with the words: 'If I am condemned, people will remember me as well as Brutus and Cassius', Cremutius walked out of the Senate and starved himself to death. His books were ordered to be burnt; but they were hidden and survived to be published in happier times. In these happier times nearly a century later Tacitus commented: 'This makes one deride the stupidity of people who believe that today's authority can destroy tomorrow's memories. On the contrary, repression of genius increases its prestige. All that tryrannical conquerors, and imitators of their brutalities, achieve is their own disrepute and their victims' renown.' Today's authorities have not yet learnt Tacitus' lesson and even at the time of writing a Soviet historian has been expelled from the Communist party for writing too critically of Stalin, Soviet writers are in gaol for publishing their works abroad, and Pasternak's *Dr Zhivago* cannot be published in his own country; and each year new tyrannies arise to commit similar follies.

This problem of the legacy of tyranny and the rewriting of history recurs repeatedly in the Roman Empire and is bound up with the problem of the succession. Even when there is no revolutionary break, the despot has no wish to be over-shadowed by his predecessor. In the Roman Empire the break was as often as not violent. When the hereditary principle worked and there was a peaceful succession the results were often disastrous. Caligula succeeds Tiberius. Marcus Aurelius is followed by his degenerate son Commodus. The stern Severus censures the stoic Emperor for his partiality to his family, and then bequeaths the Empire to his even more monstrous son Caracalla. More often however the ingredients in the succession were the swords of the Praetorians, the poison of the assassin, the plots of concubines and catamites, and the intrigues of those formidable imperial matrons, ranging from the high born Livia Augusta and the haughty Agrippina in the first century, through the Syrian Mamaea who ruled through her son Alexander Severus down to the prostitute Theodora who shared the imperial power with her husband, the wise Justinian. These ladies owed their power to the dynastic principle, and as long as that principle of succession prevailed, women played an important part in the history of despotism – Lucrezia Borgia in the Renaissance for example and Madame Mère and the Empress Josephine under Napoleon, the last great tyrant to try to found a dynasty. With the disappearance of the hereditary principle women have ceased to play an important role in tyrannical life, although the case of Evita Perón in Argentina and the vindictive part played by Chairman Mao's wife in the great Cultural Revolution should warn us against regarding this change as permanent. Eva Braun, whom Hitler married in order that she might share his funeral pyre, deserves only a footnote in history; and Clara Petacci, the mistress who shared Mussolini's fate, may be chiefly remembered by the discredit which the corruption associated with her family brought on the *Duce*'s rule; the amours of President Sukarno served during his reign to advertise his virility and after his fall to illustrate his extravagance. The stern castigators of 'the monstrous regiment of women' might expect some improvement in the tyrants' behaviour from this decline in female influence; they would be disappointed.

Unsatisfactory as hereditary succession proved, it had the virtue of keeping the struggle for power within the family. When it broke down, the legions were called in and there was civil war or the threat of it. The armies of the frontier outdid the Praetorians in the bloody work of making and breaking Emperors. For these were no longer the old Roman legions recruited from Italy and officered by the ruling caste of Rome, but barbarians and peasants from the frontier areas disciplined by officers who had risen from their ranks, like the Thracian Maximin who became Emperor in A.D. 235. 'After the murder of Alexander Severus, and the elevation of Maximin,' writes Gibbon, 'no Emperor could think himself safe upon the throne, and every barbarian peasant of the frontier might aspire to that august, but dangerous station.'

This was the situation which Diocletian sought to remedy by associating first one then three Caesars with the purple, thus hoping to train suitable successors. The remedy proved as bad as the disease and a fruitful cause of rivalry and civil war, eventually dividing the Eastern from the Western Empire, and saddling the unfortunate citizens with the burden of four competing imperial courts instead of one. The conversion of the Empire to Christianity brought another element into the succession problem, that of theological orthodoxy which prefigured to some extent the role of ideological correctness in Communist states today.

The surprising feature of the Roman Empire is not so much that it failed to solve the succession problem, as that it survived so long the failure to do so. Few modern dictatorships have had the opportunity of tackling the problem seriously and few recent tyrants have applied their minds to it. By the time they face death it often happens that their egotism is so inflated that they either, like Hitler, consider the state or nation as unworthy and indeed incapable of surviving its leader, or, like Chairman Mao in recent years, they try to project their egos beyond the grave by inspiring the young with their revolutionary spirit. Besides, with the increasing paranoia and megalomania which often attend the failing years of tyrants, there comes suspicion, hatred and fear of their courtiers until in their latter days they are the loneliest of men. Their courtiers, however, do think of the succession as much as courtiers always have; and the elements they have to manoeuvre with are roughly the same as in the past except that since Napoleon the dynastic principle as been lacking. The three main elements are the Praetorian Guard or its modern equivalent the Secret Police, the army and the ideology; to these must be added in the highly organized modern state the interlocking bureaucratic machines of party government with the propaganda and communication systems. Let us see how these elements have been manipulated in recent succession crises.

In Mussolini's case, when the time came, there was nothing to succeed to. The same was true of Hitler's last days, but his court deluded themselves. The feedback system of misleading information predigested to suit the taste of the leaders, which is common enough in dictatorships, was highly developed in Nazi Germany, and, by the end, it was largely centred on Himmler. We do not know at what stage the Reichsfuehrer S.S. conceived the bizarre idea that he might be the man to succeed Hitler and negotiate peace with the Western Allies. He knew of course that many unkind things were said about him in the Western press, as being the overlord of the Gestapo, of the concentration camps and the gas chambers; but since he felt no guilt about these matters and knew himself to be a good German bourgeois family man, he supposed that they were merely propaganda and would not reflect the reality of Allied attitude towards him, particularly if he could offer them a separate peace with a strong National Socialist Germany ready to resist the Bolshevik flood. 'Der treue Heinrich', the loyal Henry, did not of course consider any disloyalty to his Fuehrer. He had, it is true, known a good deal about the conspiracy before 20 July and had not stopped it. He probably intended to give the army chiefs enough rope to hang themselves, since this would add to his power. It did; after the July plot he became Commander-in-Chief of the Home Army and – very unsuccessfully – commanded an army group on the East Front. He had now nearly all the qualifications needed for the succession; the control of the Praetorians and thirty divisions of the Waffen S.S. or rather their remnants – and no effective opposition from the army command; he knew himself to be the bearer of the pure National Socialist ideology; his agents, particularly the vain and tortuous Schellenberg, had established contacts with the West. True, he did not have control of the party; that was in the hands of his enemy Bormann. But he was far away with Hitler in the Bunker, and the Fuehrer had said he was going to die there. So Himmler made his bid for a separate peace with the West and, even when it failed, deluded himself that he could join Doenitz's government to negotiate an armistice. To such depths of self-deception could the lust for power and the flattery of toadies and charlatans bring the man who controlled the most numerous intelligence and secret police force outside the Soviet Union.

Beria's bid for the succession to Stalin was more realistic. There is no evidence that Stalin in his last lonely years, when he had achieved quasi-divine status, gave any thought to what was to come after him. He occasionally talked of death and his courtiers hastened to reassure him. At the end he was, if we are to believe Khrushchev, planning a purge of his oldest comrades – Molotov, Mikoyan and Voroshiloff, and possibly even Beria himself. Such apparently was the motive of the fantasy of the Moscow doctors' poison plot. But death forestalled him. Svetlana Alliluyeva describes how a moment before his death her father suddenly raised his left hand in a terrible menacing gesture and how, the moment he was dead, while the other leaders stood weeping and silent around the deathbed, Beria was on his feet calling for his car. We know too how the tanks of the security forces rumbled into Moscow to forestall any trouble. Beria had perhaps the most vital weapon of all in the succession struggle, the Praetorian Guard. But he lacked the support of the army and of the Party and State bureaucracy, in which his name inspired only terror. It appears that he tried to overcome this by forming an alliance with Malenkov and associating himself with his policy of relaxation of tension and an easier life for the people. Khrushchev later said that he was planning a Soviet abandonment of Eastern Germany and this may have had something to do with the East German rising. However that may be, his colleagues suspected him of planning a *coup*, detaining him at a meeting of the Presidium, and, not having enough evidence to bring him to trial, shot him on the spot; such at any rate was Khrushchev's version, although it was announced at the time that Beria was tried and executed. Whether he was, in fact, planning a *coup* is immaterial. He had the power, and his colleagues had reason to fear that he might; as chief of secret police he was also in a position to blackmail them. So he was shot. In this action his colleagues must have had the support of the army. But it was not the end of the struggle for the succession.

Malenkov, who had accepted Beria's support, was now on the slippery slope. He had to resign as secretary of the Party and Khrushchev took over. Since the K.G.B. had had its wings clipped and was now under strict Party control, Khrushchev was now best placed in most of the elements for the succession. Ousting Malenkov, his long-standing-rival, from the Premiership, he worked to get the support of the army under its Minister Marshal Zhukhov, brought back from the obscure command to which the jealous Stalin had sent him. In 1956 by his speech at the twentieth Party Congress attacking Stalin he made a bid both for the reformist elements in the Party and for the army, whose leaders he started (posthumously) to rehabilitate from their disgrace by Stalin. But as he sought to consolidate his power by reorganizing the Party, his colleagues realized somewhat late their danger and combined to outvote him in the Politbureau, using, according to one report, Prime Minister Bulganin's bodyguard to cut him off from his supporters. He riposted by calling on army support to fly in members of the Party Central Committee, in which he could rely on a majority of his supporters. Marshal Zhukhov was therefore the kingmaker and when Khrushchev's main rivals had been defeated the Defence Minister very soon suffered the fate of kingmakers and followed them into disgrace and retirement. But even now Khrushchev's position was not as strong as it appeared and when he blundered in the quarrel with China and the Cuba adventure and when he became more and more irritated by the strait jacket of the Party line, and more and more impulsive in trying to break loose from the restraints imposed by his colleagues, the latter brought him down by the same methods by which he had consolidated his position – a majority vote in the Central Committee. This time the instrument by which it was mobilized, unknown to Khrushchev, was the secret police and their chief Shelepin was rewarded for his part by rapid promotion.

The components in the power struggle in the Soviet Union, therefore, remain the same although they have been used with restraint, since the leaders have not killed each other. Nevertheless the apparatus of tyranny is still to hand and as long as it is not dismantled there is always the danger of a new tyrant taking advantage of it.

The fall of Khrushchev is remarkable in two respects. First, he survived it, which indicated some softening of the power struggle since Stalin's time; for this Khrushchev himself can claim some of the credit: since he had routed his own opposition in a relatively civilized and constitutional manner, he was rewarded by a lighter fall himself. However – and this the second remarkable fact – it was a fall into complete oblivion as far as his own countrymen were concerned. Except for his death announcement the name of Khrushchev has been neither printed nor publicly spoken in the U.S.S.R. Thus, of the two leaders who have ruled over that great country for forty years one is unmentionable and the other, since it is impossible to ignore the fact that Stalin existed, may be referred to only in carefully defined stereotyped formulae, and any writer who tries to tell the truth about him is in trouble. One is 'un-person'; the other is 'semi-person.' This illustrates the fact that the first tool of tyranny – the complete suppression of information – still lies ready for some new Soviet dictator to pick up; secondly it shows the evanescence of what is now called the 'charisma' of leadership.

When we consider the so-called 'charismatic' leaders who were banging about and making a great noise in the world a few years ago, where are they now? Sukarno of Indonesia dead in dishonoured retirement. Nkrumah of Ghana in exile, Ben Bella of Algeria in gaol; and all, it would appear, unmourned in their own countries. What, then, is this 'charisma', this aura of greatness which is so easily dispelled? All that is necessary is the initial success in seizing power and the total control of all means of propaganda to project the leader, as a supernatural figure with whom the mass of the people can identify themselves.

To the dictator himself and his contemporaries this 'charisma' is a very real thing; it is like the good fortune which the Roman's valued so highly in their generals (and Napoleon in his marshals). But its durability depends on his real achievements for good or ill. Thus the credit which Hitler built up in years of fanatical struggle and the mystique of his early victories enabled him to lead the German people through defeat after defeat to total disaster, still exercising ascendancy when, isolated in his Bunker, the reality of his power had slipped from his hands. Similarly, despite the attempts at de-Stalinization, the great shadow of Stalin still looms over the Soviet Union, a ghost that could only be exorcized by a total honesty which none of his successors has dared to practise.

The more recent dictators present a flimsier aspect. Sukarno fell after twenty years of leadership. He had established himself in a national liberation struggle, but not in such a desperate and hard fought struggle as had, for example, rendered

Marshal Tito's ascendancy so durable. He maintained his power by mob oratory, and by a skilful balancing act between the army, the nationalist and religious forces and the Communist Party. The balance was represented by the cloudy ideological mixture NASAKOM, a combination of nationalism, the Islamic religion and Communism. As long as he could show some success, when for example West Irian (Dutch New Guinea) was handed him by the United Nations the precarious balance could be maintained. The confrontation with Malaysia could then be used to divert public attention from the increasing chaos of Indonesia. But when no success was forthcoming the balance was upset. The Indonesian Communist Party exploited the confrontation to build up a force of armed 'freedom-fighters' and to infiltrate the propaganda and information services. The Prime Minister Subandrio used his growing influence with the President to push him in the direction of the Communists and against the Army. The generals became increasingly alarmed. Sukarno himself sought refuge from the chaos around him in megalomaniac schemes to change the world, to set up another United Nations of the 'newly emergent forces'. Every 'ism' he had presented to the Indonesian people – and he was a prolific author of 'isms' – was, he declared, of God Almighty. His megalomania and paranoia grew, as his health failed. And it was apparently his collapse at a public meeting and reported death that precipitated the *coup* of 30 September 1965.

The ingredients of the *coup* are familiar, even if many details are in doubt. The principle actor was the chief of the Praetorian Guard, Colonel Unting, commander of the Palace Regiment. Behind him apparently stood the Grand Vizier, Prime Minister Subandrio and the Communists, who planned to use him and Sukarno, if still alive, as the front for communist seizure of power, and on the military side the commander-in-chief of the Air Force. The victims of the *coup* were the generals, six of whom were slaughtered in atrocious circumstances; whether the generals themselves were plotting a *coup* and were anticipated is doubtful. Finally the President himself may have approved the *coup* in order to release himself from the threat of army control. In any case, he subsequently gave what cover he could to Subandrio and the Communists, and made accusations of a planned army *coup*.

When the surviving generals struck back, their vengeance for their tortured colleagues was terrible. The Communist attempt to raise civil war in central Java was quickly suppressed and there followed throughout the villages of Indonesia a holy war against the infidels in which perhaps 300,000 lost their lives, the greatest disaster that had ever befallen a communist party. Whether or not Peking had actually inspired the *coup* which incurred this terrible revenge, it certainly gave its approval to it afterwards.

While this massive slaughter was going on, President Sukarno was refusing to ban the communist party and giving his support to Subandrio who was seeking the means of counteracting the army's power. The President still relied on his mystique to re-establish his power and tried to follow the policies, such as confrontation with Malaysia, which had brought Indonesia to disaster. But he had a subtle opponent in General Suharto, who had led the army's counter-*coup*. His instruments were the rioting students and school children, the very people who should have been completely indoctrinated by Sukarno's 'isms'. In their riotous demonstrations, they sacked the Foreign Ministry and blockaded the palace, while the troops stood by. The President and his cabinet manoeuvred obstinately up to the last moment, but finally had to surrender power to Suharto's ultimatum. To have liquidated the President at one blow would have made a martyr of him. Now he had been destroyed by his own excesses and follies, and by the next generation of the intelligentsia which should have been the bearer of the mystique.

The end of another 'charismatic leader', Kwame Nkrumah, was less catastrophic. Like Sukarno, he had increasingly in his latter years diverted his attention from the urgent domestic problems of his country to his world-wide Pan-African mission. Increasingly, in his latter-day utterances and in his obsession with the neo-colonialist menace, he identified himself with the communist international position. Fearful of assassination he had withdrawn into paranoiac seclusion. The resources of Ghana were wasted on expensive prestige projects and on Communist-run training camps for the future guerrillas of the Pan-African movement. When he set out on a journey which could well have ended with his open adherence to the communist camp, the army struck. The *coup* proved easy, the support of 'the Redeemer' negligible, nor in his exile in Guinea is there any sign of a popular demand for his return. Apparently the 'charisma' which was easily gained in the peaceful struggle for liberation from the British, has been as easily lost.

Other 'charismatic leaders' survive; and the greatest of them Chairman Mao, is at the time of writing making an extraordinary effort to secure immortality by perpetuating his thought and inspiration beyond the grave. On all past evidence, he will not succeed.

However the legacy of tyranny even after its fall is a dangerous one. Too often the military leaders who overthrow tyrants have neither the skill nor the will to establish or re-establish constitutional government. Even where it is re-established, there is a danger, in times of stress, of a nostalgia for imaginary past glories. In Rome the delusion that the infamous Nero had returned from the grave was welcomed by the populace; we have noted the Messianic expectations which accompanied hopes of a return of Frederick II Hohenstaufen from his mountain fastness; and not surprisingly the French people, exasperated by the bumbling incompetence and lack of glamour of democratic governments have craved the glory and excitement of Napoleon the great law-giver and war-maker. The tyrant gets the reputation – often undeserved, as we have seen – of the efficient man who gets things done. It is scarcely imaginable that men anywhere should remember Hitler's autobahns and abolition of unemployment and forget the gas chambers and holocausts of war. But which of us, frustrated by the inefficiency and muddle and unnecessary contention of government by consent, has not on occasion thought: 'What could not I do, if I had dictatorial powers? The problems are all so simple. Just remove a few crooks and incompetents. Oh no! No question of concentration camps or secret police, let alone gas chambers or nuclear bombs.' Yet it only needs enough people to think that way at the same time for long enough and with sufficient ferocity, and that is where it would lead.

13. The Tyrant and the Future

Tyranny is, so to spreak, a nervous breakdown of the body politic. Society succumbs to stresses that are too great for it. In considering the progress of any given community, it is necessary to estimate both the stresses to which it is subjected, and its stress threshold – the point at which the stresses become unbearable.

Modern society, as we have seen, is subjected to a high degree of stress of the kind that normally leads to tyranny. Rapid technological progress breeds a sense of insecurity; a newly learned trade or skill is out of date in half a generation, and those who have learnt it are liable to be flung on the scrap heap. Similarly with institutions; they soon fall out of step with the giant stride of technical progress; yet man is a creature of habit; all morality, custom, law is based on habit and, if habit is broken once or twice in a generation, morality, custom and law collapse, and society becomes atomized into a 'lonely crowd' of insecure individuals ready for the word of command of a master who can exploit both their lack of cohesion and distrust of each other, and also their craving for the 'togetherness' of the mass movement. Technological progress brings with it also a rapid growth of population and a rush to the cities. Such demographic changes and rapid urbanization have commonly led to tyranny in the past; indeed we are told that chimpanzees, who in their natural habitat behave reasonably and unaggressively, when crowded together in zoos become aggressive and, instead of maintaining a natural and recognized hierarchy, submit to the biggest bully. However, here perhaps we are in danger of substituting the myth of the noble monkey for that of the noble savage.

Another consequence of rapid technical progress, with its ease of transport and communication, is the mingling and clash of cultures, which has commonly caused deep perturbation in man's mind and a sense of the need of Messianic deliverance from catastrophic disaster. These emotions, previously often sublimated in religious fervour, nowadays find their outlet in extravagant secular expectations. At the same time men of one culture aspiring to political unity among themselves, but finding themselves unable to achieve it, as is now the case, for example, with the Europeans, the Arabs and the Africans, become tempting bait for the conqueror tyrant.

This juxtaposition and clash of cultures also produces another fruitful source of tyranny, envy and the disappointment of great expectations. The peoples of newly independent nations are led to believe that the deliverance from foreign rule will bring them the same kind of benefits as were enjoyed by the foreign ruler. When this does not happen, their leaders, the young intelligentsia, whether in university or army, feel humiliated by their inferior standard of living and impotence *vis-à-vis* greater powers.

The pressures are highest where the stress threshold is commonly lowest, among the newly independent peoples. This threshold is low where there is a past-history of earlier tyranny, or where an alien culture is grafted on a more primitive and simpler one or, indeed, on a more ancient and complex one. In these circumstances, under stress, society is liable to relapse into bad childhood habits. Thus it is in no way surprising that some African nations, scarcely emerged from tribalism should, shortly after achieving independence and having experienced the problems and disappointments that attend it, relapse into dictatorship or tyranny, which is a more modern and fashionable form of tribalism.

Least of all should it surprise the nations of Europe, which after the collapse of empires and dynasties developed an unprecedented epidemic of more or less tyrannical dictatorships. These include Germany and the Soviet Union, the prototypes and exemplars of all modern dictatorships. The degree of

modern tyranny can indeed be measured by their approxima-
tion to these two – the one which sought infamous ends that
could only be secured by violent and evil means, and the other
which has sought noble ends that cannot be secured through
the Communist means of violence and class hatred.

Tyranny is the obverse of the coin of constitutional government, which Western civilization has sought to make the
common currency among its former dependencies. It is in no
way surprising that many of them choose to gamble on 'tails'
rather than 'heads'. In doing so they naturally choose from the
models set before them, mixing the ingredients in accordance
with their national circumstances. Most of these new dictatorships call themselves socialist and may in a sense be so, for a
variety of reasons. There is the genuinely idealistic belief that
'socialism' is the best means of benefiting the people. The fact
that the Soviet system has brought Russia in a generation from
relative underdevelopment and exploitation by foreign capital
to a position of complete independence and great power is
bound to inspire emulation. Above all, nationalization of the
economy involves the greatest possible concentration of direct
control in the hands of the ruler. On the other hand, new
dictators tend to exploit the nationalist and racist appeal of the
National Socialist type, even if like Fidel Castro they profess
Communist internationalism as a means of extending their
power and influence.

It can be argued with some justification that dictatorship is a
phase through which many, if not most nations must pass in
order to become modern states. The part of Oliver Cromwell,
the first such dictator, in laying the foundations of modern
Britain, is often cited as an example. Just as, according to
Engels, force is the midwife of every old society in labour with
a new, so, it might be added, tyranny – or at any rate dictatorship – is the wet-nurse. Both these Sarah Gamps, however,
must be regarded as out-of-date, and unhygienic in the nuclear
age, since they are likely enough to prove fatal to both mother
and child. They need not prove lethal to the rest of mankind, if
the victim is an underdeveloped country; but if such a break-

down were to occur again in a modern, highly industrialized state, the human race would not get off so lightly as it did last time. Civilization was damaged, perhaps irreparably, by the Second World War; it would not survive a nuclear conflict.

It is no part of the purpose of this study to predict whether this will or will not occur. The medical analogy of the nervous breakdown is not intended to suggest that diagnosis or prognosis is possible; that would be to mistake a literary device for a scientific hypothesis. The comparison of society to an organism may – as it did with Plato and St Paul, Hobbes and Spengler – inspire valuable insights, but if the analogy is treated as a fact of nature and a basis for prediction, it can only result in a misleading and dangerous idolatry. It is part of our argument that large scale prediction about human society is not only generally futile but often harmful and dangerous, since the prophet, like Jonah, tends to develop a vested interest in the verification of his prophecy, and only by the grace of God helps to avert it. Thus if Marx or Lenin or Stalin predicts a whole epoch of wars and violent revolutions it becomes the business of Communists everywhere to make dreams come true; if a Nietzsche or a Hitler predicts that a war will bring about a higher civilization, a great nation will devote itself to the preparation of such a war. This is the danger of ideological thinking which seeks to explain and chart the human condition in terms of a single all-embracing, allegedly scientific theory.

This study of tyranny offers no such certainties. However it does point to the signs to be looked for, the questions to be asked. In examining the signposts for our time, it is natural to turn first of all to the United States. For it is there, more than anywhere else, that the future of liberty is likely to be decided, both because American strength provides the main physical defence of freedom and because the United States is already far advanced in the social revolution of automation, on which other nations are only somewhat nervously embarking. Such social revolutions test a society in its most sensitive area – in the case of the United States, the area of race relations. Automation contributes to a rapid rise in prosperity, accompanied by corresponding high expectations. These expectations tend to be disappointed – and even to be replaced by fears and frustrations – in one section of the population, namely those engaged in unskilled labour. Since, in the U.S.A., a large proportion of this section is distinguished by the colour of its skin, a distinctive minority is suffering just that set-back to rising expectations which commonly leads to revolutionary feeling, and this at a time when society is trying to reform its treatment of the Negroes – a perilous moment for any régime. The danger is the more acute because of the revolution which has brought Negro governments to power in many countries. It is true that American Negroes enjoy far greater prosperity, better education opportunities and even greater freedom than the people of most self-governing African states; but in politics men tend to count their disadvantages rather than their blessings, and the fact that most Africans in one way or another control their own destinies makes the underprivileged position of the American Negro all the more offensive to his self-respect.

The fact that a very substantial minority is in a violent and revolutionary mood does not in itself threaten tyranny, since it is not conceivable that the Negroes should seize power; nor need it be doubted that North American society, which has absorbed so many waves of immigrants, should be able, by a supreme effort, to deal with its own internal immigration now knocking violently at the door, were it not for other stresses. The chief of these is the United States' changed position in the world. Not since Rome, with a form of governmant suitable to a small Italian city-state, became ruler of the inhabited world has there been such a rapid climb to great power. The exercise of this power, the obligation of defence against Communist expansion, has not only involved the United States in great expenditure, thus impeding the solution of domestic social problems, but also carries with it the threat of a militarization of American life.

The Vietnam war with its frustrations and sacrifices has increased both this threat and the protest against it. The combination of the youthful protest with the movement for civil rights for Negroes – particularly as the latter takes the form of violence on the streets – is liable to arouse a more violent reaction from the other extreme. The insecurity and anxiety created by domestic violence and foreign war or cold war is a mood which could be exploited by a would-be dictatorship. During the Korean War Senator Joe McCarthy showed how the system of checks and balances on which freedom in the United States depends could be partially paralysed by a skilful appeal to men's fears and prejudices. The impatient desire for quick solutions and the suspicion of a hostile conspiracy when these are not achieved are not confined to the United States. But the rapid transition from isolationism to supreme international power and responsibility in conditions of great danger and difficulty is liable to aggravate such feelings. McCarthy was able to exploit this combination of impatience, fear and suspicion to secure considerable power, despite the opposition of successive presidents. It is not difficult to imagine the danger, if the powers of the government were to be put behind such a movement; if, for example, a presidential candidate were to harness the white backlash against the violence of the Black Power campaign, the nationalist reaction against criticism of the war and cold war effort, the disciplinarian reaction against the excessive licence of the young. The assassinations of President Kennedy and Robert Kennedy and of Martin Luther King were not the result of terrorist conspiracy. But they and the undercurrent of violence of which they are symptoms do make the paths of moderate reform and conciliation more difficult and dangerous, if more necessary. War and the danger of war, the colossal powers concentrated in the central government as a result, the mood of impatience, the fear of Communist conspiracy, the search for violent solutions – many of the classic conditions for a breakdown of constitutional government do exist in the United States.

However, the stress threshold of American society is a high one. The democratic tradition, which could survive even the horrors of civil war, is extremely strong, the institutions through which it expresses itself are flexible, varied and deeply entrenched in people's loyalties. The machinery of peaceful change is highly developed. American observers have themselves often drawn attention to the dangers just outlined, and this self-awareness is of the safeguards of liberty. Never has a nation engaged in war allowed such freedom of criticism and protest as the United States during the Vietnamese conflict. The extremes of wealth and poverty are tempered by a high general level of prosperity and – except in the case of the Negroes – by a reasonable equality of opportunity. Such a society should be able to stand against the assault of any would-be tyrant, unless its fortifications are shaken by some extreme shock, such as humiliating defeat in war or crippling economic crisis; and if freedom stands in the United States, its chances are by so much the better elsewhere.

Britain is exposed to equal stresses. Whereas the United States is struggling with the problems of a sudden access of international power and responsibility, Britain faces the results of the loss of imperial power, a fruitful source of tyranny in the past. This loss of power has been partially masked by victory in war, by the peaceful nature of the de-colonizing process and by the creative alternative of the Commonwealth. The postwar economic recovery confounded the prophets of economic doom resulting from the loss of Empire; indeed it was accompanied by an unprecedented rise in the standard of living. Therefore it is only recently that most Britons have come to face the reality of their country's changed position in the world and the search for a new role. There is disillusion with the alternatives of the Commonwealth and the United Nations, to which high hopes were originally pinned, and frustration at the failure to find a new solution in Europe. At the same time recurring economic crises, even if cushioned by a generally high standard of living, generate a mood of discouragement. A ruling class trained for the exercise of power in a great Empire now lacks purpose and has failed to pass on a sense of identity to a younger generation, which is increasingly self-conscious and critical as a result of the spread of higher education. There is therefore disillusionment, disappointment of high expectations, a mocking and sometimes violent contempt for established institutions among the young. The permissive society is in some danger of lapsing into the kind of anarchy which tempts an authoritarian reaction. To these stresses immigration from the Commonwealth has added a racial problem, much smaller in scale than the American one, but serious because of its novelty and because, owing to its association with the loss of Empire, it can easily be exploited by nationalist extremists. Any would-be tyrant needs a butt, one that is sufficiently close at hand and sufficiently distinctive to inspire anxiety and aggression among a large section of the population who feel themselves to be threatened by the foreign body in their midst. The coloured immigrants serve the troublemakers' purpose well, since those whose interests are immediately threatened by them are just those who have most reason for discontent anyway.

The exaggerated reaction to Commonwealth immigration is a warning to Britain that 'it could happen here', but probably only in the event of a massive new economic crisis, with runaway inflation and mass unemployment. It is a timely warning which should enable the nation to deploy the resources for peaceful change derived from three centuries of immunity to invasion and civil war and the British genius for clubbing together for all sorts of purposes and adapting old institutions to new ends. The temptation for Britain, on shedding her Empire, is to fall back into an old-fashioned and restrictive tribalism; the coloured immigrants form a present and visible incitement to yield to this temptation. However, this is balanced by the widespread conviction that Britain cannot survive or thrive in isolation. The nation which more than any other spread the movement of nationalism throughout the world has now more obviously than any other outlived it. Britain, forced in upon herself, now turns back to Europe and raises the question, whether that continent, the cradle of modern nationalism, can become its grave, with Britain acting the role of first grave-digger.

Europe above all has experience of the self-destructive

nature of nationalism and of its tendency to produce the tyranny of the foreign conqueror or the domestic dictator; but the Continental peoples, who have known the humiliations of invasion and defeat, have perhaps greater temptation than Britain to relapse into tribalism. Nowhere has this temptation been stronger than in France. This great nation had the bitter experience of being on the winning side in war, yet suffering the humiliation of defeat, of losing an empire while fighting two unsuccessful wars to retain it. By 1958 France found herself on the brink of civil war and of an army *coup* of the type which later overcame Greece. From this fate she was saved by General de Gaulle. His function was that of the dictator in the original Roman, rather than the modern, sense of that term. He had to overcome an emergency, to provide a period of strong and stable government, to bind up the wounds of the nation and overcome its antagonisms and class conflicts, to restore its self-respect. For this a period of authoritarian and paternalistic rule was necessary and cannot be described as tyrannical. National self-respect was indeed restored, but largely by a series of high-handed gestures at the expense of France's allies which were irrelevant to the fundamental problems of the nation. The period of stability was used not to solve these problems, but to put them into cold storage. The institutions which could have been strengthened and used to bring grievances into the open and to work for agreed solutions – the National Assembly, the political parties, the trade unions, radio, television, the press and the universities – were weakened by atrophy and inertia. Consequently when a new generation arose, oblivious of the peril and humiliation which had brought the General to power, the grievances which had long been bubbling beneath the bland surface of Gaullist paternalism could not emerge through constitutional channels, but had to erupt in anarchic disorder. The government and the forces of law and order on the one hand and the extremes of youthful anarchy, idealism and nihilism had to face each other on the barricades, without the shock-absorbers of free speech and debate which could have cushioned the collision.

Thus ten years of authoritarian rule brought France to the brink of the kind of anarchy which is often the precursor of tyranny. This enabled President de Gaulle to exploit the threat of totalitarian Communism to frighten people to seek refuge again beneath his paternalist wing. Thus having come to power through the fear of a military *coup*, he maintained it through the fear of a left-wing *coup*, the classic left–right combination gambit which raised the question whether authoritarian rule might not degenerate into tyranny. However, the constitutional manner of the General's departure from power has answered this question in his favour.

If, in international affairs, President de Gaulle's pursuit of an outdated version of national glory has had a less disruptive effect, it is because France's powers are limited. The fabric of collective security so laboriously constructed since the Second World War has survived France's virtual defection. The steps taken towards a united Europe have at least not been reversed, even if its expansion and consolidation have been hindered. The risk is that Gaullist nationalism might awake in other countries of Europe an equally nationalistic reaction – in Britain, for example, as a result of the European Economic Community's rebuff and, more dangerously, in Germany. Indeed de Gaulle's example may have contributed to the recent growth of the right-wing nationalist movement in that country. Many of the conditions for a recurrence of tyranny do indeed exist in Germany – defeat in war, a sense of humiliation repudiated by the young, an unusually wide generation gap between those who have lived under Nazi rule and those who have not, a tradition of authoritarian government rather than ordered freedom, the division of the country which could be so easily exploited to whip up nationalist passion. Against these must be set the very recent experience of the consequences of tyranny and the contrast of yesterday's misery with today's prosperity, yesterday's devastation with today's security, assured by an international collective security system, and the cautionary example of Ulbricht's tyranny next door. Short of an extreme economic crisis or immediate danger of war, these factors should operate against a recurrence of tyranny in the land where it has brought the greatest ruin to Europe.

However, Western Europe, which up to the early 1960s seemed to be advancing confidently towards a more secure and well-integrated future, has now been checked in its stride by the recurrent spectre of nationalism. This is the more unfortunate at a time when this same nationalism shows signs of breaking up the tyranny which has held most of Eastern Europe in cold storage for over twenty years. During the past decade Romania, apparently the most supine of satellites, has broken away from Soviet tutelage. Its dictator, Gheorghiu-Dej, followed the pattern of puppet tyrants by asserting his independence as soon as he felt it could be done with impunity. His successor, while denouncing his memory, has gone further along the same independent path, though in doing so he has done little to relax the iron grip of dictatorship. More significantly Czechoslovakia has thrown out its puppet dictator, Novotný, in an effort to show that Communism without tyranny is possible. The Yugoslavs have long been trying to prove the same, but have left a doubt with their Communist colleagues whether in dispensing with the police state they have not given up Communism too. However if any state should be able to combine Communism with democracy it should be Czechoslovakia, with its tradition of orderly and constitutional government. Other peoples under Communist rule have been watching the Czechoslovak experiment with eager expectation. There, as in the Hungarian rising of 1956, it was the intelligentsia supported by the students, a generation raised entirely under Communism, who were the pioneers of the reform movement; at the same time the Polish students have expressed similar aspirations; and, if the Soviet Communists are proceeding in an opposite direction, their repressive policy is a reaction to similar stirrings among their own intelligentsia and younger generation – a generation, which knew nothing of the Stalinist terror, ruled by people who gained all their training in government in that brutal school. Indeed, the brutality of the Soviet leaders' reaction to the Czechoslovak spring rising is proof alike of their fear of the infection of liberty and of the force of the movement for freedom both in Czechoslovakia and in neighbouring countries.

The 1960s have indeed been a bad decade for dictators. Chairman Mao, in his attempt to immortalize the revolution, has plunged China into chronic chaos, exploding the Communist claim to lead the underdeveloped countries on the road to modernization. Three of the greatest 'charismatic' leaders, Sukarno of Indonesia, Nkrumah of Ghana and Ben Bella of Algeria, have fallen leaving little trace except the impoverishment of their countries. From this, however, one can draw little comfort, except that, as in Aristotle's time, tyranny is a short-lived and unstable form of government. The requirements of modern technological society are stability, continuity and predictability; tyranny is, by its nature, violent and arbitrary, sudden and unpredictable in its actions.

However, the 1960s have been a bad decade for freedom and constitutional government, too. Africa had outstripped Latin-America in military *coups*. Its greatest state, Nigeria, has fallen apart in civil war and tribal massacres. India, the most numerous democracy the world has ever seen, has been threatened with disruption into its linguistic states, with communal strife and extremism. Dictatorial régimes which called themselves anti-imperialist or socialist could rely on economic and military support from the Communist powers; in consequence the Western powers often found themselves supporting right-wing dictatorships in order to check the spread of Communism. The great powers, unable to strike at each other directly for fear of nuclear destruction, sought to injure each other through their dependencies in various parts of the world, thus becoming involved in local conflicts and rivalries in Asia, the Middle East and Africa; and there was the chronic fear that any local war might escalate into nuclear conflict. The arms race was consequently intensified, consuming the resources which could otherwise have been used to counteract the effects of an unprecedented population explosion.

If one were to try to cast a nation-by-nation balance sheet of tyranny the result would not be too bad. As long as India remains a free country, it can be argued that more people are under free and democratic government than ever before in history. If certain old-established democracies show signs of falling under dictators, certain Communist countries are haltingly emerging from tyranny. And the tyrannies under which many newly independent countries have fallen give no evidence of stability. However such a nation-by-nation analysis leaves out of consideration the most distinctive feature of the modern world, namely the crisis of confidence which affects the most advanced technological societies – a crisis of confidence deeper than that arising from racial conflicts or from the Cold War or from the war in Vietnam – a loss of nerve, just when the blessings which men have coveted down the ages seem within their grasp.

The nature of this crisis is hard to comprehend when one is in the midst of it. It arises from a sense of impotence when all things seem possible, a lack of freedom in the midst of unlimited licence, a loss of purpose when too many purposes are set before us. It is a crisis of identity in the sense that a man's identity is largely determined by the goals which society sets him, and by the image he has of himself as either achieving these ends or failing to, accepting them or rejecting them. Complex modern society presents no such clear patterns. In most traditional societies the ruling class at least has a clear image of itself and of the functions of men in society and, through commonly accepted moral and religious principles and assumptions about the meaning of life, through upbringing, education and religion, acceptance of this image becomes, as it were, part of the air which men breathe. If it is a pattern which they can accept with self-respect, the society is stable; when it ceases to minister to men's self-respect, a revolutionary situation arises; when an alternative more acceptable pattern of images and values is offered there is a revolution, either peaceful or violent. This is what happened in the religious revolutions of the Renaissance and Reformation; it has happened again in the nationalist and populist revolutions of the past two centuries. Modern industrial societies, when they have developed beyond the stage of primitive nationalism, offer no such pattern. In capitalist and pluralist societies the mass media and the advertisers thrust on the individuals a random and bewildering jumble of fragments for a pattern. In Communist totalitarian society an obligatory image only acceptable to bureaucrats is imposed by bureaucrats.

From this arises the sense of alienation from society which Marx observed over a century ago. It is the sense of being a cog in a great machine, a means and not an end, which results in the loss of human dignity, purpose and identity. It was this feeling of frustration and humiliation as well as fear of unemployment and starvation which drove the Luddites of the early nineteenth century to smash the machines. Since then this sense of frustration and alienation has found increasingly articulate expression through the growing intelligentsia which modern industrial society has to educate, without in many cases offering them any clear purpose in life or role which satisfies their self-respect. But if the feeling has been most clearly expressed by the intelligentsia it is diffused throughout society. The rioting student is very often expressing in extreme form the frustration which most people feel when confronted with their income tax returns and the many other forms which give the right to breathe in modern society. We resent the tyranny of vast impersonal organizations, which, despite all democratic rights and representation, we feel powerless to influence. The age of automation is liable to bring with it even vaster and more impersonal organizations, since without them we cannot maintain vast masses in the relative affluence which we have come to expect. Lenin looked forward to the day when the government of men would give way to the administration of things; in modern affluent society the tyranny of men seems too often to give way to the tyranny of things; in Communist society the tyranny of men is superimposed on the tyranny of things.

Against this, the young protest. In communist societies they claim elementary rights of freedom of expression, freedom from censorship and ideological indoctrination, freedom to travel. But the young in the universities of the West, who enjoy these liberties to a degree unknown in any previous society, protest too. Many demonstrate from idealistic motives against a society which does not practise the values which it professes – against nuclear weapons, the Vietnam war or racial discrimination. With the mass media bringing the ills of the world instantaneously into the homes of all, there is plenty to complain about; and if there were not, the students have grievances enough of their own. The university population is growing at an unprecedented rate; many of the students come from families in which there is no tradition of higher education; they go to universities which are either new, with no traditional discipline, or old, with traditions which need adapting to new demands. Their expectations from their studies are high; but they find themselves worse off than their brothers and sisters in jobs; and their prospects of suitable work are uncertain. Their teachers are, in many universities, too few and too remote. They are, in any case, not in a position to give clear-cut answers to the many problems that press in on the young from the world and the university, since they themselves often share the moral bewilderment of their students.

The university if a microcosm of society; it is to some extent even a caricature, because of the concentration of some of its features, and of the sensitivity of the young to such distortions and their impatience with them. In any society the kind of situation just described sets men looking for leaders and provides opportunities for the demagogue. This is as much the case among the young as among their elders. The great majority of the students may want to continue quietly with their studies, but the tone is often set by the extremists. These, although they may exploit bread-and-butter problems, are more concerned with ideas and principles. The interesting result has been a revival of ideological thinking among the youth of western democracies at just the time when it has discredited itself in those societies where ideologies are practised. This indeed is the great difference between the students' revolt in

the Communist world and in the West. One is a revolt against
the ideological strait-jacket in favour of freedom of choice; the
other is often an attempt to impress an ideology on a society
which, enjoying substantial material well-being, shows little
sign of wanting any ideology. Without accepting Marxism–
Leninism as practised in Communist countries, the young
dissidents accept Marx's destructive analysis of capitalist
society and of the illusory nature of the so-called 'bourgeois'
freedom which in fact allows them a liberty of expression and
agitation scarcely enjoyed in any other society. To this they
add a programme of action drawn largely from the writings of
the Cuban guerrilla leader Ché Guevara and his disciple Régis
Debray, and from Chairman Mao. Now, the guerrilla techniques suitable to the peasant societies of Latin-America evidently have little relevance to the conditions of Paris or Rome
or Bonn; still less has Chairman Mao's permanent revolution
from above, designed as it is to eliminate all opposition and to
brainwash a nation, anything to do with the rather anarchistic
aims of the young revolutionaries. But to them this irrelevance
is, in itself, irrelevant. For the 'Revolution' has become an end
in itself, a way of life, and not a means of bringing about any
well-defined ends; for the young romantic revolutionaries, like
their nineteenth-century forebears, it has become in fact a substitute religion.

As we have seen in the preceding pages this confusion of
means and ends, this deification of certain of the techniques of
power, is almost by definition a recipe for tyranny. Not that
'student power' itself is ever likely to extend beyond the limits
of the universities. Even in France, where the students' revolt
brought into the open certain deep-seated tensions in society, the
moment the workers seized their factories the leadership passed
into other hands. The young revolutionaries may act as the
fuse for an explosion that goes far beyond their control, or as
an irritant of a disease far more serious than that which they
seek to cure. The danger is that the nihilistic use of power
from below may provoke the far more effective use of power by
authority. One of the aims of the extremist leaders is to

provoke police violence as a means of fanning flames of protest. In countries where the police have a tradition of ruthlessness and brutality, not very much provocation is needed. The assumption of the young revolutionaries that such disorders will crack the present frame of society and lead to something better will not convince an elder generation which has seen a similar cycle of action and reaction leading to dictatorship and world war.

It is possible to argue that this student malaise, which affects only a minority, is preferable to political apathy. It may also be a passing phase which will pass into oblivion with 'flower power' and the now forgotten struggles between the young 'mods' and 'rockers'. But it is significant because it reflects the sense of alienation of a great part of the younger intelligentsia in the face of the impersonal forces of modern bureaucratic societies, their sense of anxiety in a Kafkaesque world in which the sources of grace and of judgement are equally problematical. Religion is generally rejected as unworthy escapism. Odd scraps of discredited ideologies are put together as a substitute. At a moment when the wars of ideology begin to seem as irrelevant and outdated as the wars of religion, the youthful search for a faith shakes the complacency of the affluent society. We are living, in fact, in an age like that of the Renaissance or the Enlightenment when men are seeking a new image of themselves. Such ages, as we have seen, tend to combine enormous advances with exemplary disasters. The possible antidotes to the latter will be our final theme.

14. Remedies against Tyranny

To describe the remedies against tyranny it would be necessary to write a history of liberty, a task before which even the great Lord Acton quailed. However, since I have defined tyranny as the 'exercise of arbitrary power beyond the scope permitted by the laws, customs and standards of the time and society', the reader may reasonably ask: 'What is the scope of politics in our time and society?' So it is necessary now to try to define summarily the political values of our society and to deduce a few maxims against tyrants from them.

The great aims of man as a political animal are self-preservation (or security) and self-respect. These may conflict. To preserve his life a man may have to sacrifice his self-respect; to preserve his self-respect a man may have to sacrifice his life. We admire the man who does the latter rather than the former; thereby we admit that the supreme aim of the political animal is human dignity, self-respect. This has been confirmed in recent colonial struggles, in which people have often preferred to be mismanaged by their countrymen to being more efficiently governed by an alien ruler. Self-respect as a political emotion is valued above economic well-being, security and law and order.

However, self-respect or human dignity is by itself an empty formula. It means so many different things to different people and societies. What makes a man respect himself is not the same for a head-hunting Dyak as for Mr Smith of Ealing. The Dyak's self-respect may depend on the number of heads he cuts off; Mr Smith's – in peacetime, at any rate – may depend on having as good a car as Mr Jones next door. Why do we prefer the second state of society first? Because in Ealing the

two great aims of self-respect and self-preservation are combined; in Borneo under the head-hunters they were not. This is
why we prefer peace to war. Further, our Dyak either has to
behead or be beheaded. But Smith does not have to live up to
the Joneses. He may choose not to have a car in order to
concentrate on buying plants for his garden or a better tape-
recorder or writing poetry. His self-respect in fact lies in his
freedom of choice. This is not to say that freedom is a means
to self-respect; indeed, as de Tocqueville said: 'If we seek
freedom as a means to any other end, we have already lost it';
it means that in the highest forms of society freedom and
human dignity are identical.

The highest form of society is therefore the one in which
most people enjoy self-respect in freedom and security. This
definition may be accepted in Western society at present but it
is by no means universal or self-evident. Our Dyak may well
object that, if we stop him head-hunting, we are depriving him
of the freedom that has been common to his society, of his self-
respect, in fact; so, for that matter, may others nearer home
than Borneo. For Hitler, watching the brown-shirted masses
marching past at Nuremberg, could argue that they achieved
their self-respect in the greatness of the *Volk*, and of its per-
sonification, the Fuehrer. Many certainly did; so it is not an
easy argument to deal with. One may point to the ruins of the
Third Reich and say: 'I refute it thus.' But this will not persuade any future Fuehrer and his followers, who start out
convinced that they have a better chance of success. We cannot, in fact, obliterate Nietzsche's vision of the Superman –
and its debased elaboration in Nazi and Fascist and racist
society – by the argument of power, but only by a different
view of man, of human dignity and of society; this is not
surprising, since Nietzsche set up his Superman image as a
challenge to the different, Christian, view of man and society.
When we say, then, that tyranny, the indefinite extension of
one man's freedom at the expense of everyone else's, is the
worst form of society we are making an ultimate, perhaps
religious, judgement about the nature of man. When a tyrant,

Caligula for example, exercises unlimited arbitrary freedom using all within his reach as means of gratifying his whims, we call him a monster or a madman, not a human being any more.

Freedom, then, implies limits. Rousseau's great lie, 'Man is born free; but everywhere he is in chains', may have been a salutary counterblast to the notion that all men's chains were God-given and irremovable and that self-respect consisted in wearing them with resignation and a good grace. But the attitude which it represents and the sort of people to whom it appeals, these have been the most fruitful sources of the radical tyrannies of our time from Robespierre's reign of virtue to Mao's attempt to write beautiful thoughts on the blank sheet of the Chinese peasant, from Napoleon's new order, to Goebbels exulting in the Bunker: 'Now that everything is in ruins, we are forced to rebuild Europe.'

This attitude of radical nihilism can lead either to revolutionary tyranny, when men seek to tear up people and societies by the roots in order to make all things new, or to reactionary tyranny, when men are driven to take refuge in old tribal loyalties. The climate of nihilism proceeds from certain assumptions, sometimes avowed, sometimes unavowed, sometimes conscious, sometimes unconscious. To sum them up: God is dead, therefore anything is permitted; where anything is permitted all will be well. Men will become like gods. The historical study of past civilizations, the anthropological study of contemporary societies demonstrates that there are no absolute moral standards. Man makes himself through his institutions. Therefore it is only necessary to reorganize society according to certain scientific laws in order to recreate men in the required image. Then the evolutionary process will establish the superior race, class or group and all will be well. When all is not well, it can only be due to the survival of reactionary institutions and traditions. One great exercise of power will eliminate these and liquidate the rule of force once and for all, put an end to history, ring in the millennium, the classless society, the world of supermen, of men become gods.

The creators of this climate of opinion are the revolutionary or radical intelligentsia, not people of any particular class, but an *élite* from every class which is growing with the spread of mass education. In all highly developed societies where men seek to reshape their own destiny, the intelligentsia plays the role, not perhaps of Plato's philosopher-kings, but the nearest to it that history has seen. It is a dangerous role. For Hegel and Nietzsche might well have disapproved of Hitler and Mussolini, and Marx, who aimed at a society in which 'the freedom of each would be the condition of the freedom of all', might well have been shocked at Stalin; but they were the fathers of these monstrous offspring, as surely as Marcus Aurelius sired the vicious Commodus; and they are the more to blame, because man cannot control his chromosomes, but he is the master of his ideas.

One may perhaps forgive these great men for not foreseeing where their ideas would lead. But for us, their successors, there is no such excuse; we know from ample experience that, human nature being what it always has been, the rulers of this world will pick up those of the philosophers' ideas that conduce to their own greater power. We know, too, that whereas our ancestors' ideas might take several generations to reach a wide audience, the impact of ideas through the mass media of today can be almost instantaneous. It is then to this great and growing group, at once the promoters of tyrannies and their natural victims, often the first to revolt against the crimes and follies of which they have sometimes made themselves unconscious and unwilling accomplices, that these maxims against tyrants are addressed.

The intellectual can have but two great ideals – truth and freedom; freedom, without which truth cannot be sought, truth, without which all his activity is a mere enslavement of men's minds. There are many temptations to treason against these ideals. The distinctive seduction of our age is the idolatry of the 'ism'. We abstract and generalize in order to understand; we use portmanteau words in order to describe. Such portmanteaux are a necessary shorthand in a complex world. But then we are tempted to reify our abstractions, to treat them as things; the next stage is to deify them, to treat them as gods – or devils, as the case may be. Hence we say that Communism does this or Imperialism does that and Neo-Colonialism the other; and we attach a fanatical devotion or detestation to these 'isms'. But, as Camus wrote: 'Politics is not religion, or, if it is, it is nothing but the Inquisition.'

When Julien Benda wrote *Le Trahison des Clercs* in the heyday of Fascism, the main seductions to treason were those of nationalism, They still exist even for western intellectuals, but still more for the intellectuals of the newly independent countries, who may with the best will in the world feel compelled to suppress truth in the national interest and to condone the suppression of freedom in the interests of efficiency and prestige; and their western colleagues, who supported their fanatical liberation struggle, are apt to condone their equally fanatical use of power, forgetting the distinction made by Victor Hugo: 'Le fanatisme, hideux quand il persécute; auguste et touchant quand il est persécuté.'

Some of the more subtle temptations towards a double standard of judgement arise from a guilty conscience. We feel guilty about our colonialist past and therefore inclined to condone acts of tyranny in the newly independent countries; but this involves a condescension not less patronizing than those who say: 'I told you so. What can you expect of such people? We ought never to have given them independence.'

We feel guilty about our imperialist past; therefore we condone the Soviet seizure of the Baltic states and the transportation of hundreds of thousands of the oppressed peoples, ignoring the fact that though imperial rule by a free people is a form of tyranny, imperial rule by a tyrant is a worse form, as the records of Hitler and Stalin show.

We feel guilty about the sufferings and exploitation of the British working-class during the industrial revolution and the enclosures under a free system of government; therefore we make excuses for the total tyranny by which Stalin pushed through the industrialization and collectivization in the

U.S.S.R. We are even tempted to listen to the Marxist–Leninists who tell us that the freedom we enjoy is a purely formal, bourgeois liberty based on the exploitation of the workers, who despite free votes, free speech and free trade unions, are not really free because their livelihood is controlled and their opinions are formed by capitalist monopolies. Therefore we condone the suppression of freedom in 'socialist' states, because the workers there have freedom from capitalist exploitation, which is 'real' not 'formal' or 'bourgeois' freedom. The left-wing intellectual therefore tends to take up a more tolerant attitude to the suppression of freedom by left-wing dictatorships; even though it may be more thorough, it is for ends of which he approves. However, there is no 'bourgeois' freedom or 'proletarian' freedom, but just freedom; to deny this is to take up an intolerably patronizing attitude to the workers who know it as well as anyone else, as they showed when they demanded free elections and free trade unions in the Kronstadt rising in 1921, in the Berlin rising in 1953 and in the Hungarian rising in 1956.

Instances of a double standard arising from a sense of guilt could be multiplied indefinitely. For example at the time of writing we feel so guilty about the bombing of North Vietnam that we tend to condone the action of the Vietcong in launching a civil war which is usually the most savage form of war. Such self-criticism is necessary and healthy in a free society; but it can obscure the issue of tyranny, by leading to the 'mote and beam' fallacy – that is to say, concentrating on the mote that is in our own eye to the point of ignoring the beam in our opponent's; we may be sure that the tyrant will come to our help in this, by magnifying our 'mote' into a 'beam', while maintaining a total self-righteousness about himself.

However, the intellectual's greatest temptation to treason in the eternal struggle between freedom and tyranny is the Utopianism which makes the best the enemy of the good, the perfectionism which demands all or nothing, the quest for certainty in an uncertain field and for a perfect freedom without limits. The tyrant's ideology will offer him all this: the comforts of religion without supernatural belief, the excitement of a radicalism that destroys the roots and makes all things new, the sanctification of the basest motives by the loftiest aims.

Against this all that rational freedom can offer is a few dusty maxims. Do not seek a greater certainty than the subject matter permits, says Aristotle; and, since the subject matter of politics is human behaviour, there are precious few certainties. Do not generalize from too few instances; Marx extrapolated from the very peculiar circumstances of mid-nineteenth-century Britain, France and Germany a general scheme of history and human destiny which was to become the opium of the intellectuals. Do not worship history, like the Hegelians; do not ignore it, like the anarchists; learn from it. For the exercise of power is the great subject of history and the taming of power is the great object of politics; it is the hard art of reconciling what is with what ought to be. We must study, therefore, the chains in which we are born into the world, not only the genetic chains of heredity, but the institutional chains, the family, the class, the nation, and see where they can be eased and adapted to modern living. For that is the true radicalism, not tearing up the roots, but studying them and pruning where necessary. Freedom may not mean the acceptance of necessity; but it does mean a choice among fairly limited options, the limits being set by man's own nature and the society into which he is born, the various institutions to which he belongs by nature, tradition or choice, and the various relationships accepted or chosen by him. It is precisely these relationships which form the field of his freedom, and the independence of the various institutions he is associated with is the guarantee of it.

To these considerations may be added certain well-tried recipes: 'close alliances with despots are never safe for free states' (Demosthenes); 'a tyrant, the more he is tolerated, the more he becomes intolerable' (*Vindiciae contra Tyrannos*); and certain maxims from more recent experience: take seriously a tyrant's threats but not his promises, particularly when he promises peace; when he accuses you of a crime, believe that he is either preparing or executing the same himself; but do not let your suspicions make you act like him; it is better for a free man not to believe in a conspiracy that does exist than to imagine one which does not.

Finally, the price of liberty is eternal vigilance. As the author of *Vindiciae contra Tyrannos* puts it: 'Tyranny may be properly resembled unto a hectic fever, the which at first is easily to be cured, but with much difficulty to be known, but after it is sufficiently known becomes incurable. Therefore small beginnings are to be carefully observed, and by those whom it concerns diligently prevented.' We are all, in a democracy, those whom it concerns; and some small beginnings of tyranny in Britain are easy to observe, but difficult to prevent.

The first and obvious symptom is the growth in the power of government, Whether it goes beyond its legitimate scope is very hard to determine, although it would certainly have seemed so to any previous generation. The trouble is that the scope of British government is very ill-defined. The Crown and people in Parliament are in theory all-powerful; this implied originally a certain division of powers – between Crown and Parliament, between Lords and Commons, between Government and opposition. But now all power is with the Government, since the opposition may indeed criticize its actions, but cannot, if the majority is substantial, throw it out; and the upper House can only delay action for a short time – a power which it is reluctant to exercise and may not long retain. This puts immense power in the hands of the Prime Minister who, once he is appointed leader of the party by a party caucus, is in an unassailable position. Thus we get many of the disadvantages of a presidential system without the compensation of restraining checks and balances, These checks and balances are to be found, if anywhere, outside Parliament, in the courts, in the great corporations and private concerns, in the trades unions and the various voluntary organizations and clubs which have always been a great guarantee of British liberties. But their independence is in danger of erosion.

These threats to freedom are in part the result of a rapidly changing technological society. An unprecedentedly rapid rate of change very soon renders old institutions out of date, with the result that either they fail to fulfil their functions and thus tempt tyrannical meddling by the government, or they go beyond their scope and become tyrannical themselves. The latter alternative may be preferable, in so far as many smaller tyrannies are less harmful than one great one; but the one big one can very easily spring from a number of smaller ones. Therefore both are to be avoided, and only we, the citizens of Britain, can avoid them by constant, vigilant and self-critical activity in those institutions which are no more than ourselves in society.

Similarly, if it is generally agreed that the powers of government have increased, are increasing and ought to be diminished, then we, the electorate of Britain, are to blame. Every five years or less, we sit back and listen, while our prospective rulers make promises which every sensible man knows they will not be able to keep. Then we normally elect the party which makes the more implausible and self-contradictory promises. When they fail to fulfil these promises, we become disillusioned with the whole democratic process. The government then turns round and says that it is for us, the people to put things right; this we know to be true, but the reminder comes ill from those who during the election campaign have been promising us Utopia by Act of Parliament. It would perhaps be well if, during all election broadcasts the caption on the T.V. screen were to be Tom Payne's dictum, 'Government is at best a necessary evil, at worst an intolerable one' – except, of course, that in attending to the promises, we should ignore the caption.

The disillusionment proceeding from the disappointment of exaggerated hopes of Government is increased by constant, comprehensive and mocking criticism of the entire hierarchy of society which is summed up under that convenient term, the Establishment. It is not surprising that an Establishment which has for generations been at the centre of a great Empire, and has had to adapt itself to the exercise of restricted power in a medium-sized island, should present certain out-of-date and ludicrous features, which deserve ruthless criticism and biting satire. But much of the current assault on the Establishment seems to be based on the assumption that it is an uniquely British institution; that other societies can do without it and Britain could, too. This is a very parochial view. Every society has its Establishment; each varies in the cement that holds it together. If we look back a little in history or look out a little into the world, we shall see that the cement is sometimes naked power, the pecking order of bullying bureaucrats, sometimes wealth with all its corrupting influence, sometimes family with the excesses of nepotism, sometimes the pomp and pride of position. The criteria of a good Establishment are that it should distribute power in responsible hands and not concentrate it in irresponsible hands; that it should be open to the widest variety of legitimate, but not corrupt, influences; that it should attract people to the public service from a wide variety of motives and not just from lust for power or gain; that it should be flexible and capable of reform without those sudden leaps and starts which break the habits and sense of security on which social cohesion depends; that it should be seemly and satisfy the aesthetic sense of the people in a way that will not drive them to seek the glamour and excitement of politics in some 'charismatic' leader; that it should be capable of effective, but not arbitrary, action. In many of these respects the British Establishment is imperfect; in none is it the worst in the world.

Yet no society, perhaps, has presented a more disreputable picture of itself to itself, since the Weimar Republic and the French Third Republic – and we know what happened to them. The most unbridled liberty can lead to the most absolute tyranny; not that the present 'permissive' society is likely to do so. For a society with strong institutions and traditions can stand a great deal more experiment, licence and self-depreciation than a less deeply rooted community. The ancient Roman virtue of *pietas*, of respect for ancestral institutions and achievements is at a discount in an age that claims to know better, and certainly does in the field of science and technology; but it remains deeply ingrained in the British character – some would impatiently say, too deeply ingrained. Yet tyranny has more often been warded off by the appeal to ancient rights than by the demand for revolutionary liberties.

So the dangers are perhaps small, and small dangers call for small remedies. Here are a few proposals. To my fellow-intellectuals – that we cease contemplating our navels and shuddering at what we see, and lift up our eyes to consider our position in history and in the world; to trade unionists – that we attend branch meetings; to our legislators – that they consider formulating the constitutional limits on the powers of government which have so far been left unwritten; not that freedom was ever saved by a constitution, but it can prove a valuable trip-wire or warning light; to our Scottish and Welsh fellow countrymen – that they should go on agitating for home rule and their own Parliaments, as separate centres of power, provided that they are willing to pay for it; to the Church of England – that it should disestablish itself, or at least take the appointment of Bishops out of the Prime Minister's office.

These, however, are parochial matters; the great issues of liberty and tyranny are likely to be settled elsewhere. As we have seen, the failure of units that have become unviable to combine in a larger unity – the Greek city-states in the fourth century B.C. and the Italian cities of the Renaissance – have been a fruitful source of tyranny by foreign conquest. Indeed it is possible to argue that larger federations have never been forged except in the crucible of war and civil war; to which Europeans may reply: 'We have had our civil wars, and more than enough. After Napoleon and Hitler we cannot afford another conqueror; even an unsuccessful one, armed with nuclear weapons, could finish off Europe in a week.' The progress which Western Europe has made towards unity in the past few years shines by comparison with previous failures; but it is still not enough. There are those who argue – with great force – that even if the European powers were willing to surrender enough of their sovereignty to make European unity possible, the result would only be another form of tyranny, that of an unrepresentative bureaucracy in Brussels. Even if this were true, it would still be preferable to what must be, by historical precedent, the most probable alternative – a Europe united in a common ruin.

However, it is clearly not the case that such large units necessarily tend towards tyranny. Indeed, with a judicious separation of powers, they may be a safeguard against it. Because of her federal structure, the U.S.A. was able to absorb without undue danger the aspiring dictatorship of Huey Long in Louisiana. Even the fledgling and infirm federation of India was able to accommodate and dispose of a Communist government in Kerala, being the first state ever to get rid of a Communist dictatorship. Admittedly, the Communists have returned to power and the Indian federation is threatened with the disruptive perils of the linguistic states, but the point that a large federation can be a safeguard against tyranny has been made. It should not be beyond the political ingenuity of Europe to devise a representative authority, with powers sufficiently limited not to menace the national identity of the constituent states.

An equally powerful objection is that it would only be half a Europe, that the closer the integration of the West, the more final will be the exclusion of the Communist East. This is a strong argument against European integration in the short run, but it ignores the most important long-term factor, the magnetic power of freedom. For freedom remains, as it always has been, the main revolutionary force in the world today. For a time this was obscured by the appearance of Communist dictatorship as the main source of revolutionary ideas; but Communism has only been able to extend beyond the tanks of the Red Army where it has allied or identified itself with a national liberation movement. As a social doctrine it has become reactionary. The Metternichs of the twentieth century, who attempt to stifle ideas with censorship and secret police, are to be found above all in the Communist states. A twentieth-century Karl Marx would if he were honest have to say in his manifesto: 'A spectre is haunting Eastern Europe, the spectre of freedom.' It is not Communist ideas or parties that have to be banned in Western Europe, but liberal ideas which are banned in the East. It is not London and Paris, Bonn and Rome that fear ideological co-existence and competition, but Moscow and Sofia and East Berlin.

To recognize this dynamic force of freedom is not to say that it will necessarily triumph. It is true that in the interests of economic efficiency certain relaxations of the Communist strait-jacket have to be permitted. However, freedom is never won as a mere means to efficiency, nor indeed as a means to anything else. But there are many in the Communist world who value freedom for its own sake and who have shown themselves ready for supreme sacrifices to attain it. They can exploit the room for manoeuvre given by the economic reforms, and thus extend the area of free choice. The cases of Yugoslavia and Czechoslovakia show that, where freedom gets its foot in the door, it is not easily expelled. At the moment of writing it is being forced back in the Soviet Union itself. But be sure your virtues will find you out, as well as your sins. Perhaps the greatest virtue of Communist rule has been its concentration on a high standard of mass education. The purpose is to produce a new generation of indoctrinated Communists and skilled technicians, but education cannot be canalized in this way; anyone who reads the Russian classics, let alone the classics of world literature, is bound to have a wide view. For every young Russian imprisoned for publishing his works abroad or for demonstrating against his colleagues' arrest there are thousands of sympathizers, among them scientists and technicians, who are indispensable in a modern technological society. It is this alliance which makes it so difficult for the secret police to put the lid back on this ferment, although they are trying very hard.

Time is on the side of the young; so is social development. The development of modern mass society, based on a technology of closely meshed, interdependent large concerns may seem to us to threaten established freedoms. The rights of private property which were the basis for the sturdy independence of a Pym or a Hamden or a Washington are progressively eroded. A certain uniformity is required of the 'Organization Men', the new managerial class, the most powerful group in any highly developed technological society, whether capitalist or socialist; and modern mass media of communication and propaganda make for conformity of thought. Hence we feel ourselves threatened by the nightmare of a technological dictatorship. This, said Albert Speer, the most intelligent of Hitler's ministers, is what differentiated Nazi dictatorship from previous tyrannies:

Through technical devices like the radio and loud-speaker, eighty million people were deprived of independent thought. It was thereby possible to subject them to the will of one man. . . . Earlier dictators needed highly qualified assistants, even at the lower level, men who could think and act independently. The totalitarian system in the period of modern technical development can dispense with them; the means of communication alone make it possible to mechanise the lower leadership. . . . The nightmare of many a man that one day nations could be dominated by technical means was all but realised in Hitler's totalitarian dictatorship.

The danger is evident. However, that 'all but' of Speer's is vital. Hitler did not quite achieve totalitarian dictatorship and his attempt to achieve it by destroying initiative and independent thought and action made German society less efficient and thereby contributed to his defeat. Germany never achieved such efficient mobilization of the resources of the nation as the great democracies. Both Hitler and Stalin were able to remedy this inefficiency to some extent by massive use of the blunt instrument of slave labour. But such means are destructive of the higher skills of a modern technological society. These call for order, which excludes the arbitrary interference of the tyrant, for independent thought and initiative by *élites* in many fields, for contact between these *élites* and their colleagues working in the same field elsewhere. Further, the development of modern mass media, while increasing the dictator's propaganda power at home, has through foreign broadcasts deprived him of the monopoly of information which is the most dangerous weapon in the battle for the mind.

Therefore while we in free societies may fear some restriction in our liberties from the continuous technological revolution, those living under dictatorship may hope for some expansion of this freedom from the same source. Modern technology develops more naturally and efficiently in a plural than in a totalitarian society. There is, of course, nothing inevitable about the process. Independent centres of enterprise and initiative may provide bases for freedom. They are not in themselves free institutions. Nor is it easy for a country like Russia, with centuries of despotism and no tradition of liberty to draw on, to develop free institutions. The other countries of Eastern Europe with more liberal and constitutional traditions to refer back to may have a better hope of such a development.

Nothing could contribute more effectively to this development than a great European society, unified in freedom. Its magnetic attraction would be immense not only to Eastern Europe, but also to developing countries which under the stresses and strains of newly won independence have succumbed or are in danger of succumbing to tyranny. To many new nations the dictatorial short cut to modernization and self-respect has proved an irresistible temptation; and will doubtless continue to be so in the future. We have seen from the example of Latin-America how easily military dictatorship can become endemic in such countries.

However, provided the roots of freedom remain sound in the continent of its birth, provided that they can put forth new and strong growth, then despite all the omens to the contrary, a new birth of freedom in the world can reasonably be hoped for. If Europe herself can solve the problem of nationalism, then there is hope for other continents to which we have exported that great creative and disruptive force. In that case none of the gestures of liberty will prove in vain. The Speaker's book of rules and those laborious experiments in constitutional government will provide the traditions of freedom for post-dictatorial Africa. The Czechoslovak spring, the Hungarian

Revolution, the Polish October, the East German rising, even the few months between February and October 1917 in Russia, all these may come to be seen as the first signs of spring.

However such predictions are foolishly complacent without two provisos: that the roots of freedom are sound; and that the peace can be kept. But are the roots sound in liberty's native soil? It can be argued that the freedom, which has been treated here as the highest form of man's political existence, is the result of special historical circumstances which are already passing away, that it is bourgeois, formal liberty as the Marxist–Leninists say. It did, indeed, come into being at a given historical moment. As Lord Acton puts it: 'Beginning with the strongest religious movement and the most refined despotism ever known, it has led to the superiority of politics over divinity in the life of nations, and terminates in the equal claim of every man to be unhindered by man in the fulfilment of duty to God – a doctrine laden with storm and havoc, which is the secret essence of the Rights of Man and the indestructible soul of Revolution.'

The process has developed rapidly since those words were written seventy years ago. We have moved into the secular society; the concept of human rights has become separated from its origins in duty to God and religion. At first, the necessary moral consensus in which these rights could be practised survived its religious origins in a handful of national states in Christendom, and according as this moral consensus was deeply or lightly rooted in the popular consciousness, people resisted or succumbed to tyranny. But now we have moved a stage further. The liberties to which all men are entitled are codified in the United Nations Universal Declaration of Human Rights. It guarantees every possible freedom (and some which in the poorer societies of the world are impossible). Thus we attempt to transplant the results of centuries of difficult and stubborn growth to soil not always prepared for it. Can these rights be established where there is no consensus on the nature of God and man? And can they survive in the communities in which they are now most practised? These are for the most part permissive societies in which there is no longer much agreement on moral standards or on any fundamental beliefs.

This perhaps is the logical outcome of freedom. As Sir Isaiah Berlin pointed out in his inaugural lecture on 'Two Concepts of Liberty':

It is a commonplace that neither political equality nor efficient organization is compatible with more than a modicum of individual liberty and certainly not with unrestricted laissez-faire; that justice and generosity, public and private loyalties, the demands of genius and the claims of society can conflict violently with each other. And it is no great way from that to the generalisation that not all good things are compatible, still less all the ideals of mankind. . . . To admit that the fulfilment of some of our ideals may in principle make the fulfilment of others impossible is to say that the notion of total fulfilment is a formal contradiction, a metaphysical chimaera.

This is not a difficult conception for the Christian who believes that ultimate fulfilment is only to be found in a kingdom which is not of this earth and not by human endeavour but by the grace of God. The Christian, indeed, may see in the Ecumenical movement, with its coming together of Christians throughout the world, and their reaching out to the other great religions and the humanists, the possibility of establishing a rational basis for the Universal Declaration of Human Rights. But that obviously is only a long-term faith and not one to which most of those who now have to struggle with the problems of liberty would subscribe.

They are confronted with the reality of a fragmented society which has no overall vision of itself, in which men have difficulty in finding their identity or any basic principles to stand on, in which the tension of passionately held convictions – the origins of tolerance – often seems to give way to a chaos of fashionable opinions; and the toleration of indifference is not likely to survive adversity. 'It may be,' says Sir Isaiah Berlin, 'that the ideal of freedom to live as one wishes – and the pluralism of values connected with it – is only the late fruit of our declining capitalist civilization: an ideal which remote ages and primitive societies have not known, and one which posterity will regard with curiosity, even sympathy, but little comprehension.'

In these circumstances, the free man is confronted with the difficult tasks of admitting the relative validity of his convictions, yet standing for them unflinchingly. In *L'Homme Révolté* Camus wrestles heroically and desperately with the problem of how the rebel without support of religious belief, ideology or any absolute standards can combat the excesses of power. He comes up with a desperate solution in the shape of the Mediterranean ideal of moderation – expressed in such ancient Greek maxims as 'nothing in excess' and 'virtue is a mean'. To this there are two objections. It is an ideal that has been but little practised, least of all in the Mediterranean, where nearly every country has at one time or another during the past generation succumbed to tyranny or dictatorship. Secondly, the Greek ideal of moderation was based on belief in a transcendent power, in 'Nemesis, the goddess of moderation and the implacable enemy of the immoderate'. The main characteristic of our age, and precisely the one which sets Camus his problem, is the lack of any belief in supernatural justice or any transcendent power, and the confidence, which the Greeks would have called *hubris*, that science and technology make us the master of our destiny.

This presumably is what our theologians mean when they say man has come of age and can do without a transcendent God. Certainly the plural society in which we find ourselves is a far more novel and revolutionary form of social organization than any of the contemporary tyrannies, whether communist or otherwise, and therefore more difficult to make predictions about. For there has been no previous society that has shown at one and the same time such symptoms of decadence in some fields – for example the arts, religion, possibly morality – and such vigour in others – for example science, technology, social inquiry, education and organization. Such a society has far greater powers of regeneration than more monolithic unitary states; and the fact that it has the machinery for peaceful

change which is so vital in an age of rapid technological
advance gives it a great advantage in survival value over any
dictatorship – always, that is, provided that the peace can be
kept.

This is the proviso which, in the nuclear age, makes us feel
like those 'upon whom the ends of the world are come'. It is
a feeling of doom which has often haunted men in times of
crisis and revolution, as when St Paul wrote those words to the
Corinthians. No generation has had more reason for such
forebodings than this one which carries the means of its own
destruction in its hands. No one who has read the foregoing
record of atrocity, crime, and folly can have much assurance
that these terrible weapons will not be used. Already Chairman
Mao has indicated that, with China's millions behind him, he
might be able to derive some advantage from nuclear war, and
although his bark is usually worse than his bite, we cannot set
any limits to the lunacy of aging tyrants. We can be certain
that if Hitler, raging in the Bunker, had been able to press a
button and send the world up in flames, he would have done
so. However, it was President Truman who actually pressed
the button; and the fact that good men sometimes do terrible
deeds is one of the providential reasons why tyrants do not
dominate the earth. Whether the balance of terror could have
been maintained, but for Hiroshima, whether the deterrent
would have been credible in the hands of the democracies, if
they had never used it, is not a question that is ever likely to be
answered. What is certain is that a number of incidents and
crises between the Soviet Union and the Western powers,
which in pre-nuclear times might well have been *casus belli*,
have in the last twenty years passed quietly into history.

We have of course no guarantee that this luck will hold. The
great powers are taking an intolerable time in working out any
more permanent safeguards against nuclear weapons. However, in this matter there have been some evidences of good
luck or Providence; and few can have read through this sombre
chronicle of tyranny without the occasional reflection: 'There,
but for the grace of God, went we.' So we may perhaps venture

to complete the quotation from St Paul: 'There has no such temptation taken you but such as is common to man; but God is faithful who will not suffer you to be tempted above that ye are able; but will with the temptation also make a way to escape, that ye may be able to bear it.'

Bibliographical Note

A full bibliography for a work which proceeds from a lifetime's general reading would scarcely be possible, especially when it deals with a subject which has not for a long time been treated in its full scope. But the following brief notes may be useful.

The most recent work which I know to have covered a large part of the field was the late Alfred Cobban's *Dictatorship, its History and Theory*, published in 1939. Hannah Arendt's *Origins of Totalitarianism* is more limited, but stimulating.

In covering so wide a field, one must depend for the most part on standard works. *The Cambridge Ancient History* and the *Cambridge Modern History* are indispensable. *The Greek Tyrants* by A. Andrewes and *The Origin of Tyranny* by P. N. Ure (an economic interpretation) give good coverage of the first and second waves of Greek tyranny. *Alexander the Great and the Hellenistic Empire* by A. R. Burn and F. E. Adcock's Raleigh Lecture on *Greek and Macedonian Kingship* (1953) are of value for the next stage. But more modern works can only supplement the works of Herodotus, Thucydides, Plato (particularly *The Republic*) and Aristotle (*Politics*). Similarly for Roman tyranny Tacitus (for deep analysis) and Suetonius (for personalities) are indispensable. Sir Ronald Syme in *The Roman Revolution* gives great insight into the relevance of the rise of Augustus for our time. A. H. M. Jones in *The Decline of the Ancient World* provides a valuable supplement, in the light of more recent research, to Gibbon.

Ernst Kantorowicz's comprehensive study, *Frederick the Second*, foreshadows the Renaissance tyrants; Burckhardt's *The Civilization of the Renaissance in Italy* gives an indispensable background to Machiavelli's *Prince* and *Discourses*.

Of the many books on Oliver Cromwell I have found Maurice Ashley's *The Greatness of Oliver Cromwell* most useful. Moving into modern times I have drawn on J. M. Thompson's *French Revolution* and D. Thomson's *Europe since Napoleon*. See also Rudé's

Revolutionary Europe 1783–1815, Lord Rosebery's *Napoleon: the Last Phase,* Pieter Geyl's *Napoleon: For and Against* and naturally Alexis de Tocqueville's *The Ancien Régime and the French Revolution.*

For the rise of ideology and its association with the Romantic movement see *The Romantic Agony* by Mario Praz. As far as the ideologists themselves are concerned, I have been concerned more with the practical results of their works and less with the often brilliant insights that are to be found in Hegel, Nietzsche, Marx and Lenin. Hugh Seton-Watson in *Neither War Nor Peace* draws attention to the importance of the intelligentsia as the bearers of revolutionary – or reactionary – ideology. My critique of the ideological approach owes much to *The Open Society and its Enemies* by Sir Karl Popper, *The Origins of Totalitarian Democracy* by J. L. Talmon, *Le Trahison des Clercs* by Julien Benda, *The Revolt of the Masses* by Ortega y Gasset, *L'Homme Révolté* by Camus, and to the writings of Sir Isaiah Berlin, particularly to his *Karl Marx,* with its brief and finely balanced account of the relationship between the great man's life and doctrine.

Norman Cohn's notable study, *The Pursuit of the Millennium,* traces the relationship between the thought and action of messianic sects and of ideological movements.

For the chapter on tyranny and religion I have drawn among others on *The Political Ideas of St Augustine's De Civitate Dei* by Norman H. Baynes; for Calvin, on R. N. Carew Hunt and O. Wendel; on *Napoleon and the Pope* by E. E. Y. Hales; on Lord Acton's *Lectures on Modern History.*

Among the many books dealing with the circumstances leading up to the Russian Revolution I would mention *The Twilight of Imperial Russia* by R. D. Charques, *Russia in Revolution* by Lionel Kochan, *The Russian Empire 1801–1917* by Hugh Seton-Watson, *Survey of Russian History* by B. H. Sumner and *Russia 1917: the February Revolution* by George Katkov. ,

For Lenin see the excellent biographies of Louis Fischer, David Shub and Adam Ulam; for Stalin, Isaac Deutscher's *Stalin* and Robert Paynes' *Rise and Fall of Stalin,* Djilas's *Conversation with Stalin* and Svetlana Alliluyeva's *Twenty Letters to a Friend.* For Khrushchev see the biographies by Edward Crankshaw and Mark Frankland.

For Hitler I have followed above all Alan Bullock's masterly *Hitler: A Study in Tyranny*; also Hugh Trevor-Roper's *The Last*

Days of Hitler, The Nazi Seizure of Power by William Sheridan Allen and *The Rise and Fall of the Third Reich* by William Shirer. For Hitler's relations with the army, Sir John Wheeler-Bennett's *The Nemesis of Power, The July Plot* by Roger Manvell and Heinrich Fraenkel and *The Shirt of Nessus* by Constantine Fitzgibbon supply ample material. *Benito Mussolini* by Christopher Hibbert is a very readable biography and F. W. Deakin's *The Brutal Friendship* and *The Last Days of Mussolini* give a notable picture of a dictator in decline. *Franco: The Man and his Nation* by George Hills gives a balanced picture of the 'great survivor' among modern dictators.

For military dictatorships generally S. E. Finer in *The Man on Horseback* supplies the most comprehensive study, which is supplemented by E. Lieuwen's *Arms and Politics in Latin America*. Finally Stuart Schram's excellent biography of Mao Tse-tung, although written before the great Cultural Revolution, does much to explain it.

To all these and to many other authors not mentioned here, I wish to acknowledge my debt, while not saddling them with any share of responsibility for the result.

Index

More about Penguins and Pelicans

Penguinews, which appears every month, contains details of all the new books issued by Penguins as they are published. From time to time it is supplemented by *Penguins in Print*, which is a complete list of all available books published by Penguins. (There are well over three thousand of these.)

A specimen copy of *Penguinews* will be sent to you free on request, and you can become a subscriber for the price of the postage. For a year's issues (including the complete lists) please send 30p if you live in the United Kingdom, or 60p if you live elsewhere. Just write to Dept EP, Penguin Books Ltd, Harmondsworth, Middlesex, enclosing a cheque or postal order, and your name will be added to the mailing list.

Note: *Penguinews* and *Penguins in Print* are not available in the U.S.A. or Canada

Democracy in a
Revolutionary Era

Harvey Wheeler

Democracy in a Revolutionary Era is a comprehensive
study of today's political order. It opens with an
outline of the development of different political
systems; goes on to analyse how changes in ideology,
science and bureaucracy have affected the working
of democracy; and concludes with the suggestion
that 'world order is the only truly practical and
scientific alternative open to man'. Harvey Wheeler, a
staff member of the Center for the Study of
Democratic Institutions, Santa Barbara, California,
expresses optimism about our ability to achieve this goal
if governments, usually reluctant to abandon familiar
policies, can co-operate to escape destruction.

'The reader who wishes a penetrating, and insightful,
analysis of the modern democratic dilemma will be
richly rewarded' – *Los Angeles Times*

Not for sale in the U.S.A. or Canada